M000165948

SHOTS AT BIG GAME

SHOTS AT BIG GAME

How to shoot a rifle accurately under hunting conditions

CRAIG BODDINGTON

Drawings by Stuart Funk

SAFARI PRESS, Inc.

P.O. BOX 3095, Long Beach, CA 90803

Big Game and Big Game Rifles. Special contents of this edition copyright © 1993 Safari Press, Inc. All rights reserved. No part of this publication may be used or reproduced in any form or by any means, electronic or mechanical reproduction, including photocopy, recording, or any information storage and retrieval system, without permission from the publisher.

The trademark Safari Press ® is registered with the U.S. Patent and Trademark Office and in other countries.

Taylor, John

Safari Press, Inc.

1993, Long Beach, California

ISBN 0-940143-87-9

10 9 8 7 6 5 4 3 2

Readers wishing to receive the Safari Press catalog, featuring many fine books on big-game hunting, wingshooting, and sporting firearms, should write to Safari Press Inc., P.O. Box 3095, Long Beach, CA 90803, USA. Tel: (714) 894-9080 or visit our Web site at www.safaripress.com.

This one for Brittany . . .

Contents

Author's Note

I wish I had all the answers, but I don't. When it comes to shooting at game — and any other human endeavor I can think of — nobody knows everything, and nobody does it right all the time. Deep down I consider myself a pretty good shot. Some of the folks I've hunted with would agree; others might scratch their heads, because I have messed up, by the numbers, in front of witnesses. If there's a mistake to be made in field shooting, I'm sure I've made it. And if I haven't, sooner or later I will. It comes down to the simple fact that shooting, at game or on the range, is every bit as much a mental game as it is a physical exercise. I think I have enough experience to know what I have to do under virtually any circumstances to make a shot work — but *knowing* what to do and actually *doing* it aren't always the same thing.

So I make no claim of infallibility. If we meet around a campfire someday, we can talk about the ones that got away and the ones that didn't. If we're honest, I suspect we'll each have our share of both.

The thought processes that have gone into this book, the self-evaluation of what has worked for me and what hasn't, will undoubtedly improve my own field shooting in the years to come. I have done my best to evaluate not only what works for me, but *why*. Shooting is a very individual sport, however, and shooting at game is one of its most personal forms. If any of what works for me is of direct value to you, then this book will have achieved its goal. If it doesn't work for you but causes you to discover what does, then the success is equal. I think you will find here a lot of good techniques and sound concepts but few absolutes. Whether you use my ideas, your own, or someone else's, the idea is to hunt hard, hunt well, and hunt fairly, and to take your game cleanly. That's what field marksmanship is all about, and to that end I wish you well.

Craig Boddington
Los Angeles

1

Memorable Hits,
Forgettable Misses

The memory is a wonderfully selective device, and perhaps that's just as well. It's a whole lot more enjoyable to dwell on the things that have been done properly than to brood over the snafus. Hunters, it seems to me, have a memory that's super selective, and hunting writers in particular possess this gift to a remarkable degree. Now, it's quite possible that hunting writers on the whole possess an above-average level of field marksmanship; well they should, since their livelihood to some extent is based on their ability to bring home the bacon.

However—and this may come as a surprise—folks in my line of work do miss. We jerk our triggers, we flinch, we underestimate and overestimate range, we underlead and overlead, and we're subject to bouts of buck fever that reduce us to shaking globs of Jell-O.

Everybody misses—if it were all simple and mechanical every time we lifted our guns at furred or feathered game, the sport of hunting wouldn't be a sport at all. And it wouldn't be nearly as exciting or enjoyable. Unfortunately, few of the foibles, errors, and unexcusable misses seem to find their way into the sporting press. For one thing, it doesn't make good copy. For another, I suspect most of us would prefer to read about things that go right rather than things that go wrong. In the sporting press, the happy ending is definitely alive and well. Lastly, of course, is that selective memory. It's much easier to recall those happy endings—somehow the mistakes and misses aren't nearly so easy to call to mind.

I know another gun writer, a good friend that I've hunted with several times on the

1

Everybody misses, including me, and everybody misses for pretty much the same reasons—jerking, flinching, misjudging the range, buck fever, you name it. Misses will never be completely eliminated, since there are too many variables, but good shooting positions and attention to the basic principles of good shooting will minimize them.

ranch he manages in Texas. He's a meticulous note-taker, and before emigrating to America he was a very successful professional hunter in East Africa. In his bookcase is a series of timeworn notebooks that detail literally every cartridge fired in any rifle he's ever owned—and every bullet he's seen fired at game by himself, his clients, and his friends. Embodying some 30 years of extensive hunting experience, those notebooks hold one of the world's greatest references on practical field ballistics. And I suspect that individual could find a notation for every shot he's ever missed. Knowing him, I doubt there were many—but from each there's a lesson to be learned. Raw honesty can be painful, but in the

business of field shooting at game, the ability to look back and analyze all the mistakes and misses is extremely valuable. All too often, I fear, we would find that we've made the same mistakes over and over.

My own notebooks aren't nearly so precise. I wish they were. But I've rarely even kept a trip log on hunts, let alone a running diary. I do have a sort of "game log" that I've kept for more than 20 years. It's quite simple, recording dates, places, species of game, caliber and bullet weight used, shooting distances, and number of shots fired to bring down an animal. It yields some interesting data. For instance, over a 20-year total of several hundred head of big game, my average shooting distance was

127 yards. I suspect even that modest distance is a bit longer than average, probably because the majority of my hunting was done in the western mountains and plains.

There are a very few entries recorded at 400-plus yards, but a great many more recorded at 10 to 25 yards. The average number of shots per animal comes out at 1.66. There are, to be sure, a great many one-shot kills recorded, but I also noticed a couple of entries at six, seven, and even eight shots, and still writhe inwardly at the stark notation. I can well remember those frustrating occasions. . . .

Unfortunately, it's not a complete tabulation, for I made no permanent record of the ones that got away. Still, as selective as my memory is, I can't quite forget some of the classic foul-ups.

One occurred about 10 years ago in the Edwards Plateau country of south-central Texas. That region is literally overrun with whitetail deer — few monsters, but plenty of average to respectable bucks. It was a good place for me to be, because I simply had to have a decent whitetail buck; I'd promised an editor I'd deliver a story. The problem was that, though plenty of deer were around, I couldn't get a shot at one. The full moon was one problem, and a drenching downpour on one day was another. And bad luck didn't help.

After three or four fruitless days, the ranch owner directed me to a deep, rough canyon that nobody had yet hunted that season. I took my time, moving slowly and glassing carefully, and after a few hundred yards I was rewarded with the flash of sun-

It usually takes a lot of effort, often days of hard hunting, to get just one shot at a nice animal. Since the final reward for all that work rests on a single bullet, it makes sense to be completely ready — both mentally and physically — to put that bullet in the right place when the time comes.

light off a twitching ear on the opposite hillside. It was a doe, but the rut was on, so I sat down slowly and waited.

My hunch was correct—a buck was there, and he was about as good as that country can produce. The afternoon sun glinted off his antlers, and I had plenty of time to lie down and make a perfect shot. When the rifle—an accurate .243—went off, the buck disappeared. Not worried in the least, I waited a few moments, then picked my way across the canyon, expecting to find him right there in his tracks. But he wasn't there, and he didn't leave a drop of blood—only deep-cut tracks where he'd done an about-face and slipped out the only avenue that hid him from me completely. That time, it was easy to analyze what happened, once I sat down and thought about it.

I'd committed a shooting error common in rough country—I'd overestimated the range, held just on his backline, and without question shot right over him. The deep canyon, coupled with the small size of the whitetails in that area, had fooled me into thinking the buck was much farther than he was.

Usually there is no second chance, and there wasn't this time. Once in a great while, though, the fates will allow you to correct a mistake before it becomes indelibly etched in your memory.

Just a few years ago I took a very nice Dall ram. There are really two versions to the story—the one I prefer to tell, and the way things really happened. In the preferred version we bedded the rams on the opposite mountain the evening before, then moved on them at first light. They were moving as well, and in the nine hours it took to get a shot, they moved off that mountain, across a glacier, and up and over the next mountain; and when we finally put two good rams down, it took a full 24 hours to get back to camp—two hungry hunters with no sleeping bags or food and two boned-out sheep.

That's close to what really happened, but I often forget to tell that I actually got a shot on the first mountain. We had moved around laterally and come in underneath them. My ram—the one I shot some six grueling hours later—came out and stood on a point about 80 yards above us. I looked for a rest, couldn't find one, and settled into a sitting position with a tight sling. The ram was peering over a lip of rock. I could perhaps be excused by the fact that I was out of breath and knew I had limited time to shoot. I rushed the shot, and my bullet struck the lip of rock, stinging the ram with sharp fragments and spooking him badly.

Other blown opportunities haven't ended so well.

My records indicate that I've shot more pronghorns than almost any other species. I started my big-game hunting with them, and I still love their wide-open spaces and the challenge of stalking them in their sparse habitat. I've taken some good ones, but I'm not likely to forget my one and only shot at a true Boone & Crockett antelope.

It was in New Mexico, and we'd spotted the buck working his way up a brushy watercourse. The conditions for a stalk were letter-perfect, and we had closed the distance to 125 yards—certainly no problem shot, especially on an undisturbed pronghorn feeding broadside. I had crawled in behind a little bush and was lying prone with the sling tightened on my arm. I can still see the crosshairs dead steady behind his shoulder, and the strike of the bullet off to the right.

I was so dumbfounded that I didn't shoot again, and it was just as well that I didn't. I

More than 24 hours of hard walking was needed to get this Dall ram off the mountain—but it was my fault. I missed an easy shot, and didn't catch up to the ram again until he'd gone over two more mountains.

had broken my own rules about practicing with any rifle under field conditions; I had shot this rifle only from the bench, and I didn't know that, with tension from the tight sling, it shifted impact some 18 inches to the right. I should have known. . . .

Another entry in my logbook recorded a very nice mule deer taken in a remote mountain range in central Nevada. The shooting-distance entry reads 400 yards, but I don't know the true distance. I only know it was an awfully long shot. We'd

been hunting hard for a week, and this was the last day. We rode out into some new country that was steep and rough, cut with deep gulleys and canyons. I rode out to a little point, and my outfitter, Jerry Hughes, rode through a deep cut to my left. He jumped a big buck, and it broke behind him, headed for the safety of the far rim. It was clearly the only chance I would get, and we'd been working too hard and too long to forget it.

I was shooting a Ruger M77 in .30–06, a good rifle with which I was totally familiar. I jerked it out of the saddle scabbard and lay down on a flat rock on the canyon rim, scrunching up my Stetson for a makeshift rest. The buck was bounding up the hillside. I shot once, wild, then settled down and waited for him to top out. That would be the best shot. When he topped out he was walking, and I held a body height high and a body length in front. The sound of the bullet hitting carried back in the clear air, and I shot again with the same hold before he vanished into the timber. We found him there, shot twice through the lungs.

That was undoubtedly one of the best shots I ever made. On the other hand, since my little logbook only covers game taken, it doesn't recount another shot at a mule deer. This one, made just a few months ago, was one of the most spectacular misses I've ever made.

It was in the Kootenays of southern British Columbia, and we'd made a long stalk on the best mule deer buck I'd seen in years. Actually three bucks, the biggest a real dandy. They'd moved while we were stalking, so we came in on the wrong side and spotted them only by accident. Still, it wasn't a tough shot. The distance was short, and the deer were trotting casually up a knife-edge ridge.

I lay across a log, took a couple of deep breaths, and fired the only shot I would get just as my buck topped out. And I missed him clean. I can still see the crosshairs — probably because I put them in the wrong place. He was quartering to the right as he went up the ridge, but just as he topped out, he zigged to the left, and I shot past him. I don't know why I didn't correct for his change in direction. But at least I know what happened, and perhaps I learned a little bit from it.

The worst misses are the ones that simply can't be explained. Clear back in 1965, when my home state of Kansas opened its first modern deer season, I drew a tag in the central part of the state north of Russell. The second morning I got a shot at a really fine whitetail buck standing broadside. He was about 150 yards away, and I was using an accurate, flat-shooting .264 that had already accounted for Wyoming antelope and mule deer. I was quite young then, but I could shoot — perhaps better than now. I got a steady rest, put the crosshairs right behind the shoulder, and squeezed off as careful a shot as I've ever made. The buck took off unhurt, leaving neither blood nor hair.

What happened? I'm not sure. That whitetail is one of the ones that haunt me, a "mystery miss" where everything looked good but nothing happened. In a later chapter we'll explore these "mystery misses" in some detail, for we can learn much from them — if we can come up with some concept of how we blew it. On that one I might have rushed the shot or jerked the trigger — Lord knows I was one excited youngster.

Since it's so painful to recall the poor shots, our selective memory prefers to call to mind the really good ones. That is probably unfortunate. Once in a while we all make truly spectacular shots, and chances are they are shots that shouldn't have been attempted in the first place. I have a few like that, and even though they're products of doing exactly the right thing at the right time — and as such can be learned from — chances are they can't be repeated.

On my first grizzly hunt, time was running out. We were hunting a high basin so choked with snow that the horses couldn't make it in. Only in the last days of the hunt had we pushed within striking range of this grizzly haven of rockslides and timber. On the morning of the last day, we had spotted a good bear far up on a snowy slide. An old back injury was torturing my guide, and the bear was a thousand yards above us. We

Arizona's little Coues whitetails are small enough, and blend in well enough, that literally every shot that works is memorable. This little buck wasn't all that far away, but he was bedded in shade with only a tiny vital patch showing. It took a good steady position, plus an accurate rifle that was perfectly sighted in.

talked about it briefly, and I went up alone to get him.

The slope and the downhill breeze covered me until I reached the bottom of a bare snowslide, and that was the end of the line. The bear walked out far above me — too far, but it was indeed the last day. I grabbed a sapling for a rest, but the curve of the slope hid the bear. I tried to sit, but the result was the same. This was a rifle I knew well, a heavy-barrelled .375 that I'd had since I was 16, and still have today. It was an old friend that I'd shot for pronghorns, mule deer, and even jackrabbits with reduced loads. I stood, wrapped into a tight sling, and tried to hold the wobbling crosshairs on the bear's backline. Drilled exactly right through the shoulders, the bear careened downhill toward me and came to rest against a boulder 50 yards uphill.

Although it's a shot I'll never forget, today I question whether it should have been attempted. What I don't question is that I couldn't do it again today. In those days I was using that rifle for virtually all my hunting. The stock fit me perfectly; the trigger pull was light, crisp, and clean; and the extra-heavy barrel gave great stability for offhand shooting.

Too, I was 21 years old, with the best reflexes and eyesight I will ever have, and at that time I was involved in smallbore competition, which involved a great deal of shooting in the standing position, a position I considered my best. Today I wouldn't shoot at that bear. I'd wait him out, get closer, or just let him go. But back then I thought I could do it, and I did — and that's the stuff memories (but not sound field shooting techniques) are made of.

Selective memory creates a dual problem; it not only erases the misses — each of which could teach us so much — but it also emphasizes the spectacular, once-in-a-life-

time shot and pushes to the background the mundane, competent shot that, like the misses, could teach us something.

I wouldn't call any (well, almost not any) killing shot a lucky shot, for there's a great deal of air space and non-vital tissue surrounding the kill zone of any game animal. But doing something right once — like I did on that bear or that mule deer, one a marginal shot on a dangerous animal and the other well beyond acceptable shooting range — teaches little beyond the simple fact that such shooting is possible. If the misses can't be conjured to mind and analyzed, then it's far better to reprogram that selective memory and look at the normal, average shots that went right.

What's an average shot, and what can be learned from it? "Average" depends on where you hunt, but any successful shot at game can teach a great deal. For my hunting, the most average shot imaginable — and such a shot, although average, is unlikely to happen every year — came on a coastal blacktail a couple of seasons ago. In the part of the California coast range that I hunt, especially during the August season when the mercury tops 100° by midmorning, *any* buck is a very good buck, and shots are few and far between.

I was sitting on an overhanging rock just at dawn, looking down on a steep oak-grassland hillside that fell away into a poison-oak-choked river canyon. There was a good acorn crop that year, so there was a decent chance that deer might feed along the hillside at first light before retiring to the cool riverine brush. The sun was just up when I saw movement to my left, far down the canyon. It was a herd of deer, perhaps spooked by one of my partners, and they were trotting up the canyon toward me. Before losing them in the brush, I made out one very nice buck.

In broken country there's almost always some kind of steady rest available, and even at relatively close range it's foolish to be anything less than as steady as you can possibly get. This handy rock outcropping turned into a benchrest as good as that found on any range.

There was some small chance that things could get interesting; just 100 yards below me was a small clump of oaks that had littered the ground with acorns. I traded the binoculars for my 7mm magnum and relaxed, waiting.

Half an hour later the buck came striding up the hillside alone. There was no rush; the slight breeze was upcanyon to me, and I didn't want to chance a moving shot. He came into the little grove, vanished behind a sturdy oak, then stepped out again. His head was down, feeding, and he was facing directly toward me. I could have waited for a better angle, but that particular rifle is superbly accurate. While his head was down, I slowly wrapped into the sling and braced my elbows on my knees. The bullet

severed the spine between the shoulder blades, then angled down through the chest cavity. I doubt if the buck ever heard the rifle.

Simple? Yes. Mundane? So much so that, had it happened a dozen years ago, I might not remember it. But I did a whole bunch of things right in those few minutes. I didn't try a hopeless shot at a running buck when I first saw him. I calculated the odds of getting a better shot, decided that they beat the present possibilities, and I waited. I had a shooting rest all picked out, but I couldn't use it because of the angle of the slope. Instead I used a tight sling and a good sitting position, and I waited for the shot that I wanted. When it was presented, I took a couple of breaths, let the last one partly out, then finished the trigger squeeze with the crosshairs steady.

In much hunting country, the average shooting opportunity isn't quite that deliberate. Many years ago I was sitting with my back to a tree on a levee in North Carolina, listening as hounds coursed deer through the swamps. Although this was shotgun country, rifles were legal, and I carried a rifle. It was a bolt-action, scoped .270, an unlikely choice, and my host had offered me a buckshot-loaded shotgun instead as a more suitable arm. I clung to the rifle, and as the hound music got closer, I wondered if I'd made the right choice.

The baying came closer; then I heard a heavy splashing close by and saw antlers floating through the dense brush. The buck, unseen but for his rack, hesitated, then gathered himself to bound over the open levee and into the safety of the swamp beyond. The .270, a slick little Mannlicher-stocked carbine that came up smoothly and on target, could well have been a shotgun when that buck came out of the swamp. The gun came to the shoulder smoothly, and I don't know where the crosshairs were. I do know the buck was in midair when the rifle went off, and I know he crashed down on the edge of the levee with the bullet angled through the point of the on-shoulder.

What's to be learned there? The fact that, however unlikely the caliber and choice of action, the rifle fit like a good shotgun and handled as quickly. After that buck—sporting the best antlers taken in that county in this century—was hung up, the .270 was subjected to no more derision. When that buck leaped over the levee at 30 feet, the only hope was for a gun that fit the shooter perfectly and handled like lightning—whether buck, ball, slug, or bullet was chosen.

There are many memorable hits and forgettable misses in the career of any serious hunter, and we'll examine a number of each in the following chapters. More importantly, though, we'll look at the shooting techniques, the choice of equipment, and the preparation that can contribute to a memorable hit. And by the time we're finished, we should reduce the number of misses that, forgettable as they are, will still be allowed to haunt us by even the most selective of memories.

2

Shooting Basics

Shots at big game occur in endless variety. Just as no two whitetail bucks will ever be exactly alike, no two shooting opportunities will be the same. Some shots will come suddenly, others after long study and careful deliberation. Some will be in bright sunlight, others in fading twilight—perhaps deepened by fast-falling snow or wind-driven rain. A few will be at bayonet range, and a very few will be at the outer limits of you and your rifle's capabilities. But whatever opportunity presents itself, it's clear that in order to turn that opportunity into meat in the pot, you must place your bullet in the right spot.

Accurate field shooting is a unique skill, and, sad but true, the consistently successful marksman is a rare man. Ask any professional hunting guide for his No. 1 problem with clients. Almost invariably, the answer will be poor shooting. Unfortu-

nately, missed shots are part of an outfitter's business. He has to live with them because he knows most of his clients will miss. All of us miss shots.

My good friend and colleague John Wootters calls the marksmanship of American hunters a "national disgrace," and I can't disagree. Missing is frustrating, embarrassing, aggravating, and whatever other negative adjectives you care to think of. But that's only part of the story. The other part is that the vital area of an animal is surrounded by lots of non-vital areas.

When a bullet fired at game is misdirected slightly, the very best thing that can happen is a frustrating, embarrassing, aggravating—and *clean*—miss. All too often, though, the miss isn't clean, and a wounded animal escapes. A few will recover, but not many. So poor shooting is not only a matter of hunter success, but

The nationwide percentage of missed shots is undoubtedly staggering. Misses will occur, but they should be the exception, not the rule. With plenty of practice and good shooting basics, accurately shooting a rifle in the field is actually quite simple.

also a very serious conservation issue. Losses of crippled game are so unpleasant to contemplate that virtually all outdoor magazines stay completely away from the subject.

There is no statistic, but it's believed that deer hit and lost by hunters — due to poor shooting and/or hunter inability to determine when *not* to shoot — number many thousands annually. It is not possible to eliminate all misses, but it is possible to raise our proficiency so that we put ourselves in the category of hunters who consistently bring home their game most of the time.

What, then, is "average" shooting competency? From what I've seen in hunting camps around the country, I doubt whether the average hunter/shooter connects with a well-placed shot 50 percent of the time — and that's not good enough. At the other end of the spectrum, what's really outstanding field shooting performance? The competent rifleman who knows when and

when not to shoot — and knows his rifle and how to shoot it — should be dead-shot accurate at 90 percent or better.

I think it's well within the reach of most of us to attain a field shooting skill level that will put 9 shots in 10 in the vital area on game. That other 10 percent? Well, I'm happy to donate those shots to buck fever, faulty range estimation, wind drift, and all the other things that make life interesting. But I'll hope that the 10 percent goes either to clean misses or to hits that are close enough to the mark to allow follow-up shots and recovery of the game!

Field shooting is not an art, though a competent rifleman is artistry in motion. And it is not a science, for the human element defies the strict scientific approach. It's a skill composed of many diverse elements, and its hallmarks are confidence and constant readiness. It's a skill built around sound basics, suitable equipment, and experience. Only the passing of hunting seasons brings experience. All the other elements are within the grasp of all of us.

One of the problems is that field shooting is so infinitely varied, unlike all formal target shooting disciplines. Make no mistake, *any* shooting at all is an aid to field shooting, but specialization in one form of shooting may not make versatile, well-rounded field marksmen. The 1,000-yard competitor should be, and invariably is, deadly on deliberate long-range shots. The Olympic-style running-boar competitor should be awesome when a buck jumps in heavy cover. Is either good at the other's game? Perhaps, but if he is, it's due to the talent of the shooter, not the sport he follows. These and all other types of competitive shooting tend to focus on a narrow, specialized shooting situation, not the full range of opportunities that might arise while hunting.

It isn't that I don't recommend the formal shooting games — I recommend all forms of recreational shooting, from BB gun to Olympic. Many serious competitive shooters are great field marksmen, certainly better than I. Formalized competition, however, isn't an essential to good field shooting. Most formal shooting games do approximate at least one type of field shooting, but they all have something far more important in common with successful field shooting — they begin with the same set of basics.

Position and Body Alignment

Various effective shooting positions will be covered in later chapters, but first let's look at the basic premise: You simply must have the steadiest position possible to do the best shooting. Generally, this means the most comfortable position, but not always — some very steady positions, such as sitting, may always be sheer murder for muscles not used to bending and stretching that way. Also, the use of a makeshift rest in the field won't always be as comfortable as the benchrest at your local range. However, it's important to be as comfortable and relaxed as possible when preparing to shoot.

Equally important from the start is body alignment. Essentially, this means lining your body up behind the rifle so your gun barrel naturally follows your arms, hands, and eyes to the target. This concept applies to all positions, and will be covered more specifically in later chapters. For now, though, it's important to understand that successful shooting requires your entire body's assistance as well as your full mental attention. Shotgunners learn early on that you can't swing a shotgun against yourself; proper foot placement is one of the great keys to wingshooting. Surprisingly, body position is also one of the keys to consistent rifle shooting from any position, including a benchrest.

From any shooting position, the rifle's sights should naturally line up on the target. If you need to exert force to bring the sights to bear, you're "muscling" the rifle — and you're already starting a bad habit. The simplest example is the solid benchrest, seemingly a foolproof shooting platform. Sit down at the bench, and rest the fore-end on a raised cushion. Get nice and comfortable, and use your supporting hand — not the one that holds your trigger finger — to pull the butt snugly into your shoulder. Drop your cheek onto the stock, and take a look through the sights. Are they

From any shooting position it's essential that the body and the rifle be properly aligned on the target. The sights must fall naturally onto the target without your having to "muscle" the rifle into position to get off an accurate shot.

perfectly aligned on the target, or do you need to use that supporting hand to literally pull them into place? If they aren't lined up, then your body alignment is out of kilter. Rather than muscle the sights into place, shift your body a few degrees one way or the other so that the sights line up naturally, virtually on their own.

As we shall see, this concept applies equally to all shooting positions. In a deliberate situation, where there's lots of time — whether at the bench or as an undisturbed buck feeds at the end of a meadow — it's worth a few seconds to get the body into alignment behind the rifle. But, as with all the shooting basics, the time to practice isn't when you're lining up on a buck. Once the concept is understood, it can be practiced in your living room as well as at the range. Eventually it becomes habitual for the sights to naturally align on the target the instant you drop into position — and you're free to concentrate on the shooting principles that will put your bullet in the right place.

The B.R.A.S.S. Rule

Of all the U.S. armed forces, the Marine Corps prides itself most on individual marksmanship and goes to the most trouble to both train its recruits and maintain an acceptable marksmanship level among all Marines. After some 15 years of regular and reserve service, I'll admit that I've found a few things on which the Marine Corps and I don't agree. But their ability and methodology for turning out good shooters isn't among them. The Marine system is based on sound, steady shooting positions and good body alignment. But the heart of it is the "B.R.A.S.S." rule: Breathe, Relax, Aim in, check Sight align-

ment, Squeeze the trigger. We'll look at each of these concepts in more detail.

First, breath control. You can't live without breathing — but you also can't get off an accurate shot while you're breathing, so there has to be a compromise in there somewhere. The problem is that the rising and falling of your chest while breathing affects your entire body, and it creates enough movement to cause a miss at any range.

On a target, severe vertical stringing of shots, especially with a beginning shooter, is usually the result of breathing. The solution is simple. As you're getting into position for a shot, take a few deep breaths. When you get lined up on your target — paper or game — take a last deep breath, let it partway out, and take your shot. The reason for letting it partway out is that you don't want to shoot with the pressure of an expanded chest. And you don't want to let it all the way out, because you need a few seconds to finalize your sight picture and squeeze the trigger.

The key concept is: You can't shoot while you're breathing. In a hunting situation you're going to be excited, and you might well have just climbed a hill or dashed to a favorable shooting spot. You'll be breathing much harder than you would be on the range, if only from excitement. There's a better than even chance that you won't be able to get your breathing completely under control — which is why it's so important to form good habits on the range. Again, *you can't shoot while breathing.* Take a few breaths, let the last one partway out, and try to get your shot off. If you can't get the sights to steady before you need more air, exhale, inhale, and try again.

Recently I had to make a difficult long-range shot at a moose, and I'd just run a mile to get into position. I had a wonder-

It's impossible to shoot accurately while you're breathing; the up-and-down motion of your chest will do the same thing to your bullets. Take a deep breath, let most of it out, and then hold it while you squeeze the trigger. If you don't get the shot off, take another breath and start all over again.

fully steady rest, but the altitude was pretty high, and I couldn't get my breathing under control. I could see the crosshairs going up and down — and completely above and below the moose. It took several tries before I could get a shot off, but there was no point in rushing — I simply couldn't shoot until I could hold my breath long enough for a dead-steady shot.

After you've taken several deep breaths, you're in a good shooting position, and you're pretty much all set, you make a conscious decision that this is the one. You take a good, deep breath and let it partway out, relaxing your entire body as you do. You see, you can hold your breath, but you can't stop your heart from beating. Each heartbeat sends blood coursing through your muscles, causing a slight muscular tremor.

And the more rigid your muscles are, the more pronounced the tremor. Relax. Concentrate on the target, the sights, and the trigger squeeze that will get your bullet to the right place.

Aim in. You've already been aiming at the target. But you've been breathing, so your sights have been moving a bit. Now you're holding your breath, you're as relaxed as possible, and this is it. Put your sights exactly where you want them. Make certain you know exactly how the animal is standing, and visualize where the vitals lie and the path your bullet must follow to reach them.

Check your sight alignment. With military shooting, this is meant to apply to open and aperture sights, meaning that, once everything else is accomplished, you

Out in the field, when you're excited and breathing hard from strenuous walking with an unfamiliar load, breath control becomes one of the most critical items in successful shooting.

check one last time to make sure the front sight is properly centered in the rear notch or sight ring. For the hunter who uses iron sights, it's good advice. But for the scope user, it's equally good. Take a last-second check to make sure your sight picture is clear and that your crosshairs are exactly where you want them.

Now, and only now, you can squeeze the trigger. Trigger control is one of the most important concepts in all types of shooting, and vital afield; the life of an animal rests on it. Much fuss can be made about proper finger placement on the trigger, but the important thing is that it be comfortable for the shooter. Generally speaking, you want neither too much nor too little finger on the trigger. For most people the best control will be just forward of the last joint. Too much finger on the trigger can cause horizontal movement, but whatever is comfortable is best.

The words "trigger squeeze" have been used so much that I suspect they've lost their meaning. Quite possibly, the word

The best finger placement for good trigger control is usually just forward of the outermost joint — not on the tip but on the thickest portion of the finger's pad.

A crisp, light trigger pull is nice, but some of America's most famous hunting rifles—including most lever actions—have what target shooters would call awful trigger pulls. The actual trigger pull of your rifle isn't nearly as important as your complete familiarity with it.

"squeeze" isn't quite right anyway. You don't squeeze a trigger as you would a lemon, because you don't exert pressure with your entire hand. Your shooting hand is wrapped firmly but not too tightly around the pistolgrip or small of the stock. No death grip! Your index finger extends naturally to the trigger. When everything else is right, you begin exerting slow, steady, *even* pressure on the trigger with your index finger.

It's often said that you should be surprised when the gun goes off. I don't think so. With any practice at all, you know your trigger pull, and you know approximately when the trigger will break. No shot fired should ever be a surprise—that's called an accidental discharge! On the other hand, even though you should know approximately when the rifle will fire, you must not *anticipate* it. You must simply maintain your sight picture while exerting steady pressure on the trigger until the rifle fires. It's easy to say, and really not all that difficult to do. The important aspect in field shooting is that at any second the situation can change dramatically. If it does—if the animal changes position slightly, if you run out of breath, if the sight picture slips — you must be prepared to call off the shot, to get your finger off the trigger and try it again.

In serious target shooting, the weight of a trigger pull is extremely important. Depending on the event, the trigger pull is probably controlled by formal rules and specifications, and it may well be measured by ounces of pressure, not pounds. For deliberate varmint shooting, such as long-range work on woodchucks, an extremely light trigger pull is advantageous. In field shooting on big game, however, a too-light trigger pull is downright dangerous. A hunting rifle trigger requires deliberate, conscious pressure to cause the rifle to fire, for you must be able to call off the shot at any split-second until the firing pin falls.

Most custom gunsmiths tend to set the triggers of hunting rifles at about 2½ to 3 pounds. By contrast, in these days of product liability concerns, most factory triggers are closer to five or six pounds. A slightly lighter trigger is easier to control; you don't need to exert as much pressure over as long a period of time to make the gun fire. However, the exact weight of the trigger pull isn't really critical in field shooting. What is critical is that you know the trigger pull on

your rifle. "Snapping" or dry-firing does no damage to a centerfire rifle (don't do it with rimfires). Just make certain the rifle is empty by checking the chamber, and you can become thoroughly familiar with your trigger pull — and practice all the other shooting basics — right in your living room.

It used to be that most bolt-action rifles had fully adjustable triggers, but in these lawsuit-happy days, readily adjustable factory triggers are rare. Even so, the triggers of most bolt-action rifles can be adjusted — but I strongly suggest that the job be left to a good gunsmith. If you choose to have your trigger adjusted, a three-pound pull is close to minimal for a hunting rifle. Because of the nature of their firing mechanisms, the triggers of most other action types — lever actions, semiautos, and others — are not adjustable at all, and are usually downright dangerous to mess with.

Well, we've discussed the basics that apply to all types of shooting, whether on big game, tin cans, or in formal competition. In chapters 10, 11, and 12 we'll put these basics to use in various field shooting positions. But first, let's spend some time making sure we have the right equipment for shots at big game.

3

Matching the Gun to the Game and to the Shooter

Just a century ago, sweeping changes were being made in sporting rifles. Muzzle-loaders were at their absolute peak in accuracy and precision, and were still winning all the matches, but the self-contained metallic cartridge had already made them obsolete. A dozen different single shot rifles comprised the bulk of the available sporters, but the lever actions were there too, not only the pipsqueak-chambered Winchester '73, but also the '76 and the '86, handling serious hunting cartridges like the .45–75, .40–82, and a host of others. Today only the .45–70 Government survives from that era—definitely a dinosaur, but just as good now as it was then. But as popular as the lever actions were, they were expensive and relatively scarce. I think it's safe to say that 100 years ago, in the late 1880s, the single shot rifle was the favored hunting arm.

The next decade would bring incredibly rapid change. By the turn of the century, there were Savage, Marlin, and Winchester lever actions firing small-caliber smokeless cartridges. There were also turnbolt guns, an action type seen only rarely in the blackpowder era. By 1900 the Mauser existed in its current form and was becoming the world standard military rifle. The Americans had the Krag and were already experimenting with the Springfield, a modified Mauser action. The British had the Lee-Enfield, an action they would retain for half a century. The great single shots were still in the field, but "little" cartridges like the .30–30 Winchester and .30–40 Krag seemed to be just as effective as the old slow-moving blackpowder numbers—and they were available in lighter, handier repeating rifles. If anything, the transition from blackpowder to smokeless was

A century ago the single shot was America's most popular hunting-rifle action. Today, in modern rifles like Ruger's Number One, the single shot still has a lot of appeal.

Winchester's Model 1894 is one of the world's most successful and famous hunting rifles. It remains popular to this day, and the ejection mechanism of the current version has been modified so that it can be mounted with a scope.

quicker than the transition from muzzle-loader to breechloader had been.

It's another safe bet to say that in the first few decades of this century, the lever action was America's No. 1 sporting arm. Winchester and Marlin had their great saddle guns, plus hard-hitting rifles in long-gone smokeless chamberings like .33 and .35 Winchester. For the well-heeled turn-of-the-century big-bore man, there was even the Model 1895 Winchester in .405. Savage arrived on the scene late with the Model 99, but it was a revolutionary action and was quickly offered in revolutionary chamberings. These included the .300 Savage, which retains a following to this day (and in its day approximated the mild ballistics of the then-current military .30–06 load), and the hot .250–3000, the first sporting cartridge to reach the amazing velocity of 3,000 feet per second.

There were other action types out there as well. The bolt action wasn't readily available in this country, not yet. But influential hunters like Theodore Roosevelt quickly obtained Springfield actions, and the first "sporterized" bolt guns were born. A very few Mausers too found their way into this country. But the day of the bolt action hadn't dawned yet.

Instead there were slide actions from Colt and long-recoil semiautomatics from Remington—both attempting with some success to make inroads into the lever-action market occupied by Marlin, Winchester, and Savage. The Colt Lightning, a slide action, was actually quite a popular rifle in its day, and Remington also had a fine pump gun. I used a borrowed Colt Lightning in .25–20 on my first mountain lion hunt, and a slicker and faster action never existed.

Early Remington semiautos, such as the famed 1908-vintage Model 8, were distinguished by the recoil spring surrounding the barrel. They were chambered for long-gone rimless cartridges like the .25 and .30 Remington—and also the .35 Remington, which today remains a standby cartridge for close-cover hunting.

Winchester too was into the semiautomatic business early on with its Models 1905, 1907, and 1910 self-loading rifles chambered for long-forgotten cartridges like .32, .35, .351, and .401 Winchester Self-Loading cartridges. The Winchester rifles were lighter and handier, but their cartridges lacked the efficiency and versatility of Remington's offerings.

The slide actions and semiautos had their following, as they do today, but America's premier hunting rifle was a lever action until well after World War I. After that conflict, though, surplus military bolt actions became available in large numbers for the first time. Springfields and 1917 Enfields were released to the public by the thousands by the Director of Civilian

Marksmanship (DCM). The .30–06 gradually caught up to and then passed the .30–30 as *the* American sporting cartridge. Thousands upon thousands of returning GIs had been impressed with the accuracy and reliability of both the Springfield and the Enfield, and there was no doubting the long-range efficiency of the .30–06 over the .30–30.

After World War I Remington used its wartime tooling to produce the Model 30 series, essentially a 1917 Enfield action, while Winchester introduced the Model 54. The Great Depression undoubtedly slowed things down, but gradually the bolt action was taking over. Just as the nation was recovering from the Depression days and the gun industry was getting back on its feet, the next global conflict came along. World War II not only slowed things down but halted the production of sporting firearms for four years. By the time the war ended, the Springfield was out of production and the semiautomatic Garand in .30–06 was America's service rifle. The Garand was, and still is, much-loved as a battle rifle. But another wartime development, the little M1 Carbine, had been produced in the millions. Firing a straight-cased .30-caliber cartridge only slightly more powerful than a pistol round, the .30 Carbine was light, quick-firing, and dependable. It was a great favorite among GIs, though most combat veterans admitted that it was a bit light in stopping power.

With the total conversion of the military to self-loading actions, and with millions of soldiers, sailors, and Marines returning home, it would seem natural that after World War II the semiautomatic would have become the most popular sporting action. It never happened. Perhaps it was because the Garand, wonderful in combat, simply couldn't be converted to a light

The bolt-action rifle is the darling of today's gunwriters, and with good reason — it's accurate, dependable, and chambered to versatile, flat-shooting modern cartridges. This bolt-action Remington is a .30–06 — hardly an ultramodern cartridge, but it's the cartridge that turned Americans toward bolt actions, and it remains one of the best choices for all-around hunting purposes.

sporter — and because Marsh Williams' Carbine, already sporter-weight, lacked the power desired for deer. In the first two decades after World War II, the bolt action completed its ascendancy.

The bolt action is the darling of the press, and certainly seems to be America's most popular rifle action, with the lever a distant second, though well ahead of pumps, autos, and single shots.

That's just a little bit of background. There remain five action types available in sporting rifles — bolt, lever, slide, semiautomatic, and single shot. I guess you could make that six if you count the occasional double-barrelled rifle seen in this country. The fact that the bolt action is the most popular doesn't necessarily make it the best, certainly not in all circumstances. It's also worth noting that fine rifles are available in all action types today.

The bolt action pretty much rules the roost from coast to coast, but there are strong regional preferences for certain actions, and even models. Remington's semiauto and slide actions, for instance, do well in the Northeast and Southeast, where the close-cover deer hunting calls for a quick-handling rifle that offers fast repeat shots. Pennsylvania, America's No. 1 deer state in terms of hunter numbers, is undoubtedly Remington's best market for the slide-action rifle — semiautomatics aren't legal hunting arms in that state.

The Northeast too is a great stronghold for the lever-action rifle, as are the rainforests of the Pacific Northwest. But it's interesting to note that in all the years I've lived in California, I've never seen a new Savage 99 on a dealer's shelf. Lots of Marlins, Winchesters, and Browning's BLR, but not the Savage, and with its rotary or box magazine capable of handling sharp-pointed bullets, it's a perfectly sound choice for any western hunting.

To some degree, action choice is a matter of personal preference; whatever rifle gives you the most confidence is the right choice. Actually, most of the advantages one action type may have over another are more theoretical than actual. For example, the bolt-action rifle tends to have a bit more potential accuracy than semiautos, slide actions, or lever guns. But potential accuracy and our ability to put same to use in the field are two different things. All the action types offer perfectly adequate accuracy for virtually any field shooting.

It's also said that the bolt action (next to the single shot, obviously) is the slowest action type for repeat shots. Theoretically that's true, but a good man with a bolt action is unbelievably fast — and besides, the idea is to make that first shot count, not get another shot on its way quickly!

I will not recommend one action type over another. Personally, I have the most experience with bolt actions, lever actions,

single shots, and doubles. But there's a reason for that. All of the sporting slide actions and semiautos eject to the right. As a left-handed shooter, I've never been comfortable having that ejection port in my face.

For lefties, that's a point worth considering. For the rest of us, any action type is fully capable of performing any task you ask of it in the field. Here's a more detailed rundown on modern sporting actions.

Slide Actions

The slide action is a time-honored American tradition, and in shotguns it remains extremely popular. In rifles, well, there's never been a great proliferation of pump guns. Colt dropped out of the slide-action-rifle business many years ago, and since then this segment of the market has pretty much been owned by Remington. Other than Remington's long series of slide actions, the only other recent centerfire I

Remington's slide-action rifles have a long and glorious history. The current Model 7600, shown in .35 Whelen, remains a standby for close-cover hunting — a role it fills as well as any rifle can.

can call to mind is the Savage 170. It was dropped a number of years ago, but was actually a very slick-handling little rifle. But even though it's a one-company race, there seems little danger that the slide action will vanish; those Remington pump guns are much loved by those who use them.

Over the years, I've seen them used and used well in a lot of different places from Pennsylvania deer camps to Alaska and Africa. An interesting observation is that for most of the hunters I know who use slide actions, that action gun is the *only* rifle they hunt with. And that generally means they know it well and can shoot it.

There are a couple of good reasons for owning a pump gun. Perhaps the best one applies to a serious shotgunner who uses a slide action but also wants a rifle to do some casual big-game hunting. For a guy like that, the pump gun is a familiar and logical choice — and there are millions of bird hunters who prefer a pump gun. A second reason is fast second and subsequent shots. As I said, the most important shot is that first one, but once in a while everybody needs more than one.

The slide action is indeed very fast, but it also offers another advantage. In a fast-breaking situation, such as a whitetail buck jumped at close quarters, the slide action actually helps get you back on target for the second shot. After firing the first shot, your supporting arm snaps the fore-end to the rear, then pushes it back forward to complete the cycling of the action. The forward motion is toward the target, and with that forward motion you're actually unconsciously pushing the rifle into alignment with the target. Any shotgunner who uses a pump gun is aware of this; for second and third shots, all you have to do is watch the birds and follow your arm. That's where the

speed of the pump gun comes in — not in cycling the action, but in getting back on target.

Slide actions do not have the mechanical leverage for extracting spent cases that a bolt action offers, but neither do levers or semiautos. This factor means nothing to shooters of factory ammo, but for handloaders it means that all cases must be fully resized and loads kept on the conservative side. The serious handloader would probably not choose this action type, but beyond that I simply can't think of any reason not to select a slide action.

Today's Model Six, Remington's latest and most improved slide action, is a beautiful rifle. It shoots well, and individual rifles make you question the adage about the bolt action's accuracy supremacy. It allows a scope to be mounted low over the receiver, and it's offered in a wide variety of versatile, powerful hunting cartridges. I think it's at its best in close cover with only the occasional medium to long-range opportunity. Its cartridges are primarily deer cartridges, but hunters who swear by it have proven to me that it isn't out of place anywhere!

Semiautomatic

There are certainly more semiautomatic sporting rifles available than slide actions, but surprisingly not all that many more. As an action type, the semiautomatic (at least, today's semiautomatic) is extremely reliable and certainly fast. Modern semiautos are also extremely accurate. Browning's BAR and Remington's Model Four are usually fine shooters, and Heckler & Koch's .308 and .30–06 sporters are often real tack-drivers. There's also a slight recoil reduction obtained from a gas-operated semiauto like the Browning or Remington.

Since Americans' choices in sporting rifles have historically followed the current military arms, it's amazing that the semiautomatic isn't more popular than it is. John Falk, public-relations director for Olin-Winchester, still prizes his Winchester Model 100—but it was one of several fine semiauto sporters that never gained popularity.

The semiauto's lack of accuracy is largely a myth, and the same can be said of pumps and levers. All the action types offer plenty of accuracy for virtually all field shooting. This Remington semiauto was plenty accurate for precise shot placement on a wild turkey, and you can't ask for more than that.

As with the slide action, there is really no reason not to select a semiauto as a hunting rifle. The same consideration regarding careful resizing of reloads applies, and the semiauto might not be legal to hunt with in your area, but other than that, today's semiautomatic is a fine hunting rifle. It's offered in more makes and models than the slide action, so chances are there's a rifle out there that will appeal to almost anyone. And it's available in more chamberings, from Ruger's fast-handling little .44 Magnum carbine and "Mini-.30" in 7.62x39 Russian all the way up to Browning's .338 Magnum BAR.

There is one caution, though, that should be mentioned. The semiautomatic

can't be babied. When you chamber a round, it's important to let the bolt snap forward to make certain it seats fully. That's noisy. I was on a deer stand in New Hampshire with a Heckler & Koch .30–06 semiauto one time, and I'd forgotten that little message. After sneaking into position, I quietly eased a cartridge into the chamber and sat down to wait. A buck did come along, and I waited until he was broadside at about 35 yards. But when I squeezed the trigger, nothing happened.

Well, there wasn't much choice, especially for a lefty. I had to take the rifle down from my shoulder very slowly, get hold of the operating handle, pull it rearward, then turn it loose and hope it worked. It fired that time, but the deer knew exactly what was happening; instead of a broadside shot at bow range, I had a running shot in heavy cover. I got him, but I was pretty upset with that rifle.

Actually, though, it wasn't the rifle's fault. It was strictly mine. I had forgotten that you simply can't ease cartridges into a semiauto's chamber. That brings up some important safety considerations inherent to this action type. For the stand hunter, it's no problem. Take an empty rifle onto the stand, load it up once, and you've made all the noise you're going to make. When you leave, unload.

The still-hunter in rough country has a bit of a problem, though. I don't know about you, but I won't negotiate rough country with a round in the chamber. With a semiauto, if you unload (and you should) to climb down an embankment, over a boulder, or through a fence, accept that you're going to make a bit of noise when you load up again. For this reason, I see the semiauto at its best for the stand hunter or for open-country hunting, where that mechanical noise might not be so critical. But again, there's really no reason not to select this action type for virtually any hunting.

Lever Actions

Perhaps if John Wayne had used a slide-action Colt Lightning, we'd feel differently about lever actions than we do. But he didn't. He chose a Model 92 Winchester, as have three generations of western actors, and even though the Western movie is out of fashion on the silver screen, the feeling American hunters have for their lever guns is deep-rooted and virtually unshakable. We can talk about bolt actions all we want, but no bolt-action sporting rifle will ever approach the production figures of Winchester's Model 1894. And at this writing, Marlin *is* America's largest producer of sporting rifles.

The lever-action rifle's claim to fame is as a short, light, fast-handling carbine for close-cover hunting. As such, it has been chambered for modest, short-range cartridges—the .30–30 and .32 Special in Winchesters, the .30–30 and .35 Remington in Marlins. There's simply no way of reckoning the deer that have fallen to these rifles, but that's only part of the lever-action story.

As mentioned earlier, lever actions were available in powerful cartridges suitable for any big-game hunting 100 years ago—the 1886 Winchester was even chambered for the huge .50–110. In 1936 the last incarnation of the '86 was introduced as the Winchester Model 71, and its only chambering was the brand-new .348, a powerful large-capacity cartridge that pushed heavy bullets at surprising velocities.

In recent years there's been a surge of interest in more powerful lever-action chamberings—Marlin's .444 and .45–70, Winchester's .375 and .356 Winchester, and Browning's reissue of the Model 71 in .348. The limitation of all of these has been and is the tubular magazine. "Traditional" lever actions are limited to flat-pointed bullets since the nose of one cartridge in a tubular magazine rests against the primer of the one ahead of it. Sharp-pointed bullets can cause detonation in the magazine under recoil—a most unpleasant situation. Flat-pointed bullets have poor aerodynamics; they lose velocity very quickly and limit the ranging capabilities of the rifle firing them. There's a plus, though. Flat points and extremely rounded points do set up more quickly in game than spitzer bullets, and I believe they transfer energy (and resultant shock) more quickly. It wouldn't

The Savage 99, though it boasts a 90-year history, is a non-traditional lever action in that its box magazine will handle sharp-pointed bullets, which are unsafe in the tubular magazines of the traditional saddle gun. Scope-mounted and chambering flat-shooting cartridges, the 99 is suitable for virtually any type of hunting.

surprise me to learn that the blunt shape of the .30–30 bullet has a lot to do with its effectiveness on deer-sized game. It certainly isn't its paper ballistics!

However, with apologies to John Wayne and the Ringo Kid, the tubular-magazine rifle isn't the only lever action. Starting with the Model 1895 Winchester and continuing on to the great Savage 99, there's a long tradition of lever actions suited for flat-shooting cartridges handling spitzer (sharp-pointed) bullets. The Model 1895 (recently reissued by Browning) was the only successful lever gun chambering .30–06-length cartridges, but the 99 Savage has been offered in a host of flat-shooting chamberings.

More recently there have been several excellent developments. Sako had a wonderful little lever action, the only European lever gun I'm aware of. For some reason it was not successful, and hasn't been made for years. Winchester had one of the best in its Model 88, and it was offered in superb cartridges like the .284 and .358 Winchester. Why this rifle didn't last is beyond me, but it didn't.

Browning seems to stand alone with a successful modern lever-action design, and the BLR is a dandy. Perhaps the secret is its traditional lines; it looks like John Wayne's rifle, but mechanically there's little com-

parison. It has a short-throw lever and a box magazine, and is chambered for flat-shooting rounds like the .257 Roberts, 7mm–08, .308, and .358. So long as the Browning BLR stays in production, there's still a lever action suited for almost any hunting situation.

Claims about inaccuracy have long been hurled at the lever action. It's true that the two-piece stock doesn't allow for the best bedding, and trigger pulls on lever guns are usually horrible. They also can't be adjusted and retain any measure of safety. However, I've found a large degree of variance among individual lever guns. All offer plenty of accuracy to get the job done, and occasionally you'll get a rifle that is a real surprise. I've had Savage 99s that were superbly accurate. Marlins usually shoot well. And right now I have two Winchesters in my gun safe — one a Model 94 in .30–30 and the other a Model 71 in .348 — that shoot as well as any production bolt action I've owned. In any case, at the ranges lever actions and lever-action cartridges are at their best, tiny groups from a benchrest aren't important.

In the past a very real criticism of some lever actions has been their top ejection, meaning that mounting a scope low over the receiver was nearly impossible. This applies primarily to Winchesters; Marlins and Savages have been "scopable" for generations. Today's Winchesters have been modified to eject at an angle to the right, so that problem exists only with older rifles.

The great strength of the lever action is said to be its fast-handling capabilities, and I agree completely. The lever action is often a short-barrelled carbine, and in that configuration is light and compact. You can carry it all day—its receiver offers a perfectly balanced carrying point—and at day's end it will still come up like lightning. Even in longer-barrelled models, the lever action puts a lot of metal between the

Winchester's Model 71 in .348, recently revived by Browning, is a classic hard-hitting close-cover lever action. This one, a Deluxe version with peep sight, is surprisingly accurate, and its big, flat-pointed bullet hits like a freight train.

hands, offering exceptional balance and fast swinging.

However, unlike the other action types discussed so far, the lever action does not offer the most versatile cartridges. The traditional tubular-magazine lever gun, whether in .30–30, .35 Remington, or the big Marlin .444 or .45–70, is a 150-yard rifle. The newer .307 and .356 Winchester cartridges will add 50 yards or so. In rifles like the Savage, Browning, and Winchester 88, cartridges such as .308, .250 Savage, and .284 Winchester will add another 50 to 100 yards. At this point we're reaching out pretty well, beyond the distance most of us should be shooting at game. Even so, the lever-action rifle is limited by its cartridges, and is a bit out of place for true open-country hunting.

It does have the advantage of being incredibly fast for repeat shots, and the action can be cycled without interrupting the shooter's concentration or sight picture. However, that depends a bit on the shooting position you prefer. If you happen to be lying down or resting across a flat rock, you may need to go through some interesting gyrations to cycle the action!

Honest, I really like lever actions. But I don't use them in open country. I tend to use them in close cover, or for game such as black bear and wild hogs where I know the shots will be reasonably short. To me, the lever action isn't a rifle to use where deliberate, precise shooting is called for. Instead, the lever action is a rifle for fast shooting in close cover. Under such circumstances you won't be handicapped by a heavy trigger — you won't even be aware of it. You won't have to worry about holding a bit high because of the rainbow trajectory. And it won't matter that your rifle's best group ever was 2½ inches at 100 yards. What matters is that you get that rifle up fast and on target, and that's what the lever action is all about.

Single Shots

The single-shot rifle vanished from the American hunting scene more than 50 years ago, and there was every reason to believe it was gone for good. Bill Ruger, one of the truly great firearms geniuses of all time, thought differently. He modified and modernized a falling-block single-shot action and introduced the Ruger Number One — a great action on a great rifle, and a great success story.

One of the beautiful things about the single-shot action, especially one as strong as the Ruger, is that it can digest virtually

When Bill Ruger redesigned a century-old action and brought out his Number One single shot, some knowledgeable people thought he was crazy. He wasn't; more than a quarter century later, the rifle remains extremely popular. The single shot's only drawback, in my view, is that it must be either completely empty or fully loaded, making it a questionable choice in some situations.

anything. From the factory the Ruger has been offered in virtually every cartridge imaginable, from .22 Hornet up to .458 Winchester Magnum. I've seen Number Ones rebarrelled to .470 and other big Nitro-Express rounds. It offers the utmost in cartridge versatility, and because the action is simple and compact and there's no magazine, it can be built quite light.

The Ruger, of course, isn't the only modern single shot, but it was the first and has remained the most popular. Browning has a fine single shot, an exposed-hammer gun similar to the Winchester Hi-Wall of the last century. Thompson/Center too has a superb break-open that offers interchangeable barrels.

As a hunting rifle, the single shot has a lot going for it. It's simple, goof-proof, and light in weight; and all three modern single shots have great handling abilities. There's also a tremendous amount of appeal to the "one-shot" concept. One shot, one animal—the way it's supposed to be. Indeed, carrying a single shot does make you extremely careful with that one shot.

I have a Ruger in .243 that's a favorite pronghorn rifle. I had another in .270 that I hunted deer with quite a bit. And I even used a Number One Tropical Rifle in .375 H&H on an African hunt. They're great rifles, and I do believe the one-shot capacity makes better hunters.

There are a couple of drawbacks. The two-piece stock can make accuracy unpredictable from one rifle to another, especially with sporter-weight barrels. My .243 has been a tack-driver since the day I owned it, likewise a heavy-barrelled .22–250. That .270, though, was a problem rifle. It provided adequate hunting accuracy, but it was erratic enough that I worried about it in open country.

There is one other problem that the hunter should take into account. The single shot is either fully loaded or fully *unloaded*; there's no magazine, so either the chamber has a round in it or the gun is completely empty. For most hunting this is not a problem, and certainly the chamber can be loaded and unloaded quickly and silently. But on horseback hunts, where the rifle must have an empty chamber but might be needed on short notice, it's a potential problem that requires some advance planning and practice to solve.

There are two other situations in which the single shot might not be the best choice—in extreme cold and for use on dangerous game. In subzero weather you simply don't want to fumble around for shells any more than you have to, and if you need a second shot from a single shot, you will have to come up with a cartridge from somewhere and manually get it into the chamber. Hunting dangerous game speaks for itself; the one-shot concept is a good one, but if an angry bear is coming your way, it isn't concepts that will stop him.

Doubles

The double-barrelled rifle, in both side-by-side and over/under form, is popular in many parts of the world but has always been a rarity in America. There are a couple of good reasons: Americans, with their wealth of good firearms publications, tend to be pretty knowledgeable about firearms, and they place a premium on accuracy. Because of the difficulty of getting two rifle barrels to shoot to the same place, double rifles simply aren't accurate by our standards. Yes, the very rare one is, and Valmet's system of adjustable barrel hangers allows that gun to be regulated by the shooter to a high degree of accuracy. Doubles will offer more than adequate hunting accuracy, but even at their best they can't compete with bolt actions.

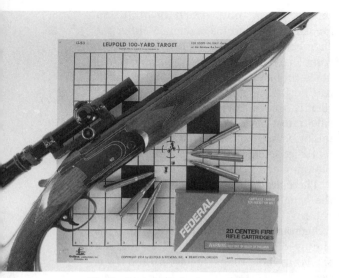

The double-barrelled rifle is a real rarity in America. Although nothing offers a faster and more reliable second shot, doubles are extremely costly and not particularly accurate. The Valmet over/under, with adjustable barrel hangers, solves both of those problems.

The other problem with doubles is cost. Double rifles are tremendously expensive, primarily because of the handwork required to get those barrels to shoot together. In that regard, the Valmet is a tremendous breakthrough; a Valmet over/ under rifle can be had for the cost of an over/under shotgun, while a traditionally regulated double rifle will cost about as much money as a car.

I've messed around with a Valmet over/ under .30–06 on quite a variety of game, and have used three different side-by-side .470s on dangerous African game. The advertised strength of the double, and it's very real, is that nothing is as fast for a second shot when you need it the most. "Needing it the most" is usually defined as stopping a charge, but there's absolutely no reason the Valmet, Browning Continental, Beretta, Winchester Double Xpress, Heym, or any of the other modern doubles in deer-sized calibers wouldn't be perfectly at home in the whitetail woods.

Bolt Actions

We come at last to the bolt-action rifle, the most common action type wherever big game is hunted today. Like most and perhaps all modern gunwriters, I have to admit to a bias for the bolt action. I do use most of the other action types, but the bolt action has occupied most of my writing—perhaps because it gives me so much to write about. With its sturdy lockup, one-piece stock, and easily altered bedding, it

The Weatherby Fibermark, featuring a synthetic stock that's strong, stable, and impervious to the elements, is a state-of-the-art bolt action. One of the bolt action's strong points, besides its strength and accuracy, is that it can be chambered to the most powerful and flat-shooting modern cartridges.

tends to be extremely accurate. And if it isn't, you can usually play with it until it becomes so. You can work up different loads for it to your heart's content, and it can be chambered for literally anything. There are no restrictions on the bullet shapes it will handle, and it will usually feed almost anything.

It is probably this versatility, plus the proliferation of makes and models, that led to the ascendancy of the bolt action. Actually, its drawbacks are very few. It is potentially a bit slower for the second shot than a lever, slide, or semiauto. However, once you learn to operate a bolt action properly—from the shoulder with your cheek remaining in place—it is very fast. And in any case, very few shooters are good enough and quick enough to realize the rapid-fire potential of any action type. At one time it could be said that the bolt action was heavier, but with modern synthetic stocks and today's lighter barrels, bolt actions can be built as light as anyone would want.

It is true that a bolt action has a hard time matching the quick-handling capabilities of a lever-action carbine. But a well-stocked bolt gun can and does handle like a dream. It also generally has a trigger that is more readily adjustable than is the trigger on other action types, and with its powerful camming action it is literally impossible to jam. It can be short-stroked, meaning that the bolt is not pulled far enough to the rear to eject the fired case, thus causing a double-feeding jam. But so can a lever or pump, and these are shooter errors that practice should prevent.

The bolt action is available in cartridges ideally suited for any type of hunting the world over, and in rifle configurations so diverse as to boggle the mind. All these factors help explain why it has become so popular.

The modern bolt action is available in cartridges suited for hunting literally any type of game anywhere in the world. Its accuracy and strength, coupled with this versatility, have made it popular today—but it certainly isn't the only suitable rifle action, regardless of where or what you hunt.

Summing Up

What, then, is the best rifle for you? That depends entirely upon the type of hunting you plan to do and, more importantly, the type of rifle you are most comfortable with. If your hunting is entirely in the deep woods or thick brush, you will be more than adequately served by a traditional lever action. On the other hand, if you hunt more open country—or if you intend to hunt different types of game in different parts of the country—one of the other action types might serve you best. Choice of action is to a large degree tied to choice of cartridge—so we'll turn to that next.

4

Cartridge Selection

When you're punching holes in paper, the rifle that will print the tightest group is the best choice. When you're rolling a tin can down a hill, the rifle that will hit it the fastest and most often and roll it the farthest is the one to use. But in big-game shooting, the rifle chosen doesn't really matter all that much, so long as the shooter has confidence in it. Cartridge selection is another matter; all the faith in the world won't turn the trick if the cartridge and the bullet it fires aren't adequate for the game.

In the blackpowder era, velocity as we know it simply didn't exist. Most rifle cartridges coasted along in the 1,400-feet-per-second range, and a few ultra-high-velocity rounds produced in the vicinity of 1,750 fps. The only way to achieve more power was through more bullet weight and more frontal diameter (larger caliber). The smokeless era turned the world topsy-turvy.

Suddenly the tiny .30–30, pushing a 170-grain bullet at 2,200 feet per second, seemed to kill game more surely than old favorites like the .40–65, firing a .40-caliber 260-grain bullet at 1,420 fps.

As smokeless cartridges developed further, it seems two schools of thought evolved with them—the proponents of small-caliber, high-velocity cartridges; and those who favor larger calibers and heavier bullets at lower velocities. Mind you, it's really the same campfire argument Teddy Roosevelt might have had over which was best for grizzly—his newfangled .30–06 Springfield or his favorite old Winchester '76 in .45–75. In today's format it's probably typified by the 50-year war of words between Jack O'Connor and Elmer Keith. O'Connor stressed bullet placement, and his favorite cartridge was the .270 Winchester. Elmer also believed in bullet placement, certainly, but he loved to write about "raking shots," and he wanted something on the order of a 250 to 275-grain .33-caliber bullet, with velocities in the 2,600 range—which is about 500 fps slower than O'Connor (or anybody else) could push his 130-grain .270 bullet.

There is clearly a big difference between the two viewpoints, but by the standards of the blackpowder era, both Keith and O'Connor were touting smallbore cartridges and ultra-high velocity. It's likely too that both of them went a bit too far. Keith's .333 OKH wildcat was undoubtedly everything he said it was, but he also rated the .270 as a marginal coyote rifle. It's a bit more than that. On the other hand, O'Connor used the .270 for game such as

elk, moose, and grizzly. It did the job for him, but under today's hunting conditions I'm a bit uncomfortable taking the .270 up that far.

So what do you look for in a hunting cartridge? Velocity, energy, caliber, bullet weight? Let's take a brief look at each before we talk about modern hunting cartridges.

First, velocity. On game, it's quite possible to have too much of a good thing as well as not enough. Velocity does indeed do wonderful things for you. It flattens trajectory, simplifying long-range shooting. At a certain level that seems to be unknown, it apparently imparts devastating shock to a hit animal. Velocity, in conjunction with resistance from animal tissue, also causes

A few decades ago the published velocity figures from ammunition manufacturers had a lot of "blue sky" optimism in them. These days, with so many handloaders using accurate chronographs, the ammo makers have cleaned up their acts considerably; you can count on your rifle developing velocities that are very close to the ammo makers' claims.

bullet expansion. And there's the bullet-makers' big problem — too much velocity, and expansion is too rapid; too little velocity, and expansion is too slow. And since bullets begin to slow down the instant they leave the muzzle, no bullet has ever been or can be designed that will function uniformly at all ranges and at all velocities.

The most uniform bullet performance will be at lower starting velocities — let's say, just for argument's sake, 2,200 to 2,400 feet per second. These velocities seem to be low enough so that explosive bullet expansion will not occur with most jacketed soft-points, but reliable, consistent expansion can be achieved.

On the other hand, something in the neighborhood of 3,200 feet per second seems to be the upper limit of hunting-

Left to right, 7mm Remington Magnum, .270 Winchester, .280 Remington, .30–06, *and* .300 Winchester Magnum — *a fine selection of flat-shooting, versatile cartridges suited for a tremendous variety of hunting needs.*

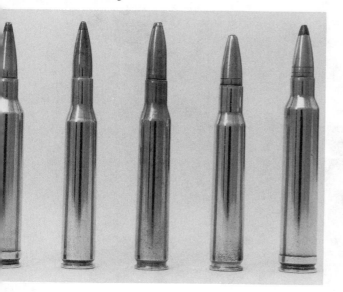

bullet controllability. There are cartridges that go faster, but they're generally loaded with varmint-weight bullets designed to virtually disintegrate on impact, not penetrate as a big-game bullet must. A quick look at a ballistics chart will reveal that the few hunting cartridges with starting velocities over 3,200 feet per second are viewed almost exclusively as long-range propositions. They have to be; consistent performance at point-blank range and at 250 yards (when the velocity is 600 fps or so less) is virtually impossible for a bulletmaker to achieve. Those cartridges in the 2,400-fps or less category are usually your short-range woods cartridges. And everything else — the full spectrum of general-purpose hunting cartridges — lies in between.

Kinetic energy, expressed in foot-pounds, is one way to measure the raw power of a cartridge. It's a good tool for comparing one cartridge against another, but it probably doesn't tell the whole story. Without going into the mathematic formula, energy as expressed in foot-pounds is heavily weighted toward velocity. For example, the old 405-grain load for the .45–70 produces 1,330-feet-per-second muzzle velocity and 1,590 foot-pounds of energy at the muzzle. The newer, lighter 300-grain bullet is much faster at 1,880 fps, about a 40 percent increase, and produces 2,355 foot-pounds of energy, more than a 50 percent increase. And yet the heavier bullet, without flashy paper figures, is favored by many .45–70 fans.

The other thing to keep in mind is that hunters have a bad habit of looking at muzzle energy only. What's really important is *remaining energy* out there where the bullet strikes. There isn't a great deal that can be done about the muzzle energy of a given cartridge, but bullet shape is critical to retained velocity and hence retained energy.

For instance, most of the factories offer 180-grain .30–06 bullets in both round-nose and aerodynamic spitzer shapes. Both start at 2,700 feet per second, so both have an initial muzzle energy of 2,913 ft-lbs. At 300 yards the sharp-pointed bullet has retained velocity of 2,222 fps and energy of 1,974 ft-lbs. The round-nose will have retained velocity at 300 yards of 1,769 fps, and energy of only 1,251 ft-lbs.

How much energy is enough? That's impossible to quantify because bullet placement is so critical. However, more than half a century ago Colonel Townsend Whelen, one of the all-time great gunwriters, suggested that 1,000 ft-lbs of energy *at point of impact* was the minimum for deer-size game, and 2,000 ft-lbs of energy *at point of impact* was a sensible minimum for elk-size game. Fifty years later I can't disagree with that rule of thumb.

Caliber is the diameter of a bullet, sometimes expressed in hundredths of an inch (.30 caliber), in thousandths of an inch (.308), or in millimeters (7.62mm). We refer to caliber a bit loosely sometimes; it actually means only the bore or bullet diameter, and there might be many different *cartridges* based around the same caliber bullet — like .30–30, .30–06, .308, .300 Winchester Magnum. All of these are called .30-caliber cartridges, and all fire .308-inch bullets, but clearly they're not the same cartridge.

Caliber — the diameter of the bullet — is not a factor in determining energy or velocity. However, it does determine the size of the wound channel and so does play a major role in the initial effect of the bullet. Frontal area is a term used to describe the surface area a bullet occupies — and displaces when it hits. The thing to remember is that as caliber increases, frontal area goes up exponentially. A .308-caliber bullet

has a frontal area of .0745 square inch, while a .338-caliber bullet has a frontal area of .0897 square inch. Not a huge difference, but note that by going from .30 to .338, there's a 10 percent increase in caliber and a *15 percent* increase in frontal area.

Now, if you were looking for a woods rifle and chose the .30–30, you'd still have that .0745-sq.-in. frontal area. But if you chose the .45–70 with a .458 bullet, and used the formula for figuring the area of a circle (area = 3.14 × radius squared), you'd come up with a frontal area of .165 sq. in. — more than double the frontal area for a 50 percent increase in caliber. And thus more than double the size of the wound channel.

Frontal area isn't something to get all wrapped up in. But it is a factor that the ballistics charts are unable to show, and it does have an effect on game. It also shows in part why the slow-moving blackpowder cartridges (and today's slow-moving woods cartridges) and the shotgun slug are so devastating in the field.

The other factor to which ballistics charts are unable to give full credit is bullet weight. Any given cartridge has its limits, both in the powder capacity of its case and in the breech pressure at which it can safely operate. Thus it stands to reason that a lighter bullet in any given cartridge will be driven faster than a heavy one.

American hunters went through a phase in the late 1950s and 1960s that I call "magnum mania," and it isn't entirely over with. Many years ago the British began using the term "magnum" to denote a cartridge that was larger, faster, and more powerful than a "standard" cartridge of the same caliber. But it was the Americans who further refined the concept, and it came to mean a belted high-velocity cartridge. In fact, in

Left ro right, *.300 H&H Magnum, .300 Winchester Magnum, .300 Weatherby Magnum, 8mm Remington Magnum, .338 Winchester Magnum, .340 Weatherby Magnum, .375 H&H Magnum. To most Americans, the term "magnum" means a powerful, fast, belted cartridge like one of these—and there was a time when a new cartridge simply had to wear a belt and offer a lot of velocity to sell well. Those days seem to be over, but there's nothing wrong with the magnums. This selection includes virtually all the modern cartridges that are ideally suited for hunting large game such as elk and moose.*

those magnum-crazed days, if a cartridge wore a belt and produced unusually high velocities, it was going to be a success—at least initially.

The sporting press by and large went along with the gag, and so did the public. For a while, if a cartridge wasn't fast, it wasn't any good. One way to make a cartridge fast, to give it impressive ballistics, is to use a lighter bullet. Remember that high muzzle velocity is the best and easiest way to achieve high-muzzle-energy figures, since velocity figures so heavily into the equation.

During the late 1950s and 1960s an incredible number of "magnum" cartridges were introduced—.264, .300, .338, and .458 Winchester Magnums; 6.5mm, 7mm, and .350 Remington; .308 and .358 Norma. During this period too, Roy Weatherby rounded out his line of magnums with the huge .378 and .460 Weatherbys. Some of these cartridges are better than others, but all were and are sound cartridge designs, and collectively they made *velocity* a watchword among American hunters.

I certainly succumbed to it. My first rifle was a .243, but my second was a .264 Winchester Magnum, and I thought it was a real death ray. It was too—it's a magnificently flat-shooting, hard-hitting cartridge that I still believe to be one of the all-time greats for open-country hunting. However, it never was quite as good as I thought it was. If you take a careful look at the ballistics charts, you'll see that the .264's advantage over the "standard" .270 Winchester is very, very slight. And the .264 burns a great deal more powder and makes a lot more noise achieving that advantage.

When first introduced, the .350 Remington Magnum was touted as a real terror. Introduced in a lightweight carbine, it was, recoil-wise. It was also one of the most devastating close-cover cartridges to come down the pike. But it never was as powerful as the ancient .35 Whelen wildcat, a "standard" cartridge based on a necked-up .30–06 case. Not until 1988 did the Whelen see the light of day as a factory round, long after the .350 Remington Magnum's star faded.

Through the magnum craze, though, the "standard" cartridges hung in there pretty well. The .30–06 and .270 have remained popular, and today the .280 Remington — after languishing for 30 years — is becoming very popular. The .30–30 and .35 Remington seem to be gradually slipping, but part of the reason is certainly the increase in the bolt action's popularity.

Virtually across the board, *bullet weight* has been the major casualty of the velocity craze. It's true that to a degree ballistics charts tell you what you want to hear. For any given cartridge they will tell you that the lighter bullets go a bit faster. And if the velocity difference is significant enough, they will tell you that the light bullet hits harder than the heavy one. Well, they won't tell you that exactly, but they will tell you that the lighter bullet develops more energy, and you can interpret that as you choose. Most hunters read "velocity = energy = stopping power on game."

Thinking like this has led to lighter bullets being the favorite in virtually any hunting cartridge you can think of — and usually that lighter bullet isn't the best choice. For proof of this, you don't need to look to the magnums. Take a look at the good old .30–30. The 150-grain bullet develops 2,390 fps of muzzle velocity and 1,902 ft-lbs of muzzle energy. The 170-grain bullet is a good deal slower, 2,200 feet per second and muzzle energy of 1,827. Which bullet is the more popular? The 150, of course. But which one seems to hit game harder and penetrate better? And which one has more retained energy at 200 yards (989 ft-lbs versus 944 ft-lbs)? The 170-grain bullet, of course. This last is because longer, heavier bullets are more stable in flight, more aerodynamic (even with flat-points like the .30–30!), and retain their velocity better.

The magnums will tell you the same story. The bullet weight that gives the highest initial muzzle energy in the .300 Winchester Magnum is the 150-grain, and it's a big seller in that cartridge. It's also too light a bullet for .300 Magnum velocities, and just might expand prematurely. At 100 yards both the 180 and 200-grain .300 Winchester Magnum bullets have caught it and passed it, offering more retained energy. And at just 200 yards the 200-grain bullet in the .300 Winchester Magnum offers *500 ft-lbs of energy more* than the 150-grain bullet.

Given a choice, I'll always go for bullet weight over muzzle velocity. Down range, where it matters, those figures will be reversed. In the .270, the 140 or 150-grain bullet is often a better choice than the favored 130. In the .30–06, the favorite 150-grain bullet is almost never the best choice. Take a look at the newer 165-grain loads for all-around use, and the 180-grain loads for heavier game. Fortunately, all of these

A magnum cartridge is no substitute for good shooting and proper shot placement, but the flat trajectory and striking power do have advantages. This big Colorado mule deer was taken at very long range with a .300 Weatherby Magnum, easily one of the world's best cartridges for that kind of work.

cartridges offer a wide variety of choices. Unfortunately, some of America's greatest (though not flashiest) game-getting cartridges have been literally emasculated by the demand for velocity.

The three great casualties that come to mind are the .348 and .358 Winchester and the .350 Remington Magnum. These cartridges made their reputations on game with a 250-grain bullet, but in terms of sales the 200-grainer was always more popular. So as these great cartridges decreased in popularity and a bullet weight had to be dropped, in all three cases it was the 250-grain load. So today only a 200-grain factory load is available in all three of these great close-cover cartridges. The lighter

bullet does go faster and kicks a good deal less, but a light bullet won't make any of these cartridges a long-range affair. In fact, you can't get any real velocity out of them, so all you have going for you is lots of frontal area and lots of bullet weight.

I don't have much experience with the .350, but I've used both the .348 and the .358 on a number of deer, black bear, and wild hogs. With the light bullet they're great deer rifles — but you need that heavy bullet to allow these cartridges to do what they're supposed to do on the game they were designed for. Unless you handload (and handloading is well worth the effort), you should think twice before investing in any of these calibers.

We haven't really discussed the specifics of picking a rifle cartridge. The first consideration, I think, is the type of country you will hunt. If you know you will spend your hunting career in close cover—be it Pennsylvania's laurel tangles, Michigan's forests, or coastal Washington's jungles, you may as well look to the family of short-range, hard-hitting cartridges designed for that type of hunting—and the guns that chamber them.

If you're planning to hunt a variety of country from heavy cover to wide-open, your choice will be a bit different. And it will be different yet again if all of your hunting will be done in wide-open mountains, plains, or deserts.

Close-Cover Cartridges

Close-cover hunting means deer hunting to most of us, but actually the range of game is much broader than that. Much moose hunting in Maine and eastern Canada is in very close cover, and elk hunting in western Washington and Oregon is often at bayonet range. Black bear hunting is almost always a short-range affair. Wild hogs, an up-and-coming game animal in many parts of the U.S., will be a short-range, heavy-cover affair in most areas.

There used to be an incredible number of excellent short-range deer calibers, but the field has narrowed tremendously. Except for those on used-gun racks, gone are the .25–35, .30 Remington, .32–40, .32 Winchester Special, and many more. Remaining today is just one, the great .30–30. It doesn't have flashy ballistics, but it has done a great job on deer since 1895. Over the years it has also been used against almost every creature that roams this continent. I've shot a number of good-size wild hogs with the .30-30, and I wouldn't hesi-

A SELECTION OF CLOSE-COVER CARTRIDGES
Factory Ballistics

Cartridge	Bullet Wt. (grains)	Velocity (feet per second)				Energy (foot-pounds)			
		Muzzle	100 yds	200 yds	300 yds	Muzzle	100 yds	200 yds	300 yds
.30–30 Win.	150	2390	1973	1605	1303	1902	1356	944	651
.30–30 Win.	170	2200	1895	1619	1381	1827	1355	989	720
.348 Win.	200	2520	2215	1931	1672	2820	2178	1656	1241
.35 Rem.	200	2080	1698	1376	1140	1921	1280	841	577
.356 Win.	200	2460	2114	1797	1517	2688	1985	1434	1022
.356 Win.	250	2160	1911	1682	1476	2591	2028	1571	1210
.358 Win.	200	2490	2171	1876	1610	2753	2093	1563	1151
.35 Whelen	250	2400	2066	1761	1492	3197	2369	1722	1235
.375 Win.	200	2200	1841	1526	1268	2150	1506	1034	714
.375 Win.	250	1900	1647	1424	1239	2005	1506	1126	852
.444 Marlin	240	2350	1815	1377	1087	2942	1755	1010	630
.444 Marlin	265	2120	1733	1405	1160	2644	1768	1162	791
.45–70 Gov't.	300	1880	1650	1430	1240	2355	1815	1355	1015
.45–70 Gov't.	405	1330	1168	1055	977	1590	1227	1001	858

tate to use it on mid-size black bear. But I still think it's essentially a deer cartridge.

If you have larger game in mind, there are a host of other close-cover cartridges available. These start with the new .307 Winchester, sort of a rimmed .308 Winchester or "super .30–30," and the newer 7x30 Waters, a .30–30 case necked down to .284. Actually, although they are lever-action cartridges, both of these new numbers shoot flat enough to extend into our next category, "mixed-cover" cartridges. From there you go up to the ancient and deadly .35 Remington, still a fine choice that kills game out of all proportion to its modest ballistics. In the .35-caliber arena you also find the .348, .358, and .356 Winchester cartridges. Ballistics on these three are very similar, and actually all three of these are much more than just close-range numbers, offering plenty of power for anything short of grizzly and relatively flat trajectory out to 200 yards or so.

The next step up in caliber would be to the .375 Winchester. With both 200 and 250-grain bullets, this cartridge has the frontal area and bullet weight to be devastating on game, but velocities are extremely low. This one is a short-range cartridge only.

In the "over .40" group, there's the .444 Marlin and .45–70. The big Marlin is a very fine and much-underrated game cartridge, especially with the newer 265-grain bullet. A friend of mine hunts elk in a brushy part of Colorado, and he uses the .444 exclusively. He has taken 19 elk in 19 years with his .444 — and none has gotten up after he flattened it with the big Marlin.

The .45–70 is simply an amazing cartridge, and it just keeps rolling along. With the strong, modern actions it's available in today, handloaders can do interesting things with it. In fact, it can be loaded to levels just below the .458 Winchester Magnum! But factory ammo might be used in

Left to right, .35 Remington, .358 Winchester, .356 Winchester, .348 Winchester, .444 Marlin, .45–70 Government, .35 Whelen, .308 Winchester, .30–06 Springfield, 7mm Remington Magnum. The six cartridges on the left are "pure" close-cover cartridges—hard-hitting, but not possessing a flat trajectory. In that role they're extremely hard to beat. The four cartridges on the right, with proper bullets, will reach out in open country and, loaded with heavier bullets, perform admirably at close range in heavy cover.

The .35 Whelen was a 65-year-old wildcat when Remington brought it out in factory form in 1988. It's a classic close-cover round, firing a 250-grain .35-caliber bullet at about 2,400 feet per second. I used one of the first factory rifles on this Alaskan moose, and its performance was devastating.

110-year-old trapdoor Springfields as well as modern Rugers, so factory loads are extremely mild. The traditional 405-grain loading duplicates the military load of a century ago, while the lighter 300-grain bullet increases velocity significantly without increasing pressure. The 300-grain bullet is a deer load. It's a hollowpoint and gives good expansion, but on game heavier than deer it may not give the needed penetration. If you decide to use the .45–70 for close-cover elk or moose, and you don't handload, ignore the paper ballistics and use the old 405-grain bullet. It still hits things like a Mack truck!

The .44 Magnum also shouldn't be ignored, as it's available in a number of short, light, close-cover rifles. Actually, the .44 Magnum is a fine close-range deer cartridge, whether fired from rifle or pistol. Velocities are pretty good, and the broad, heavy bullet hits hard. It is not a good choice for anything larger than deer, and its range is very limited, but within those limitations it's a dandy.

Cartridges for Mixed Cover

There are a whole lot more general-purpose cartridges than there are special-purpose ones. And I suspect there are a lot of hunters today who want and need some degree of versatility. Today you may comb the laurel thickets for a buck, but tomorrow you might sit and watch 300 yards of cutline. Several of the cartridges just mentioned — the .307, .348, .358, and .356 Winchester — are actually much more than close-cover rounds; all of them take the lever action into the realm of versatile big-game hunting, and all of them are quite effective on game up to moose or elk.

What is "mixed-cover hunting?" One moment you're going through a thicket where you might jump a buck any second;

the next you break onto an open hillside where the closest shot will be 200 yards. This is the most common type of hunting for most of us, and it's demanding of a rifle and cartridge. Whatever setup you choose, it has to be fast-handling for the close-in shots, but it also has to offer the accuracy, flat trajectory, and downrange power to get the job done at a distance. The lever-action cartridges just mentioned will do the job nicely out to 200 yards or a bit beyond, and there are a host of cartridges chambered for bolt actions, single shots, pumps, and semiautos that were created for just this kind of versatility.

In general, magnum velocities (and magnum recoil) aren't required for this type of hunting. The family of cartridges based on the .30–06 case is near-ideal for general mixed-cover hunting. If the game is deer and the country tends to be open, the .25–06 and .270 are good choices; the .280 is a fine all-around choice, suitable for the biggest deer; and the .30–06 re-

Left to right, *.243 Winchester, 6mm Remington, .240 Weatherby Magnum, .257 Roberts, .25–06 Remington, .257 Weatherby Magnum, .264 Winchester Magnum, .270 Winchester, .270 Weatherby Magnum, .280 Remington. This selection of cartridges is well-suited for "mixed-cover" hunting of deer-size game. Obviously, some are also ideally suited for open-country hunting, especially from the .25s on up.*

mains America's most versatile all-around cartridge.

Also not to be overlooked is the "new" .35 Whelen, now available in factory form. With a 250-grain bullet, this .30–06-based cartridge is fine for elk and moose, and I wouldn't hesitate to tackle the largest bear with it.

A companion family of cartridges is based on the .308 Winchester case. The .308 (called 7.62mm NATO) replaced the .30–06 as America's military cartridge primarily because it could be put into a smaller, more compact action with only slightly less velocity. The same is absolutely true in sporting rifles. The much shorter

A SELECTION OF MIXED-COVER CARTRIDGES
Factory Ballistics

Cartridge	Bullet Wt. (grains)	Velocity (feet per second)					Energy (foot-pounds)				
		Muzzle	100 yds	200 yds	300 yds	400 yds	Muzzle	100 yds	200 yds	300 yds	400 yds
.243 Win.	100	2960	2697	2449	2215	1993	1945	1615	1332	1089	882
6mm Rem.	100	3100	2829	2573	2332	2104	2133	1777	1470	1207	983
.250 Sav.	100	2820	2504	2210	1936	1684	1765	1392	1084	832	630
.257 Roberts	100	2900	2541	2210	1904	1627	1867	1433	1084	805	588
.257 Roberts	117	2780	2560	2360	2160	1970	2010	1710	1445	1210	1010
.25–06 Rem.	120	3010	2749	2502	2269	2048	2414	2013	1668	1372	1117
.270 Win.	130	3110	2849	2604	2371	2150	2791	2343	1957	1622	1334
.270 Win.	150	2900	2632	2380	2142	1918	2801	2307	1886	1528	1225
.284 Win.	150	2860	2595	2344	2108	1886	2724	2243	1830	1480	1185
7–30 Waters	120	2700	2300	1930	1600	1330	1940	1405	990	685	470
7mm Mauser	140	2660	2435	2221	2018	1827	2199	1843	1533	1266	1037
7mm Mauser	175	2440	2137	1857	1603	1382	2313	1774	1340	998	742
7mm–08 Rem.	140	2860	2625	2402	2189	1988	2542	2142	1793	1490	1228
.280 Rem.	140	3000	2758	2528	2309	2102	2797	2363	1986	1657	1373
.307 Win.	150	2760	2321	1924	1575	1289	2538	1795	1233	826	554
.307 Win.	180	2510	2179	1874	1599	1362	2519	1898	1404	1022	742
.308 Win.	150	2820	2488	2179	1893	1633	2648	2061	1581	1193	888
.308 Win.	165	2700	2440	2194	1963	1748	2760	2180	1763	1411	1119
.308 Win.	180	2620	2393	2178	1974	1783	2743	2288	1896	1557	1269
.30–06 Spr.	150	2920	2580	2265	1972	1704	2839	2217	1708	1295	967
.30–06 Spr.	165	2800	2573	2357	2151	1956	2873	2426	2036	1696	1402
.30–06 Spr.	180	2700	2348	2023	1727	1466	2913	2203	1635	1192	859
.338 Win. Mag.	225	2780	2572	2374	2184	2003	3862	3306	2816	2384	2005
.350 Rem. Mag	200	2710	2410	2130	1870	1631	3261	2579	2014	1553	1181
.35 Whelen	200	2675	2378	2100	1842	1606	3177	2510	1958	1506	1148

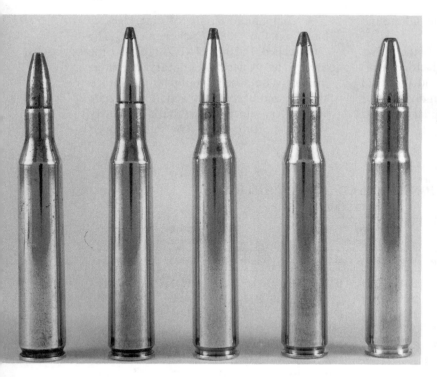

Left to right, *.25–06 Remington, .270 Winchester, .280 Remington, .30–06 Springfield, .35 Whelen. The "family" of cartridges based on the .30–06 Springfield case is comprised of some of America's most versatile hunting cartridges; all are prime candidates for mixed-cover hunting of a variety of big-game species.*

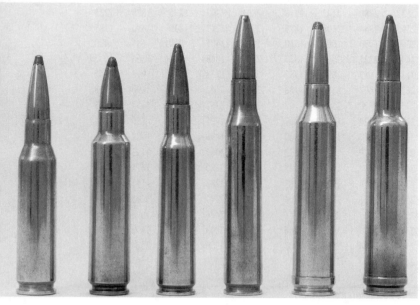

Left to right, *7mm–08 Remington, .284 Winchester, 7x57 Mauser, .280 Remington, 7mm Remington Magnum, 7mm Weatherby Magnum. The 7mms are another extremely versatile "family" of cartridges; the three to the left are nearly perfect for almost any type of deer hunting, while the three to the right are classic cartridges for open plains or high mountains.*

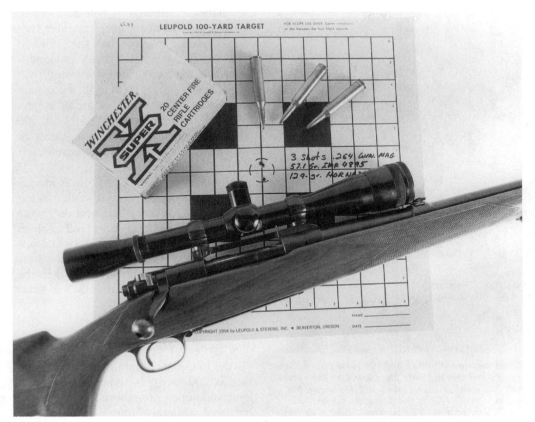

The .264 Winchester Magnum, long maligned as a noisy, barrel-burning cartridge, remains a classic long-range choice for deer and antelope. In my experience the .264 is also extremely accurate—and long-range shooting at smaller big-game animals is one of the few places where accuracy like this can come in handy.

.308, and the cartridges derived from its case, can be built into lighter, more compact rifles such as lever actions like the Browning and Savage, or bolt actions with a significantly shorter action and thus shorter bolt throw.

The .308 is the daddy of this family, and though it will lag a bit behind the .30–06 with any bullet weight, the difference is slight until you get to bullets of 180 grains and heavier. The .308 is a superb hunting cartridge, and with heavier bullets at moderate range it will do a bang-up job on game up to moose and elk.

The .243 Winchester is one of its offspring, a fine, low-recoil cartridge. It has been called a long-range cartridge, but it really isn't, not for big game. It is a superb long-range varmint cartridge, and an excellent medium-range cartridge for deer and antelope. Its little 100-grain bullet simply doesn't have the retained energy for shots

Elk are among the world's toughest game pound for pound — and they're plenty big. Cartridges from the 7mm magnums or .30–06 on up will do the job, but my favorite elk rifle is this fiberglass-stocked .338 Winchester Magnum. It's a powerful rifle, but for elk I believe the power of this type of cartridge is needed.

much beyond 250 yards. But that's not what it was designed for; it was designed to bridge the gap between varmint hunting and big game, and it does that job flawlessly. For "mixed-cover" deer hunting and pronghorn hunting in rolling terrain, it's simply superb.

In the case of the .30–06 family, I'm not sure anything beats the old '06 itself. But with the .308 family, I wonder whether the newest member, Remington's 7mm-08, may be the best of all. This little cartridge fires a 140-grain bullet at excellent velocities with a factory load, and it has turned out to be a handloader's dream. It isn't an

elk cartridge, although it will do the job, but it is a magnificent deer cartridge that reaches out a bit better than the .308 and doesn't kick as much. I can't imagine a better first big-game rifle for a youngster.

Last in this family is the .358, a compact powerhouse. Because of its arcing trajectory, it's impractical much beyond 200 yards, but it's devastating on any deer or black bear that walks, and has proven itself extremely effective on elk.

The belted magnums do fit in as mixed-cover cartridges, but only if your hunting includes a steady diet of elk and very large northern deer, and your shots tend to be on the long side. Rifles that specialize in dropping elk-size game at some distance start with the .300 magnums and go up to the .338 Winchester, .340 Weatherby, and 8mm Remington Magnums.

Long-Range Cartridges

True long-range hunting, where shots start at 200 yards, is somewhat unusual. Some wide-open pronghorn hunting is like that, and whitetail hunting in wheatfield country like Alberta can be that way. So can much caribou hunting, some mule deer hunting, and certainly some elk hunting.

Several standard cartridges are ideal for this kind of work, so long as the game isn't larger than big deer or caribou. The .25–06 with 117 or 120-grain bullets is a good starting point, and both the .270 and .280 are right at home under such circumstances. So is the .30–06 with sharp-pointed 165-grain bullets. Situations like this, though, are also made to order for the smaller-caliber magnums. The .240, .257, and .270 Weatherbys and the .264 Winchester Magnum were made for this kind of hunting. And so were the 7mm magnums, both Weatherby and Winchester. Of these, only

A SELECTION OF LONG-RANGE CARTRIDGES
Factory Ballistics

Cartridge	Bullet Wt. (grains)	Velocity (feet per second)				Energy (foot-pounds)				Drop (in inches, 200-yd zero)		
		Muzzle	200 yds	300 yds	400 yds	Muzzle	200 yds	300 yds	400 yds	100 yds	300 yds	400 yds
.25–06 Rem.	120	3010	2502	2269	2048	2414	1668	1372	1117	+ 1.9	− 7.4	− 21.6
.257 Wby. Mag.	117	3300	2543	2240	1978	2830	1680	1304	1017	+ 1.7	− 8.7	− 26.9
.264 Win. Mag.	140	3030	2548	2346	2114	2854	2018	1682	1389	+ 1.8	− 7.2	− 20.8
.270 Win.	130	3110	2604	2371	2150	2791	1957	1622	1334	+ 1.7	− 6.8	− 19.9
.270 Win.	150	2900	2380	2142	1918	2801	1886	1528	1225	+ 2.1	− 8.2	− 24.1
.270 Wby. Mag.	130	3375	2745	2472	2221	3289	2176	1764	1424	+ 1.1	− 5.5	− 16.3
.270 Wby. Mag.	150	3245	2684	2452	2238	3508	2401	2003	1669	+ 1.3	− 6.2	− 18.3
.280 Rem.	140	3000	2528	2309	2102	2797	1986	1657	1373	+ 1.8	− 7.3	− 21.1
7mm Rem. Mag.	150	3110	2568	2320	2085	3221	2196	1792	1448	+ 1.7	− 7.0	− 20.5
7mm Rem. Mag.	175	2860	2440	2244	2057	3178	2313	1956	1644	+ 2.0	− 7.9	− 22.7
7mm Wby. Mag.	154	3160	2634	2407	2196	3415	2373	1982	1650	+ 1.3	− 6.1	− 18.0
.30–06 Spr.	165	2800	2357	2151	1956	2873	2036	1696	1402	+ 2.2	− 8.4	− 24.4
.300 Win. Mag.	180	2960	2540	2344	2157	3501	2578	2196	1895	+ 1.9	− 7.3	− 20.9
.300 Win. Mag.	200	2830	2530	2380	2240	3560	2830	2520	2230	+ 1.7	− 7.1	− 20.3
.300 Wby. Mag.	180	3245	2698	2465	2250	4210	2910	2430	2023	+ 1.1	− 6.8	− 19.2
8mm Rem. Mag.	185	3080	2464	2186	1927	3896	2494	1963	1525	+ 1.8	− 7.6	− 22.5
8mm Rem. Mag.	220	2830	2346	2123	1913	3912	2688	2201	1787	+ 2.2	− 8.5	− 24.7
.338 Win. Mag.	210	2830	2370	2150	1940	3735	2610	2155	1760	+ 2.1	− 8.4	− 24.3
.338 Win. Mag.	225	2780	2374	2184	2003	3862	2816	2384	2005	+ 2.7	− 9.4	− 25.0
.340 Wby. Mag.	250	2850	2325	2090	1871	4510	3003	2425	1945	+ 1.9	− 8.6	− 25.7

the two 7mms edge their way into adequacy for elk. Better bets for elk, especially at longer ranges, begin with the .300s using 200-grain bullets and go up to the trio of medium magnums comprised of the .338 Winchester Magnum, the .340 Weatherby Magnum, and the 8mm Remington Magnum.

None of these suggestions is absolute, of course. A hunter who knows his rifle and has faith in it can work wonders with a cartridge that most of us would consider inadequate. There are also a great many fine cartridges that I did not mention, such as the .284 Winchester, .257 Roberts, 7x57,

and many obscure wildcats and fading factory cartridges.

Included with this chapter is a chart that lists hunting cartridges, suggested bullet weights, and their suitability and maximum ranges for various types of game. This chart is based on my own observations, not scientific research, so take it for what it's worth. I wouldn't be surprised if it sparks a few campfire arguments. You see, there really aren't any absolutes in caliber selection, and it's tough to make a wrong choice. Some choices, though, are better than others, and that's what this discussion was all about.

GAME SUITABILITY
Suggested Effective Ranges (in Yards) on Game

Cartridge	Bullet Wt. (grains)	Small Deer/ Pronghorn			Large Deer/ Caribou*			Black Bear/ Wild Boar			Elk/Moose			Grizzly/ Brown Bear	
		100	200	300+	100	200	300+	100	200	300+	100	200	300+	100	200
.243 Win.	100	X	X												
6mm Rem.	100	X	X	X											
.240 Wby. Mag.	100	X	X	X	X	X									
.250 Sav.	100	X	X		X										
.257 Rob.	117	X	X		X	X									
.25–06 Rem.	120	X	X	X	X	X	X								
.257 Wby. Mag.	117	X	X	X	X	X	X								
.264 Win. Mag.	140	X	X	X	X	X	X	X	X		X	X			
.270 Win.	130	X	X	X	X	X	X				X	X			
.270 Win.	150	X	X	X	X	X	X	X	X		X	X			
.270 Wby. Mag.	130	X	X	X	X	X	X								
.270 Wby. Mag.	150	X	X	X	X	X	X	X	X		X	X			
7 x 30 Wtrs.	120	X			X										
7mm–08 Rem.	140	X	X	X	X	X	X	X			X				
7 x 57	140	X	X	X	X	X		X			X				
7 x 57	175	X	X		X	X		X	X		X				
.284 Win.	150	X	X	X	X	X	X	X	X		X				
.280 Rem.	140	X	X	X	X	X	X	X			X				
.280 Rem.	175	X	X	X	X	X	X	X	X		X				
7mm Rem. Mag.	150	X	X	X	X	X	X	X	X		X				
7mm Rem. Mag.	175	X	X	X	X	X	X	X	X	X	X	X		X	
7mm Wby. Mag.	150	X	X	X	X	X	X	X	X		X				
7mm Wby. Mag.	175	X	X	X	X	X	X	X	X	X	X	X		X	
.30–30 Win.	150	X			X										
.30–30 Win.	170	X			X			X							
.307 Win.	150	X	X		X	X		X							
.307 Win.	180	X	X		X	X		X	X		X				
.308 Win.	150	X	X	X	X	X	X	X							
.308 Win.	180	X	X	X	X	X	X	X	X		X	X			
.30–06 Spr.	165	X	X	X	X	X	X	X	X	X	X	X			
.30–06 Spr.	180	X	X	X	X	X	X	X	X	X	X	X		X	
.300 Win. Mag.	180	X	X	X	X	X	X	X	X	X	X	X		X	
.300 Win. Mag.	200	X	X	X	X	X	X	X	X	X	X	X	X	X	X
.300 Wby. Mag.	180	X	X	X	X	X	X	X	X	X	X	X	X	X	X
.300 Wby. Mag.	220							X	X	X	X	X	X	X	X
8mm Rem. Mag.	185	X	X	X	X	X	X	X	X	X	X	X			
8mm Rem. Mag.	220	X	X	X	X	X	X	X	X	X	X	X	X	X	X

GAME SUITABILITY *(continued)*
Suggested Effective Ranges (in Yards) on Game

Cartridge	Bullet Wt. (grains)	Small Deer/ Pronghorn			Large Deer/ Caribou*			Black Bear/ Wild Boar			Elk/Moose			Grizzly/ Brown Bear	
		100	200	300+	100	200	300+	100	200	300+	100	200	300+	100	200
.338 Win. Mag.	200	X	X	X	X	X	X	X	X	X	X	X	X		
.338 Win. Mag.	225	X	X	X	X	X	X	X	X	X	X	X	X	X	X
.338 Win. Mag.	250	X	X	X	X	X	X	X	X	X	X	X	X	X	X
.340 Wby. Mag.	200	X	X	X	X	X	X	X	X	X	X	X	X		
.340 Wby. Mag.	250	X	X	X	X	X	X	X	X	X	X	X	X	X	X
.348 Win.	200	X	X		X	X		X	X		X			X	
.35 Rem.	200	X			X			X							
.358 Win.	200	X	X		X	X		X	X		X			X	
.356 Win.	200	X	X		X	X		X	X		X			X	
.356 Win.	250	X	X		X	X		X	X		X			X	
.35 Whelen	200	X	X	X	X	X	X	X	X		X	X			
.35 Whelen	250	X	X		X	X		X	X		X	X		X	
.350 Rem. Mag.	200	X	X		X	X		X	X		X	X		X	
.375 Win.	200	X			X			X							
.375 Win.	250	X			X			X			X				
.375 H&H Mag.	270	X	X	X	X	X	X	X	X	X	X	X	X	X	X
.375 H&H Mag.	300	X	X	X	X	X	X	X	X	X	X	X	X	X	X
.378 Wby. Mag.	270	X	X	X	X	X	X	X	X	X	X	X	X	X	X
.378 Wby. Mag.	300	X	X	X	X	X	X	X	X	X	X	X	X	X	X
.44 Mag.	240	X			X			X							
.444 Mar.	240	X			X			X							
.444 Mar.	265	X			X			X			X			X	
.45–70 Govt.	300	X			X			X			X				
.45–70 Govt.	405	X			X			X			X			X	

*Includes sheep and goat.
Chart is a general guide only, and is based on both energy and trajectory.

5

Scopes and Sights

Just a few decades ago, the telescopic sight was considered little more than a new-fangled gadget. It had been around since the Civil War, it's true, and by the 1920s some very good hunting scopes were available. But the optics were a far cry from what's available today, and the adjustments (if any) were crude. It didn't really matter much anyway—however good or bad the scopes were, the average deer hunter didn't trust them and didn't want anything to do with them! Iron sights were the norm, and shooters in need of a bit more precision chose an aperture or "peep" sight.

Today the situation is reversed; the telescopic sight has gained almost universal acceptance, and generations of hunters have grown up knowing nothing else. I'm a prime example. I learned to shoot with an open-sighted .22, and my first centerfire rifle was a surplus 1903 Springfield—with

iron sights, of course. But my first hunting rifle was a scope-sighted .243. Many years passed before I had occasion to use open sights in the field, and I wouldn't be surprised to learn that a great many American hunters never have.

That's not all bad. The scope is here to stay, and it has gained acceptance for one very simple reason: You shoot better with a scope, under all conditions. Period. The telescopic sight simply makes shooting easier; if you can see better, you can shoot better—and you can see better with a scope.

The scope does three basic things for you. First, it can magnify the target, which not only helps you to see it better but can also help you pick out the correct aiming point more easily. Second, it gives you a single sighting plane. With traditional open sights, such as a buckhorn rear and blade front, your eye attempts to focus back and forth from rear sight to front sight to target. It's a physical impossibility for the eye to focus on all three planes at once. With the scope, your eye can focus on the target only, and simply superimpose the reticle over the target.

Lastly, the scope can actually help you see better under low-light conditions, such as the prime hunting hours of dawn and dusk. Now, in bad light a poor-quality scope is worse than none. But a good-quality scope actually gathers available light and will give you a clear picture several minutes before you could possibly use iron sights in the early morning—and several minutes longer as daylight fades.

In terms of reliability, good scopes properly set in solid mounts are hard to beat. They will break, true enough, but I've seen a lot more factory-installed iron sights damaged in the field than I have scopes. It generally takes a vicious knock to alter a scope's zero, and I've seen iron sights and aperture sights knocked out of whack just as frequently as scopes.

For my money, one of the best things anybody can do to improve their field shooting is to get a good scope, mount it properly, and learn how to use it. Scope selection is a simple task. The important thing to remember is that there can be too much of a good thing; too much magnification is much worse than none at all.

These three Burris models represent the types of riflescopes most popular with American hunters today: from top, a 3–9X variable, 2–7X variable, and fixed 4X. Variables in this power range are extremely useful, but for virtually all hunting uses the power adjustment should be kept at low or middle magnification settings.

Nationwide, the 3–9X variable scope is the most popular. At 3X or 4X, such a scope is perfect for most hunting situations, but at 9X, where too many hunters leave the power ring set, there's far too much magnification. Variables are great, to be sure. But bear in mind that as you increase magnification, your field of view will decrease. The only occasions in big-game hunting where magnification over 6X might be useful would be a long-range shot where you have lots of time to prepare, or possibly a closer shot where only a portion of the animal is visible and you use the higher magnification to pick out the vitals. For every such occasion, however, there are dozens of times when variable scopes set too high actually cost hunters game. If you use a 3–9X or 2–7X variable, make a conscious effort to leave the setting somewhere in the 3–5X range, never higher. The power will be there if you need it.

And carry binoculars to look at game. That scope sight is only for shooting, not

Here are a few of the many reticles available in modern riflescopes. My favorite is the "plex" type, bottom left, with thicker outer wires and fine crosshairs in the center. The crosshair and dot, top right, is another excellent reticle, especially well suited for shooting at moving game.

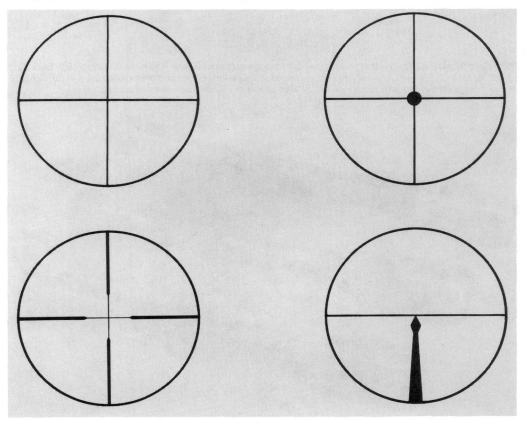

for looking. "Scoping" game with a tele-scopic sight — unless you know what you're looking at and are planning to shoot — is dangerous, shows terrible hunting man-ners, and can be downright suicidal. I can assure you it's potentially dangerous for anyone who scopes me!

I've been the variable route, and still like them. But now I tend to mount fixed 4X scopes on general-purpose rifles and 6X scopes on open-country rifles. The fixed-power scopes are simpler than variables, with less to worry about, and they save a few ounces. They also offer all the magni-fication needed. If I use a variable, it's likely to be a low-range model such as 1¾–5X or 1½–6X. Those low-range scopes, by the way, are ideal for mixed-cover deer hunting.

Reticles are largely a matter of personal preference. I like the "plex"-type crosshair that has become so popular in recent years, and virtually every scope manufacturer offers some version. This is a crosshair with thick wires on the outside and very thin wires in the center. On game, the eye just naturally seems to follow to the center. I much prefer that reticle to a standard cross-hair, especially in low light — the bold outer wires remain visible long after you've lost the thin center wires.

The dot, with or without crosshairs, used to be a lot more popular than it is today. Finding the dot can be a problem on dark animals in dark shadows, such as a black bear coming onto a bait at last light. On the other hand, there's something about a dot that is magnificent on running game.

Thanks to modern technology, a whole new class of optical sights today includes illuminated reticles and centered illumi-nated dots. I've used both, and they work like a charm. Bushnell's illuminated reticle is powered by a little camera battery, and

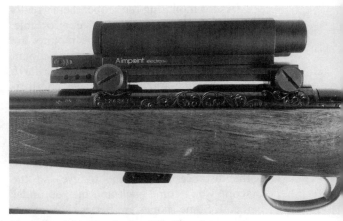

Electronic sights like the Swedish Aimpoint operate from batteries and offer an illuminated dot as an aiming point. Such a sight generally has no or very little magnification, so is a poor choice for long-range work — but makes a fine sight for quick shooting in close cover.

until you turn it on, it functions like a nor-mal scope with a "plex"-type reticle. When you hit the switch, a small red dot appears at the junction of the crosshairs. It will not assist you in seeing your target, but it does give a very fast reference point in fading light. I particularly like it for dark animals in dark shadows, and I've always thought it would be perfect in a leopard blind.

The Swedish Aimpoint and Tasco's Pro-Point are a bit different in that they're cen-tered, projected points of light. Once the rifle is sighted in, all you have to do is look through the tube, place the point of light on your target, and squeeze the trigger. They work, and they're quite durable. Neither offers magnification, although extenders are available that do give low magnifica-tion. As ranges increase, the dot starts to subtend a bit too much of the target, but such a rig makes a very fine close-cover sight.

As for mounting the scope, there's really no right or wrong, just what's comfortable. Dozens of good, solid scope mounts are available. The important thing is to mount the scope so that when you bring the rifle to your shoulder and put your cheek comfortably on the stock exactly the way you want it to be when you squeeze the trigger, you have a full and complete field of view with no adjustment of the head needed.

You also must have enough eye relief — the distance from scope to eye — so the scope won't come back and hit you under recoil. Some scopes are better than others for this, but if you can get four inches of eye relief, you should never get hit — provided your scope is mounted so your cheek is tight to the stock and you don't have to crane your neck.

The various "see-through" mounts are an excellent idea, but that's their basic problem — you must either lift your head virtually off the stock to see through the scope, or grind your cheek into the comb to see the irons. They're a great idea, but you'll shoot better by making a mental commitment to use either scope or irons and sticking with it. If a buck jumps in heavy cover, the last thing you need is to try to decide which to use!

It's often stated that iron sights are better than scopes at close range and on running game. Not true. You see better, and faster, with a scope. Period. One company, Tasco, even makes a scope with *no* magnification for woods shooting. It gives great light-gathering potential and provides the scope's single sighting plane with no magnification whatsoever.

However, there's a catch to all this. For a scope to be fast, especially on running game and at close range, you simply must learn to keep both eyes open. With both eyes open, your non-shooting eye will catch

This 1¾–5X Redfield is a fine example of a low-range variable, an ideal choice for the close-cover or mixed-terrain hunter. The mounts are the sturdy, dependable Brownell detachables made by Kimber of Oregon.

the big picture, while your shooting eye concentrates on the reticle and on putting it in the right place. If you can't learn to keep both eyes open — and you may not be able to if your dominant eye isn't your shooting eye (this is rare, but it happens) — you do have a serious impediment to speedy scope shooting.

A detachable scope has always been an attractive concept — iron sights on the rifle just in case, and a scope that can be slipped on and off at will and not lose its zero. The concept is every bit as good as it sounds. I have detachable mounts on three different rifles right now: a .375, a .416, and a 7x57. The funny thing is that I've never taken a scope off a rifle in favor of iron sights, not even to go after wounded dangerous game. But that's me — I'm more comfortable with a scope. Nonetheless, it's very comforting to have those iron sights handy and know that you can slip the scope off if something happens.

Good detachable mounts used to be as scarce as hens' teeth, but today there are some good ones. Gun South has been importing some super German mounts, and Kimber of Oregon makes the attractive double-lever Brownell mount. There's also a slick, inexpensive little gadget from Pilkington that turns any Redfield-type scope base into a quick-detachable setup.

Yes, I'm biased toward the scope sight. However, millions of hunters use open sights, by both habit and preference, so it's important to spend a few moments discussing them. A great many bolt-action rifles come from the factory today without any iron sights at all. I think that's fine; if you're going to scope a rifle, iron sights are really excess baggage, just something extra to hang up in brush. The only exception might be a rifle you're planning to take on extended hunts into really rough country, and then a detachable mount begins to make some sense.

Open sights are usually available as an option on a factory bolt gun, and they're usually supplied with other action types. The truth is, though, that most factory-supplied iron sights aren't very good these days. Too many of them are fragile and poorly installed — apparently put on for "looks," and not intended to be used as the primary sight.

Make certain both front and rear sights are good and solid. I once had a factory rear sight literally jump off the barrel on a mild-recoilling 7x57. Also take a good look at the front sight; too many of these are very hard to see. Personally, if I'm going to use iron sights, I prefer the express-type — a fairly broad, shallow V in the rear and a

Too many modern open sights supplied on factory rifles tend to be flimsy affairs. If you intend to use the open sights on your rifle, whether as a primary sight or a backup, take a good look and make certain they're both sturdy and solidly attached. This standing express sight with one additional folding leaf was installed to replace a factory-supplied open sight.

good, bold bead in the front. A sight like this lines up very quickly, but it is not a precision sight. I have sights like this on a couple of big rifles, and past 100 yards, I'm all done. The traditional American open sight is either a buckhorn — as supplied for decades on the Model 94 Winchester, with a fairly fine notch at the bottom of the "horns" — or a U-notch. Both are a bit more precise than the British-style express sight, but they're also slower to line up.

I had a lot of fun with an open-sighted rifle recently. I saw a lovely Westley-Richards .318, sort of a British equivalent to a .30–06, in a gunshop at the right price, and simply had to have it. It had the original bent Mauser bolt handle and had never been drilled and tapped for a scope. The sights were 1920s-vintage precision long-

I shot this wildebeest at about 225 yards with the original open sights on an old Westley-Richards .318. With practice, it's amazing what you can do with open sights, but they're no substitute for a good scope.

range sights—a narrow V rear, additional folding leaves marked to 500 yards, and an exceedingly fine bead up front. Heck, I had trouble seeing it!

Anyway, I shot quite a lot of game with the rifle, mostly at close range. But one day in Botswana we had a herd of wildebeest, including one very fine bull, far out across an open, burned plain. There was no way to get closer. I lay down, rested over the top of an anthill, and worked out the range as best I could. It was something over 200 yards, but not 300—much too far for open sights. I put up the second sight leaf, the one marked for 200 yards, and when our chosen bull stood up and turned broadside, I held a bit high on his shoulder. At least I thought that was where I was holding—the

sight covered most of the animal at that range! The bullet went exactly where it was supposed to go, and that wildebeest dropped in his tracks. So iron sights do work—if you practice with them.

The aperture or peep sight is actually a better option than traditional open sights. In fact, the aperture sight is an optical sight like a scope, but it has no glassware. It consists of a small rear opening located near the eye, and a front sight that's either a blade or a bead (I prefer a bead). The eye looks through the opening and naturally centers the front sight in the circle. Then it's simple to place that front sight where you want to hit.

Most aperture sights have interchangeable eyepieces with openings of different sizes. For hunting, you want the larger opening—and you just might want to unscrew the eyepiece and throw it away. With the eyepiece gone, you'll be left with a good, big opening that makes for one of the fastest field sights going, possibly faster than a low-power scope.

There's another situation where the peep sight (or irons, for that matter) has an advantage, and that's in extremely wet, rainy country. In the rain, a scope is useless without scope covers—and it takes precious moments to get the covers off when a shooting opportunity arises. With an aperture sight, your range is more limited and you aren't gathering any light—but you needn't worry about the weather.

I've always preferred peep sights on my lever actions, for some odd reason. I took an old Winchester Model 71 in .348 black bear hunting one year, and had to make a fairly long stalk at last light. By the time I got to the bear—and I got within 60 yards—it was getting dark. With a scope, there would have been plenty of light. With that peep sight, though, it was tough. Finally I aimed at the bear, now little more than a black blob, then raised the rifle to the skyline so I could see the sights and make sure of the sight picture, then went back to what I thought was the front third of the bear. That big bullet lifted him clear off his feet, and he never moved—so I guessed right. But as much as I enjoy fooling around with that kind of sight, those few moments brought home to me once again how much better a scope is than any other hunting sight.

With the aperture or "peep" sight, the eye naturally centers the front sight in the center of the aperture. Although the peep sight offers no magnification and no light-gathering ability, it is a very fast and accurate sighting device.

6

Sighting-in and Field Accuracy

Let's suppose you've selected a rifle chambered for the cartridge that will be just right for your hunting, and you've topped it with a good scope. The next step, once you've familiarized yourself with all the mechanical aspects of the rifle, is to get it sighted in. Sighting in is a pre-season ritual that ensures that your barrel and sights are properly aligned so the bullet will land where you want it to.

Exactly where that spot lies is up to you. In later chapters, as we discuss specific types of shooting, and in the chapter I call "Getting Ready," we'll cover specific recommendations for sighting-in. But for now, let's just assume that you want your bullet to land where you're aiming at a specific distance. The accepted sighting-in distance for scoped rifles has long been 100 yards; for open-sighted rifles, 50 yards might make more sense.

But right now the last thing you want to do is step out to the range and start shooting. Few things are more frustrating than sitting down at a bench, getting good and steady, taking a shot, and then looking at a clean target with no holes. No matter how carefully you or a gunsmith scoped the rifle, there's absolutely no guarantee that the scope (or sights) will be aligned closely enough with the barrel to ensure your initial shots will be on paper. In fact, there's a good chance they won't be—and nothing wastes ammo, heats tempers, and destroys confidence quicker than fumbling around on the range just getting shots on the target.

The best tool for getting started sighting in is an optical gadget called a collimator. Several scope manufacturers offer them, and the guy who owns several scoped rifles shouldn't be without one. If that advice doesn't apply to you, it's a sure bet that your local gunshop has one. The collimator has a spud that will fit the caliber of your rifle; you insert it into the muzzle. Attached to it is a little scope with a grid in the field. You align that little scope with your own scope and look through it. The position of your crosshairs on the grid will tell you everything you need to know. Just use the turret adjustments on your scope until your crosshairs center on the grid.

Generally, it's a good idea to collimate your rifle so that it looks like you'll be a bit low; since your scope is about 1½ inches above the barrel, a bit low is just right. If you collimate dead-on, chances are you'll be significantly high at 100 yards.

If you can't locate a collimator, the next best thing is bore-sighting. You can do this at home or at the range, but it takes a steady hand. First remove the bolt. Then place the rifle in some kind of steady rest. At home I often use the arms of an easy chair, bracing the rifle in place with pillows. Pick a clearly defined circular object at least 25 yards away. A knothole on your

A collimator is an extremely useful device that enables a scope to be roughly zeroed before the rifle is fired. All it can do is get the scope and bore in approximate alignment—the actual sighting-in must still be done.

back fence is perfect, and if your house is big enough, a doorknob is great.

Look through the barrel, and center that round object in your field of view. Now brace the rifle carefully and tightly in place. Without touching the rifle, look through the barrel again and make sure that round object is perfectly centered. If it isn't, shift and rebrace until the object remains centered without you touching the rifle. Now look through the scope (or the iron sights). Again, your scope picture should be just a bit high, perhaps an inch, but it should be basically centered on that object. If it isn't, adjust your scope or sights until it is.

Now, here's the tricky part. On the range, when you're adjusting your sights, you move the sights in the direction you want the strike of the bullet to go. Whether it's a scope, an aperture, or an open rear sight, to move the strike of the bullet to the left, you move the sight to the left. To move it up, move your sights up. But in bore-sighting you do *exactly the opposite!* The reason is that on the range, you're trying to shift the strike of the bullet. In bore-sighting, the barrel remains constant and you're moving the sights to match it.

Bore-sighting is not as exact as using a collimator, but you can come surprisingly close if you take your time. If you have an action—such as a lever, pump, or semi-auto—that will not permit looking down the barrel from the breech, you're pretty much out of luck for bore-sighting. It's somewhat possible to do it with a small mirror inserted into the breech, but that's almost more trouble than it's worth. If you can't bore-sight and you can't find a collimator, trial-and-error is all that's left.

Unless you're extremely lucky, your rifle will not be sighted in exactly right, even with a collimator. One hundred yards is a good sight-in range, but for the first couple

*A solid benchrest is the best way to properly zero a rifle. The idea isn't to test your shooting, but to allow the rifle to shoot as well as it can. Rest the fore-end (*not *the barrel!) on a sandbagged rest, and use your supporting arm to snug the butt into your shoulder.*

of shots you're better off to start much closer. With a collimator, 50 yards is a safe bet. If bore-sighting was the method, I'd start at 25 yards. And if neither could be done, start at 25 yards with a big target and hope for the best!

Now, let's say that as far as you can tell the barrel and your sights are properly aligned, and you're ready to shoot. Almost. Take a cleaning rod and run a dry patch through the barrel. At one time new firearms were shipped so packed with grease that firing them would be extremely dangerous. That isn't common these days, but there could be light lubricant in the barrel, and it could change where the bullet hits.

Now you're ready to shoot. At this point you're simply sighting in; you're not trying to see how well you can shoot or to improve your shooting. Instead, the goal is two-fold—to get the rifle to shoot where you want it, and to get some idea of its accuracy potential. To accomplish these things, you want to take away as much of the human element as possible. Enter the benchrest.

The bench is no place to practice shooting, but it's literally the only place to sight in properly. Most public and private ranges have good benches, but if you shoot on the

back 40, a solid bench is easy to make. All you need is a firm, steady platform to rest the rifle on, and a solid stool or tree stump on which to sit. You'll need some padding. Sandbags are ideal, but rolled-up blankets will do. Sit down on the bench. You'll want something solid under the fore-end so that it's naturally raised and aimed toward the target. A section of railroad tie is every bit as good as a commercial rest.

Place a sandbag or other substantial padding on top of that railroad tie. Rest the fore-end (*never* the barrel) across the top, and align yourself and your rifle toward the target. Now take another, smaller sandbag (or rolled-up jacket) and place it under the toe of the stock. Adjust the fore-end and scrunch up the padding under the stock until the sights are perfectly aligned on the target, then adjust your body so that your position is comfortable and natural. Keep on adjusting until the sights remain on target without you exerting any pressure on the rifle.

Wrap the fingers of your shooting hand around the grip. Then take your non-shooting hand and use it to adjust the sandbag at the toe of the stock, and also to pull the buttstock more tightly into your shoulder.

With your chamber empty, dry-fire the rifle several times to get used to the trigger — and also to make certain the rifle stays on target. Now you're really ready. Almost.

From this position you should be able to do the best shooting possible. There's a down side, though. From the bench your body isn't able to give with recoil, and it will take the worst your rifle can dish out. So be a sissy. Put some extra padding between your shoulder and the butt of the stock. On heavy-recoiling rifles (and for me, from the bench, that's anything bigger than a .30–06), put a sandbag between you and the rifle. Make certain you wear hearing protection — either good, tight-fitting plugs or muffs — and shooting glasses.

Now you're ready. Remember the "B.R.A.S.S." rule — Breathe, Relax, Aim, check Sight alignment, really concentrate on your trigger Squeeze. Fire three well-aimed, well-spaced shots. Take a look. You should have a group, and you should be able to use your scope or sight adjustments to move that group where you want it to go. Make the adjustments you think will be right, then fire another carefully aimed shot. Take another look. Chances are you're closer, but probably not yet exactly where you want to be. Repeat the process. If it takes more than a couple more adjustments, however, stop and let your barrel cool. Don't rush things. If you go beyond a half-dozen shots, let the barrel cool for five minutes or so (10 on a hot day) before continuing.

Once you have the bullets landing where you want them, try to shoot nice, tight groups. Rifles are like people — they're individualists, and every rifle simply likes certain brands or types of ammunition better than others. If you're a handloader, you can have a wonderful time trying out dozens of different weights and styles of bullets, different powders and weights of powder charges, different primers, different seating depths — the combinations are endless.

If you don't handload, you can still have some fun. For most popular cartridges there are several different brands of ammo and several different bullet weights and styles.

You now have a rifle that's sighted in, and a good idea what kind of groups it will produce. What do your groups mean? Truthfully, not all that much. Tight groups give a wonderful feeling of confidence in a rifle, and that's good. However, Americans tend to be much too hung up on potential accuracy and group size, and guys in my business are largely to blame. Minute of Angle (MOA) is a term that's thrown about quite a bit. Loosely, it means a one-inch

A nice, tight group like this builds a lot of confidence in a rifle — and confidence is half the battle in field shooting. Tack-driving accuracy is rarely critical when shooting at game. American hunters tend to place undue emphasis on a rifle's raw accuracy; the rifle's handling characteristics and the shooter's familiarity with it are more important.

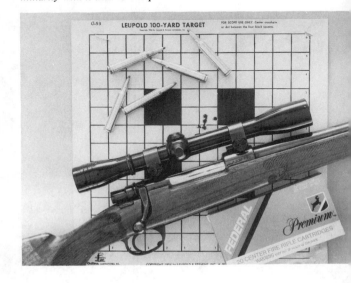

group at 100 yards, a two-inch group at 200 yards, a three-inch group at 300 yards, and so on. From what we read in the magazines, it seems as though a rifle that won't group within an inch is a real lemon.

First off, don't believe it, and second, don't worry about it. Factory rifles are very good today, and many of them will print sub-MOA groups right out of the box—especially if you're speaking of three-shot groups with selected ammo. Much fewer will hold those groups for five shots, especially with the thin barrels in vogue today, and fewer still will even come close when you pick a box of ammo off the shelf. If you have one that will, cherish it. But if yours won't, don't worry about it.

Acceptable field accuracy is whatever you need to get the job done. For most of us, that's pie-plate accuracy at 100 yards. If you seriously intend to make a habit of 400-yard shots, you need a bit more. In fact, taking some human error into account, you might have some use for one-inch groups. Truthfully, though, any rifle that will print two-inch three-shot groups is plenty good enough for 99.9 percent of all hunting applications, and three-inch groups will cover a good 95 percent.

I'm thinking right now about my own favorite hunting rifles. I actually do own two that are superbly accurate, one in 7mm Remington Magnum and the other in .30–06. Both will group around an inch on

Checking a rifle's zero is an important ritual that should mark the beginning of any hunt, especially if you've traveled a long way with your rifle. The chances are slim that a properly sighted-in rifle with good sights will go out of zero, but it pays to make sure!

any given day, and on a calm day when I haven't poured too much coffee, they'll cut that in half. The 7mm needs carefully concocted handloads to do that, while the '06 will do it with nearly anything. I'm lucky to have them, and I cherish them both. But I don't use either one very much. I'm more likely to use a fiberglass-stocked .338, and no matter what I do to it, it's a 1½-inch rifle.

When the chips are down, a real favorite is a beat-up old Model 70 in .375 that's been converted to left-hand bolt. I lie about this rifle a lot, but the truth is that groups under two inches are few and far between. And yet I've made some terribly long, difficult shots with that rifle. Just so long as I don't think about the group size too much, it gets the job done just fine.

That's the key, of course — getting the job done. Few rifles have claimed as many deer as the lever-action .30–30. Such rifles can be accurate in modern terms, but few are — and with the factory sights most of them are used with, potential accuracy is a moot point. It doesn't really matter whether they'll group in two, three, or five inches; what really matters is that they will consistently put their bullets in a deer's vital zone, call it a 10-inch circle, at the ranges for which they were intended. That's good enough.

If your rifle groups well too, all the better. But don't worry about it. In the field, that one-inch group means nothing. The only meaningful factor is your ability to put your bullet in the vitals of your game at any time, from any angle, and from any reasonable distance with which you feel comfortable.

7

Stock Fit

One of the great secrets to successful field shooting is having a rifle that fits properly. And yet there's no great mystery involved here — it's the gunstock that makes it fit. Gun fit is also extremely democratic; the plainest, least expensive off-the-shelf rifle can fit just as well — or just as poorly — as the most expensive custom rifle. The good news is that virtually any gunstock can be made to fit properly.

The objective in having a stock fit properly is quite simple: When you shoulder the rifle, quickly or deliberately, it should come up with the sights aligned and on target. In fact, the best test of stock fit is to focus all of your attention on an object perhaps 20 yards away, then close your eyes. Continue concentrating on the object, and throw the rifle to your shoulder. Open your eyes. The scope or sights should be roughly aligned

on the center of your chosen object. If they aren't, your stock may not fit you properly.

The most critical dimension, I believe, is length of pull. Essentially, this is the straight-line distance from the trigger to the butt. The so-called "standard" length of pull on most factory rifles is 13¾ inches. I'm average in size, about five feet eight inches, and that standard length of pull has always suited me just fine. But if you happen to be six feet five or five feet two, the standard dimension just might not work. Also, even if you're "standard" in size, that standard dimension could be a bit long if you customarily hunt in cold weather with lots of clothes on.

A quick way to check is to lay the butt-plate against the crook of your elbow and try to wrap your hand naturally around the grip. Then extend your trigger finger to the trigger; you should reach it naturally and comfortably, with just the last joint of your finger in contact with the trigger and the buttplate resting loosely against your bicep. If that's achieved, in most cases the length of pull will be just right.

If it isn't, there is a simple fix — so long as you aren't dealing with a piece of walnut too pretty or valuable to alter. If you are, hang the rifle on the wall and buy one you don't mind fooling with, because with a stock that's too long or too short, you're at a tremendous handicap in the field.

A gunstock is easily shortened by removing the buttplate or recoil pad and hacking off a piece of wood. It's a simple job, but it's best left to a gunsmith since the stock must be carefully taped to prevent ragged edges, and the recoil pad or buttplate must

be reset. If you do it yourself, take great care not to remove too much wood; length of pull is a critical dimension, and just a quarter-inch can make a big difference. Take care also not to alter the pitch — the angle formed by the horizontal line of the bore and the vertical line of the buttplate.

If a stock is too short, the cure is only slightly more complex. If the rifle doesn't have a rubber recoil pad, the addition of a good, thick one is usually enough to make a difference. If not, a piece of wood must be

Length of pull is generally the most critical dimension in stock fit. It's easy to check by placing the rifle in the crook of your arm, attempting to wrap your hand naturally around the pistolgrip, and placing your finger properly on the trigger. If this can be done, the length of pull is generally about right.

The primary objective of having a stock fit properly on a hunting rifle is to facilitate quick, accurate field shooting.

crafted as a shim between stock and butt-plate. It takes a little work, but isn't really a big deal.

Height of comb is the next most important item in stock fit. There isn't really a standard dimension here; it depends on whether the rifle was built for use with a scope or with iron sights. Since a scope is significantly higher (usually about three-quarters of an inch) than iron sights, the comb must be higher.

Whether the comb is right for you or not depends to some extent on the relative length of your neck and how your face is shaped — whether you have prominent cheekbones or not, and the length of your jaw. If the comb is too high, you'll find yourself having to grind your cheek down into the stock to get a good sight picture; if it's too low, you'll have to consciously lift your face. In either case, you won't be comfortable, and the rifle will kick the hell out of you. If the comb is too high, it's a simple matter to remove a little wood. If it's too low, the best thing is to try to mount the scope a bit lower. If that can't be done, you

need to build up the comb a bit with a couple of layers of moleskin.

Shooting styles come into play here, too. Americans like to position a scope just like they shoot iron sights — mounted extremely low so the neck is arched forward and the cheek makes firm contact with the stock. That's the way I like to shoot, and that's the way I stock my rifles — when I have a choice.

There's much more to stock fit than length of pull and height of comb. There are stocks without cheekpieces and with rollover cheekpieces, thumbhole stocks, Monte Carlo combs, and the list goes on. These options are mostly matters of personal preference and comfort.

There are a few more points to consider. The stock dimension called "drop at heel" defines how far below the centerline of the bore the heel of the stock lies. The so-called "classic" style of stock has a straight comb with very little drop. It tends to put the stock quite high on the shoulder during shooting, and the recoil moves back more or less in a straight line. The classic stock is

These bolt actions from Kassnar show the two most common buttstock configurations seen on modern sporters. Top is a Monte Carlo comb; bottom is an American classic style with a straight comb.

A classic-style butt with straight comb will ride high on the shoulder, and recoil will come back in a straight line.

The Monte Carlo comb places the butt lower on the shoulder, and generally the recoil will be taken away from the cheek. But it may be felt more severely in the shoulder. Butt style is really a matter of personal preference; neither type has a real advantage over the other.

generally used with scope sights; the comb will usually be a bit too high to let the shooter "get down" on iron sights.

The popular Monte Carlo comb has much more drop at heel; then the comb is raised to achieve the proper height for scope use. The Monte Carlo comb places the butt a bit lower on the shoulder. Roy Weatherby's theory about the Monte Carlo comb was that under recoil, it moved the rifle away from the face. That's true, but it might well accentuate the recoil to the shoulder. With the classic stock, the opposite is true—there's not so much felt recoil to the shoulder, but perhaps a bit more of a blow to the face. It doesn't really matter

which you prefer, so long as the stock fits you and you're comfortable with it. If that's true, the recoil will be just fine.

There are a couple of things to watch out for, though. Whether you like a cheekpiece isn't important, but under any circumstances the top of the comb should be gently rounded. Slanting, narrow combs look neat, but with every shot they'll dig right into your face. Likewise, slender butt-plates (or recoil pads) are sheer agony. A good, broad buttplate or recoil pad spreads out the recoil nicely and makes a

This stock from E. C. Bishop & Sons in Warsaw, Missouri, has the slim, elegant lines that make the classic style so popular. The cheekpiece is preferred by some and avoided by others; it's primarily cosmetic.

big difference. A nice, flat, "shotgun-style" buttplate not only reduces felt recoil, but is much faster to settle into the shoulder.

For an example of the worst stock design known to man, take a look at the Model 1895 Winchester that Teddy Roosevelt loved so well. Few rifles have ever looked sleeker, but look at the tremendous drop at heel, the crescent buttplate, and the razor-thin comb. I've never shot one chambered for the big .405 Winchester cartridge, and I don't want to.

Fortunately, modern stock designs are a great deal better than what Teddy had to live with. The vast majority of off-the-shelf rifles will fit the average man just fine. And if you aren't average, a simple if not esthetically pleasing solution can usually be found. The important thing is to do whatever is necessary to get a gunstock that fits you properly—that comes up on target with the sights aligned and won't kick your teeth out. This is one of the real secrets to consistent field shooting.

8

Recoil and the Flinch

There's no getting around it—centerfire rifles kick. All guns have recoil, but we usually don't think of a .22 rifle as "kicking." It does, but not enough to concern anyone. We do think about recoil with guns in the deer-rifle class, and most of us believe that anything much larger is sure to do us bodily harm.

First off, it needs to be understood that recoil does exist. It's a very real rearward force created as an "equal and opposite reaction" to the forward movement of the bullet. The heavier the bullet and the faster that bullet moves, the more recoil is generated. For instance, a .30–06 rifle weighing eight pounds generates just over 20 foot-pounds of recoil with a 180-grain bullet. A .300 magnum of the same weight churns up about 50 percent more recoil. Most important to hunters is how that recoil is felt, perceived, and handled.

"Free recoil" is a term used to describe the raw recoil figures that laboratory testing creates. There aren't any real surprises there; if gun weight remains constant, recoil increases with the power of the cartridge. If gun weight is increased as caliber is increased, the increase in recoil can be lessened somewhat.

Free recoil, however, doesn't tell the whole story. Far more important is what we call "felt recoil"—the actual kick the shooter feels on his or her shoulder and cheek. Many factors influence felt recoil—stock fit, design and shape of the butt and comb, gun weight, shooting position, and perhaps most important of all, mental attitude. You see, if you think you're going to get the hell kicked out of you, chances are you will.

Let's look first at the characteristics of your rifle that influence felt recoil. First is

A rifle like this .458 Lott churns up in excess of 80 foot-pounds of recoil, and you're going to feel it! There's a big difference between clinical recoil energy and "felt recoil"—the way that recoil is perceived. Gun weight, stock style and fit, and the position and attitude of the shooter have just as much influence on felt recoil as the raw foot-pounds of recoil generated.

stock fit. As discussed in the previous chapter, a poorly fitting stock is going to kick the hell out of you. To achieve a proper sight picture, chances are you'll have to nestle the butt into the wrong place, either out on your arm or in toward your collarbone. In either place, you could be in for a painful experience. In the latter case, I saw a shooter break his collarbone with one shot from a .460 Weatherby. Its owner tried to show him how to hold it and where to place the butt, but he wouldn't listen.

If you're using a scope, an important part of gun fit is ensuring that you have enough eye relief—the distance between your eye and the scope at which you achieve a full, proper field of view. On any gun in the deer-rifle class, three inches of eye relief is absolutely essential; on magnums, four inches. If you don't have enough eye relief, you'll know it soon enough; under recoil the scope will hit you between the eyes, causing a painful, messy, and most embarrassing wound. And that's the best way I know to become afraid of a rifle. Keeping clear of the scope at the rifle range, however, may not be quite enough. In the field you may have to assume some weird shooting positions, and you might get popped between the eyes when you least expect it.

I know what I'm speaking about. If we ever meet in a hunting camp, take a close look and you'll find two or three permanent half-moon scars between my eyebrows! But I wind up shooting a lot of different rifles, many of them scoped by and for other shooters. Just last year I took a test rifle in .340 Weatherby on a hunt, and I didn't have time to remount the scope. Every time I pulled the trigger, that thing hit me right between the eyes, hard. My worst scar was caused by a little .30–06 and a 3–9X scope without enough eye relief, and the specific shot was a hasty one from a loose prone position at a big mulie.

But it isn't necessary to take that kind of abuse. Buy a scope with non-critical eye relief (Leupolds, among others, are very good in this area), and mount it as far forward as you can. If you do get hit by the scope, don't be afraid of the rifle. Try to move the scope forward a bit, and if you can't do so and still obtain a full field of view, trade it for another scope.

Stock fit will go a long way toward reducing felt recoil. Stock *design* is another subject, and it's equally important in how you feel recoil. The Winchester Model 94, for example, is an all-time classic deer rifle, and its .30–30 cartridge, though adequate, is hardly a powerhouse. But that Model 94 in its original configuration, with its lightweight, narrow butt and lots of drop in the stock, just plain kicks like hell. It isn't unmanageable, but it would be with cartridges of significantly more power. The older Winchester lever guns, with similar stocks but using much more powerful cartridges, must have been real beasts in the recoil department.

A lot of drop between heel and comb seems to accentuate recoil and certainly does drive the rifle into the cheekbone, but with the vast majority of today's gunstocks being made for scope use, that problem is pretty rare. Rare, too, are the old crescent-steel buttplates that I cringe to look at. However, "classic" stocks are much in vogue today, very slim and very beautiful. Up to a point that's fine, but a good broad buttplate goes a long way toward spreading out recoil, and a gently rolling comb is critical to avoiding a bruised cheekbone.

I have a pet .30–06 with a lovely classic-style stock. It's very pleasant to shoot, with a gently rounded comb (no cheekpiece) and a buttplate 1½ inches wide. My .338, on the other hand, has a stock that appears identical. But when you put a ruler on the butt, you see that it's 1¾ inches wide —

The prone position is one of the worst for recoil; your body simply has nowhere to go. This hunter probably won't feel a thing, thanks to the intense excitement of shooting at game. On the other hand, if he doesn't have enough eye relief, he's likely to come away with a headache — the prone position is where you're most likely to get "kissed" by your scope if your eye is too close to it.

and that extra quarter-inch makes a big difference on a rifle with that much more potential recoil.

Numerous different stock designs are available that may or may not impact on felt recoil. Thumbholes were in vogue at one time, and some folks like 'em. Cheekpieces, rollover combs, Monte Carlo combs — all are acceptable features on a gunstock, but are pretty much cosmetic; their chief value is in the eye of the beholder. Basically, if you don't have a lot of drop, avoid sharp angles, and don't get carried away with slimness, you'll have a stock that will go a long way toward reducing felt recoil.

Gun weight is a subject that can be debated endlessly. Today the trend in factory rifles is toward light weight. A few decades ago an eight-pound .30–06 — probably closer to 8½ pounds loaded and scoped — would have been quite normal. Today there are a number of 6½-pound factory rifles, call 'em seven pounds all set to go.

The lightweights are a great joy to carry, no question about it. Often they wear a synthetic stock of fiberglass, Kevlar, Rynite, or whatever, and these add the advantage of being impervious to the elements. Just keep in mind that light rifles kick more, and very light rifles kick a lot more. If you go too far, you may wind up with a beast that nobody can handle.

I went too far once. I have a 6½-pound .416 Hoffman, a wildcat cartridge based on the .375 H&H cartridge that propels a 400-grain bullet at 2,400 feet per second. In a gun weighing 10 pounds, the rifle would be extremely unpleasant, but acceptable. As an ultra-lightweight, it's a joy to carry on a long tracking job after elephant and such, but a real nightmare to shoot. That rifle borders on the ridiculous.

There may be a few shooters out there who could handle that .416 with no prob-

The lightweight synthetic stocks are a real boon for carrying in rough country, and they're also impervious to the elements. On the other hand, light rifles are going to have more felt recoil. This stock has been fitted with a Pachmayr Decelerator, one of the new impact-absorbing pads that really help tame recoil.

lem. But I suspect they're rare. If a real lightweight is your desire, I'd keep it chambered to one of the mild-recoilling, ultra-efficient cartridges that will do the job on the vast majority of game. Excellent choices would be the .257 Roberts, .25–06, 7mm-08, 7x57 Mauser, .270, and .280. A .30–06 at 7½ to 8 pounds is portable and manageable; the popular 7mm Magnum is about the same. If a larger magnum is your game, you should be willing to tote 8½ to 9 pounds. The big boys, such as the .375, seem best at about 9½ pounds; 10½ pounds or more is best for a .458 — and it's still going to belt you.

Shooting positions figure heavily into felt recoil. Unfortunately, the two steadiest positions — from the bench and prone — are the worst for recoil. On the bench or lying down, your body has no place to go. However much recoil is present, you're going to get all of it. Shooting from the bench is necessary to see how the rifle shoots, and the first shots from most centerfire rifles will be fired from a solid rest.

As mentioned earlier, bench shooting has no relationship whatsoever to field shooting. So be a wimp and don't be ashamed of it — put some extra padding between you and the rifle. On the rare occasions when I bench that .416 I mentioned, I start out with a padded shooting coat. Then I put a sandbag between the butt and my shoulder. And then I put a towel or a P.A.S.T. recoil shield between the comb and my face. And I don't really care if my buddies giggle.

That's extreme, but the use of extra padding when benching any rifle above .243 is just common sense. Of critical importance, and usually forgotten until too late, is padding the elbows. Recoil will drag your elbows across the bench and scrape hell out of them.

Extra padding makes sense from the prone position, too. In fact, prone is even worse. From the bench your body can rock back a fair amount. In the prone you're held in place by your body weight, and you have quite literally no place to go. Generally, too, in the prone position your head is cocked forward at a slight angle. If a scope is ever going to hit you, it will do it in the prone position. We'll talk about that later, but keep in mind that you must assume that position deliberately and with care. Use extra padding when practicing, and make a conscious effort to get your head upright and well back from the scope.

The other shooting positions leave your body with much more flexibility; you can roll much more with the punch, and your felt recoil will be a great deal less. This is yet another reason to get off the bench as quickly as you can and practice the way you'll shoot in the field.

Of course, mental attitude is important. If you think you're going to get kicked, you will. If your body is tight and tense in anticipation of recoil, you'll feel it. Stay loose and relaxed. Wear good hearing protection — centerfire rifles are loud, and it's all too easy to confuse the bark with the bite. Concentrate on the shooting basics, not the recoil, and you won't feel it as much.

Many women I know regularly shoot rifles of a power level that most men shake their heads at. One of my wife's best friends is a slim grandmother whose favorite rifle is

When you're practicing your shooting skills, there's no reason to suffer more recoil than you have to. A rifleman's padded shooting coat like this helps a great deal, and ear protection is essential.

a Westley-Richards double .465 — and she shoots it with deadly accuracy.

Women tend to have two advantages. First, they approach shooting with fewer preconceived notions. Since nobody bothered to tell them that recoil was horrible, they don't worry about it as much as most men do, provided nobody makes the mistake of starting them off with a cannon. Second, women tend to be lighter than the average man. The theory is that they "give" more under recoil, and thus don't experience the same level of felt recoil. I think that's quite true. I'm a fairly small man, at about five feet eight inches and 160 pounds. I "give" plenty under recoil, and I seem somewhat less affected by it than a man half again my size.

But size isn't something we can do anything about. We can do plenty about mental attitude, and it's critical to all shooting activities, including recoil.

I tend more toward heavy calibers. I want to hit an animal in the right place, of course, but I also want to hit him hard. If you select a cartridge that's a great deal more powerful than you really need, you will be accepting more recoil than you have to. Chances are you won't shoot the rifle as much as you would a lighter caliber, and you won't be as proficient with it.

On the other hand, as hunters we have not only the desire but also the obligation to take our game cleanly, and adequate cartridges are just as important as proper bullet placement. An unwillingness to accept recoil is no excuse for hunting with an inadequate cartridge. And fear of recoil is an even worse excuse for not putting your bullets in the right place. If you're going to hunt, you have an obligation to yourself, your game, and your sport to attain proficiency with adequate arms. And you can do it. The deer cartridges pose problems for

few of us, but with proper practice, good padding, and a positive attitude, virtually anyone can become proficient with bear-elk-moose cartridges on the order of the .338 and larger.

It's all too easy to learn to fear the rifle before you learn to shoot it. Maybe your eyes close just before the rifle goes off, and that's easy to diagnose. More common is a slight, involuntary muscular twitch in anticipation of recoil. It's called the flinch, and it happens to everybody once in a while. It's always disastrous, especially on game.

The PAST recoil shield is one of several new products that use space-age shock-absorbing materials to reduce felt recoil. Worn in a shoulder-holster type of harness, the PAST shield is light, cool, and extremely effective.

To find out if you're having that problem, go to the range with a buddy and fire a few shots offhand. Then hand your partner some cartridges, and keep your back to him while he loads — or pretends to load — the rifle. When he hands back the rifle, you won't know whether it's empty or loaded. If the rifle barrel ducks or bobs as you snap on an empty chamber, well, you've got it.

Curing a rifleman's flinch takes a bit of work. The first factor needing attention is concentration. If you're concentrating on the shooting basics, especially the trigger squeeze, flinching should not occur. All it is, really, is an anticipation of the rifle going off. And if you're squeezing your trigger properly, that can't happen. But flinching is usually accompanied by, perhaps caused by, jerking the trigger. So the best cure is working on trigger control.

The best thing would be to go back to a .22 rimfire, a gun with no recoil, and re-learn the basics. Practice extensively without recoil, and then start all over again with your hunting rifle — this time with plenty of padding and good shooting positions.

Maybe that won't work. It's possible that you might have to consider going to a lighter caliber, one that will still do the job. Today there are more ways than ever to tame recoil.

We've discussed gun weight. A pound of lead judiciously applied to hollows inletted into the barrel channel and underneath the buttplate can work wonders; I added a full 1½ pounds to a vicious .458 in that fashion, and did it carefully enough to avoid altering the rifle's balance. But gun weight may not be desirable in a hunting rifle.

Look at the buttplate. If it doesn't wear a good, thick rubber recoil pad, it should. Installing one is a simple matter, but unless you're handy with tools, a gunsmith should do it. Some wood will need to be removed

from the stock to make sure the length of pull remains the same (unless you want the length altered in the bargain, in which case a different buttplate is the easiest solution). And the stock must be carefully taped and the pad sanded down uniformly to fit. Any rubber recoil pad soaks up some kick and has the advantage of providing a nonslip surface that holds the butt in place on your shoulder between shots. If you're having recoil problems, go for a good thick pad.

Even better is the new generation of pads made from space-age materials that absorb impact. There are several brands, but a fine example is Pachmayr's Decelerator pad made from new elastomer material.

Add to that a P.A.S.T. or similar shoulder pad. Any good gunshop should stock these, and they're available as pads that you can pin to your shirt or wear like a shoulder holster. I don't carry one in the field — with adrenaline going, it's rare to feel recoil while shooting at game — but I consistently use one on the bench.

The last item to consider is a mechanical addition to your rifle to reduce felt recoil. Muzzle brakes are nothing new; the Cutts Compensator goes back many decades and was common both on shotguns and to reduce the vicious muzzle climb of the Thompson submachinegun. Any muzzle brake or barrel-venting system uses redirected gases bled off at the muzzle to counter some of the effects of recoil. Properly installed onto or cut into your barrel, any system currently in use will have no appreciable effect on accuracy or velocity.

Initially, barrel venting's primary effect was to reduce muzzle climb. Today, though, muzzle brakes and venting systems have become much more sophisticated. They not only reduce muzzle climb but also significantly and actually reduce felt recoil. The best-known barrel-venting system

KDF's Recoil Arrestor, left, and Larry Kelly's Mag-Na-Porting are two effective means for reducing felt recoil. Both systems work extremely well, and both have the same drawback of increasing muzzle blast, making hearing protection even more important. I have used both systems, and can recommend either.

today is Larry Kelly's Mag-Na-Porting. It consists of a series of vents actually inletted into your barrel just shy of the muzzle. Cosmetically, Mag-Na-Porting is neat — you have to look hard to know it's there. If it has a drawback, it's that the system is permanent. That's OK; it works, and I can't imagine wanting to remove it once you've tried it. However, anytime you redirect gases, they must go somewhere. The big drawback to any venting or muzzle-brake system is a significant increase in muzzle blast, especially for bystanders. Hearing protection on the range, always important, is even more essential with one of these venting systems. Light earplugs should be considered for field use.

Another option is the new generation of muzzle brakes. Cosmetically, you know they're there, although they are much less bulky than their predecessors. They add a couple of inches to your barrel length. However, today's muzzle brakes are amazingly effective. A couple of good ones are KDF's Recoil Arrestor and Gale McMillan's system. I put the KDF on that beast of a .416, not really expecting much. Unbelievable! It still kicks, but about on a par with a normal .375. The reduction must be in the 40 percent range. This system also has the advantage of being threaded onto the barrel; it can be removed at will and replaced with a blued thread protector for field use.

I've never been fond of appendages on the end of gun barrels, but I have to say that both Mag-Na-Porting and the KDF brake have made me a believer! The cost is healthy, probably something over $100. But if I were having recoil problems, I'd get a good, modern recoil pad and then I'd do something to the other end. It's amazing how well you can shoot a rifle you aren't afraid of!

9

Start 'Em Out Right

If you step into a National Forest on opening day of deer season east of the Mississippi, chances are you'll believe there are too many hunters. Truth is, there aren't enough. These lines are being written in 1988, and hunting-license sales in America haven't increased in several years. There are lots of hunters—millions of us. But our numbers aren't growing, and that's scary. Even if we stay as numerous, we'll decline as a percentage of the population.

We need more hunters, for now and for the future, and it's up to all of us to make sure our ranks grow—it's really the only chance we have against the anti-hunters. Now, I don't believe that everybody needs to hunt, but if we start newcomers out right, we'll make folks who, even if they aren't out there every opening day, will at least understand why we hunt.

Everybody starts out at the same point. When we think about beginners, we generally think of kids. But wives, girlfriends, sisters, and a surprising number of adult males may also be beginners. Women and kids who are beginners *know* they are, and they'll listen. Men, beginners or not, usually won't. Which makes starting out right a bit difficult.

My daughter isn't quite three at this writing, and it's a bit early to get her started. My stepson, however, just turned 21, and when I met him at 18, he'd done no shooting whatsoever. Fortunately he's a natural athlete, and he has very quickly become a superb shot. My father-in-law, on the other hand, has been a shooter all his life but had never hunted at all until I took him out for his first big-game animal, a wild pig, about three years ago. Since then he's gotten the fever; we've done more pig hunting, he's taken his first deer, and he celebrated his retirement last year with a full-blown African safari.

The single most critical item for any beginning hunter (as well as any beginning shooter) is safety. The basics of safe gun handling must be taught, emphasized, and then checked and rechecked—and the sex or age of the beginner doesn't make any difference. For persons under a certain age, an approved hunter-safety course is required in most states today. Whether it's required or not, I heartily recommend such a course for any new hunter.

Training in gun safety doesn't stop with a hunter-safety course. We all get excited in the presence of game, but a beginning hunter has a right to get a bit more excited than someone with lots of experience. That's OK, just so long as an experienced hunter is monitoring things and can step in when needed. My stepson, Paul Stockwell, has gotten quite a bit of experience in the last three years, and he's become very competent. But it's still new to him, and I still watch his gunbarrel's direction, and I'm probably a major pain about having him clear his chamber and check his safety. I do the same with my father-in-law, although I'm probably a bit more diplomatic with him.

I'm a big fan of the late Robert Ruark's writings, and there's a marvelous passage in *The Old Man and the Boy* about the Old Man teaching young Ruark how to shoot. The boy had just missed a quail, and the Old Man, his grandfather, was showing him how to mount the gun and fire. He handed him an "empty" shotgun and told him to try it—but he'd slipped in a shell while the kid wasn't looking. *Blam!* There's nothing louder than a gun going off when you don't expect it, and no more graphic

The .22 rimfire is a marvelous instrument for beginners, and it's just as good for experienced hunters who want to keep their shooting skills sharp. With inexpensive ammo, low report, and virtually no recoil, a good .22 is the ideal gun with which to learn.

lesson in why you always have to check the chamber.

Now, I don't exactly recommend "dirty pool" like that, but I'm sure it was a lesson Ruark never forgot. Nobody did that to me on purpose—I did it to myself, and I've never forgotten it. I was probably 11, and I was tired. We'd been quail hunting, and I was walking down a dirt road with a Model 12 20 gauge. The safety was on, or so I thought, and I guess my finger accidentally touched the trigger. *Boom!* A huge crater appeared in the road at my feet, and it's a good thing I already had most of my adult height, 'cause the fright surely would have stunted my growth. It was a positive thing, really; nobody got hurt, and ever since, I've been maniacal about checking chambers and safeties. It's likely that most of us have some kind of a near-miss hidden away in our memories, but it shouldn't take that kind of a lesson if we get — and give — good training and careful supervision.

The first gun for most of us is a BB gun, probably a Daisy. It's as good a training tool now as it was in the days of the Red Ryder. There's no noise, no recoil, and little cost, and it can be shot safely in urban backyards or even living rooms with a good target frame. To start things out right, the BB gun should be treated as if it were a powerful firearm. Use it to learn or teach the shooting basics — the B.R.A.S.S. rule talked about earlier. And use it to learn safe gun handling.

The next step is usually a .22, and the .22 is a powerful firearm. At modest cost, and with low noise level and almost no recoil, the .22 rimfire rifle can teach 99 percent of everything anyone needs to know about field shooting. The little .22, judiciously applied on rabbits, squirrels, and small varmints, can even teach shot placement and stalking skills.

Regardless of the long-term hunting plans the beginner has (or you have for him or her), I think it makes sense to start out with an open-sighted .22. It's more difficult to shoot, true, but you don't have to start out at long range. With open sights, the basics of sight alignment simply must be grasped. Later, perhaps, you'll want to put a scope on that .22, if you plan to hunt big game with a scoped rifle. There's a pitfall here, though. Since the .22 has virtually no recoil, you don't worry about eye relief or bad habits such as "crawling the stock" — allowing your face to creep forward toward the eyepiece. If you mount a scope on a beginner's .22, make sure the scope is placed well forward and has the same kind of eye relief you would have on a centerfire.

Eventually beginning hunters must make the transition to the centerfire world. Start

'em out gently. A centerfire .22, such as a .222 or .223, is a great tool for this purpose. It has all the noise you need to get the point across, and just enough recoil to give an idea of things to come. A .243 or 6mm Remington is just as good, and can be used as a big-game rifle while the centerfire .22 cannot. Insist on hearing protection, and for smaller children and petite women, use some extra padding at first — even on a .243.

The bench is a good place to start. Make sure the rifle is already sighted in; you want beginners to quickly gain confidence in their ability to hit what they aim at. Paper targets are nice, but tin cans and other "movable" targets are a lot more fun for youngsters. Once the beginner has the basics, move away from the bench and practice shooting from different positions.

With adults, there's no such thing as starting too late in life. With children, though, how early to start is very much a judgment call that only the parents can make. Many states prohibit persons under 12 from holding a hunting license. A 12-year-old may or may not be ready. On the other hand, I've been in the field with 8-year-olds (under their parents' supervision, of course) who did a fine job.

It's normal to allow a youngster to tag along on short jaunts without carrying a firearm as soon as he or she wants to go. That's a good opportunity to explain things, but be careful not to wear them out. Later the BB gun will come along, then a .22, and eventually the youngster will be ready to go out and get that all-important first deer.

Choice of arms for that first hunt is extremely important. First off, the stock must fit, and if that means a bit of trimming, so be it. Second, the gun must be adequate for the job at hand. The first big-game rifle for

Although the laws of most states dictate a minimum age for legal hunting, parents are generally best able to tell when a youngster is ready to start hunting. I was with 11-year-old James North when he bagged his first whitetail, and he handled himself better than many hunters several times his age.

many of us is a .243, and for small deer and antelope it's quite adequate. However — and this may sound radical — the .243 is really more of an expert's rifle than a beginner's rifle. It doesn't kick, and that's a plus. But it also requires pinpoint shot placement on larger deer, and on good-sized animals it will not handle well the quartering shot or bad-angle shot that the beginner may not know enough to pass up.

Now, a beginner does not need to be saddled with a hard-kicking rifle; a .30–06 will probably be too much gun. But if you're picking a *hunting* rifle (not necessarily a "learning-to-shoot" rifle) for a beginner, there are some excellent choices out there that don't kick and will flat get the job done.

I started my stepson on the bench with a little .243, and he shot it extremely well. He's a big kid, half again my size, but he

didn't grow up shooting, and, like many big men, recoil is hard on him. Today he'll shoot my .375 when he has to, but he doesn't even pretend to like it. For his first deer hunt I outfitted him with a fairly heavy .270. It was a pleasant gun to shoot, and he learned to shoot it well enough to poleaxe his first deer with one shot at about 150 yards.

Like I said, he's a big guy and some extra gun weight wasn't significant. But for youngsters and women, you generally need to keep the gun weight down, so even a .270 may be too much gun to start with. I got my first wife a lovely .250 Savage bolt action on a Mexican Mauser action, a gorgeous rifle. That was an ideal beginner's hunting rifle, and she shot it well. A better choice would be a .257 Roberts or a .25-06. And perhaps the best choice of all would be the little 7mm–08 Remington. I'm a bolt-action man, and I'd put my money in a short bolt action like the Remington. But Browning's slick lever action would be another good choice. The 7mm–08 won't reach out forever, but you don't want the beginner to try long shots. It does have the bullet weight, caliber, and velocity to do the job on anything short of big bull elk (which it will handle nicely if you're very, very careful), and the recoil is very mild. The good old 7x57 Mauser, available in more rifles and currently available in surplus Mauser form, would be another fine choice.

Whatever the beginner is outfitted with, the next step is to get out into the field. Now, hunting is damned hard work under most conditions. And in many parts of the country, not all of us are going to get our deer every year, no matter how hard we hunt. So there is a very real risk that the beginner will lose interest and quit hunting if conditions are too tough or the chances of success seem too remote.

Left to right, *.243 Winchester, 7mm–08 Remington, .308 Winchester. These three cartridges based on the .308 Winchester are all ideal for beginners, giving light recoil, good accuracy, and efficiency on game. My pick as the ideal first big-game cartridge would be the fairly new 7mm–08.*

The wild hog is available as a game animal in more places all the time. Pigs are exciting to hunt and make an ideal first quarry for a beginner. There are usually opportunities to set up a good shot, and success is generally more likely than in deer hunting.

Don't count on beginner's luck—do whatever you can to stack the deck in the beginner's favor. In many parts of the country, that may mean insisting on a doe tag for the first hunt. Perhaps it means going to a different area or hunting a different animal. Here in California we're fortunate to have a year-round season on free-ranging wild hogs, and if there's a better animal for a beginner, I don't know what it is. They're plentiful, relatively easy to set up for a close shot, and exciting as heck to hunt. That's what I started my father-in-law on—but I made the mistake of letting him use his .243. It would have been fine on a sow, but wasn't enough gun for the big boar he encountered. He got it, but not easily or neatly.

Out West, the pronghorn offers a fine first big-game hunt. That's what I started

with. In much of the country, big-game hunting means whitetail deer hunting, but even with the whitetail, you may be able to stack the deck in the beginner's favor. Doe hunts are often an option, and there may be special opportunity hunts in your part of the country that are particularly good. Hunting is hunting, and every beginner must understand that success isn't assured—but if you can somehow arrange for the beginner to be successful at some point in his first few outings, you'll go a long way toward creating a lifelong hunter.

It pays dividends to sacrifice some of your own hunting to get a beginner a good shot. You might be able to stay right with your pupil, helping to locate game and then coaching during the shot—and some

When possible, an experienced hunter should go in with a beginner for his or her first few shots at game. The "coach" must keep his cool, can keep an eye on safety, make appropriate suggestions, and lend moral support.

coaching is a big help on that all-important first shot on big game.

When we encountered my stepson Paul's first buck, I was a few feet away. But my friend and colleague Bob Robb was right beside him, and I heard him take over: "Can you see the buck? OK, take your time. Get a good rest. That's it. Now get a good sight picture. Wait just a moment — he's going to stop. That's it. Now put the cross-hairs just behind his shoulder and squeeze the trigger." Perfect, and best of all, the advice was delivered in a calm, quiet voice. Coaching is great, but only if the coach can keep his cool — buck fever is infectious. If you can't keep your voice calm and level, keep your mouth shut and just lend moral support!

10

Shooting Positions

Four basic positions are in common use in formal target shooting disciplines: prone, sitting, kneeling, and standing, formerly called offhand. In target shooting, these positions are extremely rigid and inflexible—there aren't more than one or two ways to assume them properly. Field shooting is totally flexible; nobody is watching, nobody is keeping score—but a full or empty freezer depends on the outcome. In the field, these shooting positions often are (and should be!) modified with the addition of a steady rest whenever possible. And of course uneven terrain and intervening obstacles mean that the hunter's shooting position is sometimes quite imaginative.

In spite of all this, it's important to understand and be totally familiar with the four basic positions and how to get into them quickly. Improvisation in the field is not only good, it's essential, but improvised shooting positions should be an extension of good basics, not a replacement for them.

The steadiest shooting position is prone, but sitting is only slightly less so. Kneeling is very fast, but not nearly so steady as sitting. Standing is the least steady by a huge margin; in any rifle competition requiring that position, it's the one that separates the winners from the also-rans. Let's take a look at each of these positions and see where they fit into field shooting.

Prone

The prone position is assumed simply by lying down behind the rifle, elbows planted firmly, butt tight into the shoulder, head cocked upright, and cheek positioned firmly on the stock. The classic prone position has the shooter's body and out-

Formal shooting positions can be modified infinitely in the field, but it's essential to learn how and when to use each basic position.

stretched legs at a 45-degree angle to the left for a right-handed shooter, to the right for a left-handed shooter. That position continues to work best for me, but many modern coaches teach the shooter to lie more directly behind the rifle and draw partway forward the leg that's on the same side as the rifle. The 45-degree angle position allows a bit more give under recoil, but other than that, whatever feels most comfortable is just dandy.

The prone position is the slowest for the shooter to assume; most of us are unwilling to belly-flop onto rough ground. It's also the steadiest by far, and the easiest to learn. Once you're lying prone, your body simply can't go anywhere, so normal wobbles and tremors are minimized.

There are really just a couple of key points to remember. First, elbow positioning is extremely important. The tendency is to place the elbows too far out to the side. The supporting elbow, the one holding the fore-end, should be close in under the rifle

for the most direct support. If you have a choice, always support the rifle with bone, not with muscle alone. Second, be aware that recoil is a very real factor in the prone position. You're going to have to lie there and take it, and if you crawl the stock in prone, your forehead will be kissed. Lots of shooting practice from the prone with heavy-recoiling rifles is probably counter-productive, but the shooter should practice getting into a steady prone position as quickly as possible.

This position is at its best in very open country, or in mountainous country in situations such as shooting from one ridge to another. Although prone is extremely steady, circumstances that allow its use are fairly rare; usually brush or terrain won't allow you to get that low. My records indicate that I've shot most of my pronghorn antelope from the prone, but I haven't shot a deer from that position for 10 years.

It's a position that should be used whenever possible, but always make sure the bullet's path is really clear. Remember, if you're using a scope, your line of sight is *higher* than the path of the bullet. Just because the path looks clear through the scope doesn't mean that it is; in prone, you're very close to the ground anyway, and a slight rise to your front may obstruct your barrel but not your line of sight.

The prone position is best used with a tight sling, and it lends itself extremely well to use with both natural rests, such as fallen logs or boulders, and man-made shooting aids such as the Harris bipod. We'll look at these ideas in the next two chapters.

Sitting

The sitting position is the serious rifleman's favorite. It's almost as steady as prone, but can be used much more fre-

The prone is easily the steadiest of all shooting positions that don't use a rest. In this version, the body is at a 45-degree angle to the rifle. One of the real keys to this position is to keep the supporting elbow directly under the rifle.

Sitting is one of the most useful field shooting positions. It's easy to learn but takes practice to get into quickly. Notice that the elbows are extended over the knees, not rested on top, where they could slip off just as the shot is fired.

quently; it puts you high enough off the ground to allow a clear field of fire in most circumstances. It's very fast to get into, and the body has plenty of give under recoil. Once you get your rifle sighted in and are ready to leave the shooting bench, this position is the first to try, and it's one that deserves going back to at every practice session.

There are several ways to assume the sitting position; the variants involve the position of elbows and ankles. To get into the sitting position, simply plop down on your hams at about a 45-degree angle from the target. The formal target shooter will often cross his ankles in front of him, but it's faster, more comfortable, and nearly as steady to plant your feet out in front of you with your knees raised naturally. Now put the rifle into your shoulder, and rest your elbows over your knees. Don't put your elbows directly on top of your knees; they'll surely slip off at the wrong moment. Bend forward from the waist, put the backs of your upper arms *over* your knees if pos-

sible, and press them against your shins. You should be steady, if not comfortable; you'll feel a lot of muscle tension your first few times in this position.

Aim in at your target; the sights should fall naturally on it. If they don't, you may need to move your rear end a few inches to the right or left. But with a bit of practice, you'll find that the sitting position comes very naturally. You'll see an animal on an adjacent hillside, drop into the sit, and when you get the rifle up, your sights will fall naturally onto your game.

The sitting position is my favorite, and I use it more frequently than any other. The only thing that beats it is a comfortable, handy rest — and it's steady enough that I don't take more than a casual look around for a rest before dropping into it. Like the prone position, it's at its absolute best when combined with a tight sling. If it has a drawback, it's that it requires muscles to stretch in directions they might not nor-

The kneeling position is nowhere near as steady as sitting, but it is very fast—and it beats the heck out of standing. The supporting arm should be directly under the rifle, and the shooting arm stays up and helps pull the rifle into the shoulder.

mally go, so it is a position that requires both practice and keeping in shape.

Kneeling

The kneeling position gets you just about as low as sitting does, so it might seem that the two offer the same potential steadiness. Don't believe it! The kneeling position is nowhere near as steady as sitting, and is no substitute for it under any circumstances. Well, almost any—kneeling is very, very fast, and beats the heck out of trying to shoot standing up.

The kneeling position is simple to assume. The right-handed shooter drops to his right knee with that knee pointed 90 degrees away from the target. The left foot is planted firmly, pointed toward the target, and the left knee is bent at a 90-degree angle. The left arm supports the rifle, and the left elbow rests on the left knee. For lefties like me, of course, it's just the opposite.

Actually, describing the position takes a whole lot more time than getting into it. It's best thought of as a hasty position, something you use when a good shooting opportunity has presented itself and there simply isn't time to find a steadier position. In that context kneeling is extremely valuable; you can drop into it and get off a good, steady shot much more quickly than you can from standing, considering the difficulty of holding the rifle still while standing.

The last time I recall using the kneeling position, it was that kind of a deal. I'd made a stalk on a nice mulie, but had misjudged his position and come in a little close. When I eased over a rise, he was feeding in the open about 80 yards away—but I was in the open as well. It wasn't a difficult shot, nor was it a fleeting shot—he hadn't seen me yet, though he would in seconds. There was no reason to risk a shot standing up, and no reason to sit down or search for a rest. The obvious thing was to drop into a kneeling position and shoot, which I did. That buck's head hangs to my immediate left as I write these lines.

Standing

My colleague and good friend John Wootters and I were hunting the other day and talking about this book. As usual, John had an astute observation: "One of the greatest boons to wildlife conservation would be convince the American public that if an attempt is made to shoot a rifle standing up off the shoulder, with no rest, the rifle simply will not fire."

Perhaps that's a bit extreme; once in a blue moon there's a reason to take a shot at game from the standing position. But there's no easy way to learn how to shoot standing up. And there is no right or wrong way to do it. As good a way as any is to stand with your feet planted shoulder width apart, your body perpendicular to the target. Raise the rifle to your shoulder, keeping the elbow of your shooting arm out horizontally and keeping your supporting arm directly under the rifle.

The position simply isn't easy, and the tricks of the competitive shooter—such as palm rests, muzzle weights, and the elbow-supported-by-the-hip stance—simply aren't appropriate in the field. On the other hand, the hunter can use a shooting aid long since outlawed in formal competition in the standing position—the sling. I like a tight sling in *any* shooting position, but nowhere does it pay more dividends than in the standing position. We'll talk about that in the next chapter, but for now just consider the standing position reserved for emergency use only.

The standing position is most unsteady of all, and should be avoided for shooting at game. Once in a while there's no other choice, so this difficult position must be practiced as much as or more than any other. There's no easy way to shoot standing up, but getting the feet planted solidly will help immensely.

This fine whitetail was taken with a shot from the standing position at about 60 yards. There was nothing to rest the rifle on, and the underbrush prevented using a steadier position.

11

The Forgotten Sling

I'm all for good, clear riflescopes, and Lord knows I love the accuracy that today's out-of-the-box rifles deliver. But modern fire-arms and sighting equipment have made us lazy; we often allow fancy equipment to substitute for sound principles of marks-manship.

The scope does a great many things for you, as discussed earlier. Its most obvious (although not most important) advantage is to magnify the target image. The scope actually magnifies *everything* — including your wobbles. With a scope, you're in-stantly aware of any unsteadiness. And it doesn't take much; if your gun muzzle wob-bles off a target 100 yards distant by just a tenth of an inch as you squeeze off, your bullet will land 10 inches from where you aimed. A wobble of just an inch will shift your bullet more than *four feet* from the same 100-yard target. With a scope, you

can see the slightest wobble, and either cor-rect it or back off and start over.

Back in the good old days of iron or aperture sights, those wobbles weren't so easy to see, so it was essential to use every trick in the book to ensure a steady hold. One of the tricks that seems to be largely forgotten by hunters is the tight sling. I say "by hunters" because both centerfire and smallbore competitors still use a tight sling in prone, sitting, and kneeling positions, and the Marine Corps still teaches it and requires its use for qualification firing.

Oddly enough, the tight sling seems to be an American development, and our armed forces are one of the few that have adopted its use. Generations of hunters trained with the 1903 Springfield and later the M1 Garand adopted — and adapted — the military sling for use in the field. In recent decades, though, the military sling has evolved into a simple carrying strap of nylon webbing. During requalification or competition shooting on a formal range, it can be used as a tight sling, but in my 15 years in the infantry I've never seen a Marine rifleman use a tight sling away from a formal range. The trained snipers — now, that's a different ballgame. You won't see them shoot without a tight sling!

I've seen very few hunters under the age of 50 use a tight sling in the field — but those who do generally know exactly what they're doing.

The principle of the tight sling is quite simple, and it can be applied to almost any shooting position. Basically, the tension of the sling works against the tension of the body, and can add an unusual measure of stability — especially in the kneeling and sitting positions.

Unfortunately, too many hunters today believe the rifle sling is used only for carrying the rifle over one's shoulder, so let's discuss that use of the sling first. In some situations a sling is nearly essential, but in others it's a pain in the neck — if not downright dangerous. Basically, the rifle should be slung over one shoulder, muzzle up, whenever you need both hands free to negotiate obstacles or when you're hiking a long stretch where it's darned unlikely you're going to need it.

There are a couple of considerations here. First, I've seen short carbines carried muzzle down, and that's theoretically OK on level ground. However, the risk is that if you take a tumble, you're almost certain to pack the muzzle with dirt. It's a mess to get out without a proper cleaning rod. But if you happen not to notice you've plugged the muzzle, you've got a bomb in your hands. Second, when that rifle is slung over your shoulder, it's out of your direct control. A branch can knock it off or a vine can snag the safety and/or the trigger. You

could also slip and take a tumble, and the muzzle can point anywhere. So the slung rifle should never have a round in the chamber. If you're certain you're going to get a shot, hold the rifle in both hands in front of you!

The sling is invaluable for helping to carry the rifle, but it's easy to get lazy and have the rifle slung when it should be in your hands and ready to use. Using the sling as an aid to steadier shooting is an even more important role than helping carry the rifle.

For that very reason, a number of top hunters I know detest slings and won't have anything to do with them. Montana outfitter Ed Nixon is one. He loves to ghost through the timber still-hunting whitetails — a game he's better at than anybody I know — and he wants his rifle always at the ready.

He has another reason for hating slings: if he isn't still-hunting whitetails, he's on horseback in the high country. A sling is a real menace in the saddle scabbard. If the back end sticks out, it will form a loop that can catch on brush and cause the rifle to be jerked out — generally to land on sharp rocks and then be trampled by a frightened horse. If the back end doesn't stick out, the added bulk will cause the rifle to hang up in a well-fitting scabbard.

I agree with Ed on both counts; if you're still-hunting through close cover, the last thing you need is a swinging, clicking, catching sling. And you sure don't need one on a horse. But on the other hand, there's nothing better on a long, fruitless hike back to camp, or when you need both hands to haul yourself up a steep bank. And it's quite simple to have it both ways, thanks to the quick-detachable swivels that are in almost universal use today. I personally like Uncle Mike's detachable swivels with the screw-in detaching knob; no matter how rough the going, they simply can't come undone.

Of course, the problem with any gadget is that you have to remember to use it. I like to shoot with a sling, so my rifles always wear them. If I plan to slip through some timber that might hold game, I'll generally remove the sling and put it in my pocket or daypack. At least I'll do that early in the day, before I get tired. As much as I like slings, I'd trade 'em all in if somebody would give me a dollar for every shot I might have gotten if my rifle had been at

high port and ready rather than slung over one shoulder!

There are several different types of slings on the market. All will work as a carrying strap, but not all can be used as a tight sling. The true tight sling, also called a loop sling, requires either a two-piece military sling, its length adjusted by claws, or a modified one-piece sling with a single claw, often called a Whelen sling after the late gunwriter, Colonel Townsend Whelen (who always touted the use of a tight sling). The Whelen-type sling has nearly vanished; I haven't seen one for years. Two-piece, two-claw military slings are nearly as rare, but enough shooters still use them that they are available. I have two right now, a one-inch-wide sling by Boyt in Des Moines and a 7/8-inch-width sling from George Lawrence in Portland. Each has a long upper strap with a claw keeper and a short lower strap with a claw at one end and a square buckle on the other, plus two leather keepers.

In use, the long strap is passed through the forward swivel, then doubled back and secured with the claw to form a long loop. One of the keepers adjusts the size of the loop. The two straps are joined with the square, free-running buckle at the bottom end of the loop. That lower strap passes through the rear sling swivel, and its claw actually adjusts the length of the sling for comfortable carrying.

The secret to the loop sling is to have the loop the proper length for you, and that takes a little experimentation. Let's employ it in the sitting position. Sit down at an angle of about 45 degrees from the target, planting your rear end and your feet firmly with your knees cocked up. Release the rear sling swivel so the sling hangs free from the front swivel. Now, for right-handers (lefties like me need to reverse everything), open the loop of the sling, give it half a turn to the left, and put your left arm into it. Get

To use a tight loop sling, first unhook the rear sling swivel and spread the loop open. A right-handed shooter then gives the loop a half-turn to the left and slips his left arm into the loop. Get the loop well up above the bicep, then slide the keeper down to tighten the loop in place.

Pass the left forearm around the sling, and snug the hand up tight against the forward sling swivel. Get into a good, tight sitting position, and use your right arm to pull the butt into your shoulder. A good test of your sitting position with a tight loop sling is to get all set, then release your shooting hand. The rifle should stay in position without any pressure from that arm or hand — so all your shooting hand has to do is its critical work of squeezing the trigger.

the loop well up on your upper arm, above the bicep—you'll get too much muscle tremor if you put it on the bicep proper. Use the keeper to tighten it down. As a side note, proper use of the true loop sling says that it should be detached from the rear swivel; target slings don't attach to it in the first place. However, if you're lucky, you may not have to detach your sling from the rear swivel; it depends on the length of your loop and the amount of tension you want and need.

Now pass your left forearm around the sling, and snug your hand tight up against the sling swivel—a glove on that hand will help for lengthy practice sessions, but for the occasional shot afield, don't worry about it. Now rest the flats of your triceps—the backs of your upper arms—*over* your knees and against the flats of your shins. *Do not* rest your elbows on your knees; you'll wobble all over at best, and at worst your elbow will slip clear off at the last second. Get your elbows as far over your knees as you possibly can. Keep your left hand snugged up tight against the forward sling swivel; use your right hand to snug the rifle butt into your shoulder. You should be perfectly steady in this position, with or without your right hand touching the rifle.

You should feel a good deal of tension in this position, particularly in your lower back; the sling is working against your back muscles to create stability. If the tension isn't there, shorten the loop until it is.

The loop should be adjusted so that you don't have to mess with it; use the lower claw to adjust the length for carrying the rifle. The tight or loop sling will work in the prone position just as well as sitting, although for some people the length of the loop may not remain the same. It will also work extremely well in kneeling. However, for game shooting kneeling is a hasty position; if you have time to undo your rear swivel and get into the loop, you've got time to get into a good sitting position.

I'm certain that many of you who haven't used a tight sling are certain by now that I'm nuts, that animals won't stand around long enough for you to go through such machinations. Don't knock it until you've tried it. For one thing, with practice all of this can be done very quickly. For another, all too often we rush our shots. Better to sit down and take a few deep breaths while you're getting the sling ready. Of course, in some situations you don't have that kind of time; the loop sling is for deliberate situations where you have time and must have all the accuracy of which you're capable.

I've used the loop sling any number of times, and it always does two things for me: One, it gives the best stability I can get out of the sitting position—almost as good as a solid rest—and two, it occupies my mind while I'm setting up for a shot and prevents buck fever from setting in. Both reasons are equally valid in my book!

A typical situation occurred one morning in Montana, just after a snowfall. The rut was on, and we picked up fresh tracks heading out of the timber into some open sagebrush draws. It was just a matter of when we would spot the herd and how big the buck would be. We topped a ridge and saw them bedded below us, a swollen-necked four-by-four with his five does. He wasn't all that far, perhaps 250 yards—good shooting range, but much too far for a snap shot.

I quickly looked for a rest on the barren slope. There wasn't one, and time was running out. Out of reflex I had the rear swivel undone and the loop over my arm before I slid into a sitting position. I was too late to shoot him where he lay; he was already up and moving. But I shot him before he'd gone 10 yards, and he slid back into his

The hasty sling does not require a loop, and can be used with almost any carrying-strap type of sling. It's good for almost any position, but is a great aid to standing—in my opinion even better than a loop sling. First put your supporting arm through the sling. Then wrap your hand around the sling, snugging your hand tight against the forward sling swivel. When you raise the rifle, the sling will tighten against your chest, creating tension and a surprising degree of stability. With practice, the hasty sling can be assumed almost instantaneously—even while you're raising your rifle for a shot.

snow-melted bed. Could I have made the shot without a tight sling? Maybe, but why not use every advantage possible?

Well, perhaps that case wasn't really typical, since time was running out. Usually I use a loop sling when time doesn't seem to be a major issue. When you need some stability but you know you must shoot quickly, learn how to use the hasty sling. The hasty sling can be accomplished with almost any sling, plain carrying strap or military type.

I've always liked the hasty sling, and it has always worked for me. Jack O'Connor wrote that he didn't like it, and he knew more about shooting game than I ever will. But give it a try. It works in all positions, but I like it particularly in kneeling and standing. In the standing position (if you absolutely must shoot standing up!) the loop sling will not help you, but the hasty sling will draw tight across your chest and add a surprising measure of stability to an unstable shooting position.

To assume the hasty sling, leave the rear swivel attached. Simply thrust your supporting arm between the sling and the rifle, then wrap your forearm around the sling once and slam the web of your hand against the sling swivel. You're all set to go. In the sitting position it is not as steady as a loop sling, but it does help, and it's not just fast — it's instantaneous. You can get into a hasty sling as you drop into a kneeling position, or simultaneous with raising your rifle for a quick offhand shot. Generally, if you have time to shoot offhand, you have time to drop to one knee — which is hundreds of times steadier. But whether you do or not, you always have time to get into a hasty sling if you practice it a bit; it can be done quite literally while the rifle is leaping to your shoulder.

I have done a fair amount of offhand shooting at game, and I practice shooting from my hind legs religiously. I'm not very good at it, and I don't shoot at game that way unless I have to. When I have to, unless it's a snap shot at point-blank range, I always use a hasty sling. The last time I can recall was at a fine whitetail buck at about 60 yards. I'd been stalking him, and had plenty of cover. But there wasn't a tree big enough to rest on, and the underbrush was too thick even to kneel. I wrapped into a hasty sling and held as steady as I could. I knew it would be a toughie because I was shooting a new test rifle with an abominable trigger pull. I thought the rifle would never go off; it seemed I just kept squeezing and squeezing. Finally the sear broke, and the bullet went exactly where I wanted it to; the buck leaped straight into the air, heart shot, and came down with all four feet in the air.

I generally carry a rifle with a military sling in place. However, I don't use a military sling on a heavy-caliber rifle; the chances of needing, wanting, or having time for that kind of precision are rare. For a carrying sling, my all-time favorite is a 1½-inch-wide web strap that narrows down at both ends and has leather tabs to fit one-inch sling swivels. I picked it up in Spain, and I wish somebody over here would make one like it. It's light in weight, strong, and doesn't slip on the shoulder; the width reduces shoulder chafing, and it dries quickly. It's plenty flexible enough for a hasty sling, while a leather sling of that width isn't (besides being heavy as hell).

The new nylon slings, padded and two inches wide where they meet the shoulder, also work real well. These are also flexible enough to use as a hasty sling. But for real stability, nothing beats the two-claw military sling.

It's also worth mentioning that if you ever plan to shoot with a tight sling, you should check your zero with and without sling tension; sometimes it makes a big difference. I mentioned earlier that I had a Mannlicher-stocked 7x57 that shifted 14 inches with pressure from a tight sling, and not knowing that fact cost me the best pronghorn I've ever laid eyes on.

Barrel-mounted sling swivels are very attractive; I kinda like 'em myself. They're great on heavy-kicking rifles, since a fore-end-mounted swivel can come back and gouge your hand. For carrying in the woods, the barrel-mounted swivel also puts the barrel several inches lower when slung. However, there are two significant disadvantages to barrel swivels: First, you cannot snug your hand up against the forward swivel, which is one of the real keys to good shooting with a sling. Worse, a barrel-mounted swivel is almost certain to change your point of impact when pressure from a tight sling is applied. I would restrict the barrel-mounted swivel to hard-kicking rifles from which you don't anticipate needing a lot of precision.

Every serious rifleman should have a sling in his repertoire — you'll be surprised at how many times you use it, once you get used to the idea!

12

Use a Rest!

We'd been working our tails off to find a good blacktail buck in northern California's lava country, a land of deep canyons, manzanita-choked sidehills, and stretches of rolling oak grassland. It was easy country to hunt, but the weather was too mild and the bulk of the deer hadn't yet migrated down from the high country. Mike Ballew and I were working little pockets, doing two-man mini-drives where bucks had been spotted earlier in the season; it was about all we had left to try.

One very narrow oak and manzanita hillside was bordered by wide-open lava flow on both sides. We had gone a couple hundred yards, Mike on the lower edge and I on the upper, when I heard him give a holler. I had no idea what he said, but I knew it meant "Buck!" and I figured it wasn't headed my way. The strip of cover was only 50 yards wide, but it was thick. I launched myself downhill at a dead run,

breaking through vines and poison oak and leaping over deadfalls. Mike's voice guided me, and the urgency in it grew; whatever he'd seen was getting away fast. Finally I broke into the clear, and later Mike said he wished he'd had it on film.

I saw the buck as soon as I got clear, and he was a dandy. He was also gaining ground quickly; he'd crossed the boulder-strewn streambed below us and was streaking up the far hillside for all he was worth. Without slowing down, I looked for a steady rest, spotted a likely boulder a few yards downslope, and changed course for it. I whipped off my cap, scrunched it up to put under the fore-end, and slid in behind the boulder with the rifle already in position. The buck was going straight away, and I actually overshot him; the bullet entered the back of his neck just ahead of the shoulders and came out centered on his brisket. I guess it really was one of those spectacular-

Almost anything can serve as a natural rest—rocks, trees, clumps of sagebrush, you name it. The tricks are to keep your subconscious mind searching for a potential rest when you're in game country—and to practice using a field rest quickly.

looking affairs that require a fair amount of luck—but it worked, and it worked only because I took the extra half-second to find a steady rest.

The only hunting guide I couldn't get along with was a big-talking Texan who had a favorite line about hunters who couldn't shoot and always had to look for a rest. Sorry, Charlie, but looking for a steady rest under virtually all circumstances is the mark of a savvy field marksman, not a poor one. The poor marksman throws up his rifle and blazes away, generally hitting nothing. The serious rifleman plans his shot. Whether he has a tenth of a second or a matter of minutes to get off his shot, he uses the available time to get into the best position he can—and that means using a steady rest if one is available.

On that buck I mentioned, I could just as easily have dropped into the sitting position, and possibly even prone. But prone was impractical, and I didn't think I'd be steady enough soon enough in the sitting position, as I had just run 50 yards as hard as I could. Kneeling and standing were out of the question; the buck was 175 yards away when I first saw him and gaining every second. The only chance was to find a good rest, and fortunately there were plenty of boulders around.

A natural rest can be virtually anything solid that offers some measure of added stability, and such a rest can be used from any position, depending on its height and the position of the game. On the relatively rare occasions when a prone position can be used in the field, a rest of some type can almost always be found or created. Logs or low rocks are great, but even better is a daypack—and that's one reason I almost always carry one. Over the years, a great many stalks have ended with a slow crawl over the top of one ridge to shoot at an animal either on the next ridge or in the valley between. In a situation like that I shed my pack before I get to the crest and either drag it behind me or push it in front of me as I crawl to the top. Then it's a simple matter to slip it into place, rest the fore-end over it, and get a good, steady shot.

Even better, though, is to pick out a likely log or rock that will work just as well, since crawling with the pack can be a pain. A good part of picking the spot where I'll take my shot depends on where I can get a good rest—especially if the game is un-

A packframe makes a near-perfect field rest, and I often carry one for that express purpose as much as for packing out game. With a good, steady rest like this, the kneeling position is just as good as a benchrest.

disturbed and the distance is much over 150 yards.

It's a bit more unusual to combine a rest with the sitting position. The sitting position is very deliberate and is generally chosen because there isn't a natural rest. However, every once in a while there will be a knee-high rock or log that you can sit or kneel behind and rest the rifle over. If I have a choice between a good, solid natural rest and a sitting or kneeling position with a tight sling, trust me — I'll take the rest every time!

It isn't unusual to combine the standing position with a natural rest such as a vertical tree or a horizontal tree limb. When combined with something nice and solid, the standing position is something else again — and I remove all my advice against it. If you plant your feet firmly and lean into a tree with your supporting arm and hand, you've got a pretty firm foundation from which to shoot.

Sometimes you can be a bit creative, too. Once or twice I've been caught where there was too much brush for anything but a standing shot, and the range was a bit too far to attempt such a shot. If you're lucky, you might be able to bunch a half-dozen weeds or a couple of saplings into an acceptable standing rest.

The real trick, I think, is twofold — first, to accept that it's worth a few extra seconds to find a rest and get the steadiness you need; and second, having accepted that, to always be on the lookout for something that will work. A good hunter's eyes are always working, always scanning for any indication of game. But if he's also a good rifleman, a small part of his subconscious is also looking for a good place from which to shoot — especially when you get into those little pockets of habitat that put all your senses on full alert. You know the feeling

The tripod stands preferred by thousands of Texas whitetail hunters are usually built to offer a good, steady, padded rest. Tree-stand hunters should borrow this trick and place their stands so that a horizontal branch is available for a rest.

you get in a little hollow that a big buck would be likely to hole up in, or a patch of quakies into which elk would retreat. You intently look for an ear twitching, a flash of sunlight on antler, a horizontal line in vertical timber. Part of that alertness should be the rifleman's instinct to look for a place from which to shoot.

Under some circumstances, a good rest can be planned well in advance. Where permanent tree stands are legal, a horizontal branch tied into place overlooking the area where action is most likely to occur should

Africa's numerous termite mounds make ideal natural rests and also offer good cover to stalk behind and often enough height to improve visibility.

When using a vertical rest, it's important that the rifle itself not touch it directly. Instead, place your supporting hand against the rest and then hold the fore-end so the rifle is cushioned from the solid object.

be an important part of the setup. Likewise for ground blinds, and even for hillsides and trail crossings that you normally stake out during the course of a season. Your stand simply should have a rifle rest available, and if a natural one isn't present, take a few moments to build one. When a good buck appears, you'll be glad you did.

Using a rest of any kind is quite simple, and there's just one rule to follow — *never* rest the rifle barrel on a solid object. The dynamics of stock bedding and barrel vibrations will be significantly altered if you

do, and your shot could be perfectly aimed and yet fly completely wild — usually high. Personally, I don't like to rest the fore-end on a solid object, either. The risks aren't as great, but they are present, depending on how the rifle was stocked and bedded, and the recoil is likely to gouge the hell out of your gunstock, especially if you use a boulder as a rest.

The solutions are simple. Use hats, jackets, daypacks, and bunched-up fists. If I'm lacking a daypack, I'll take my hat off, scrunch it up in my hand, and rest the fore-end across the mess in my hand.

The same principle applies for a vertical rest such as a tree trunk, and there's a little trick here. With the little, ring, and middle fingers of your supporting hand, either grasp or lean firmly against the rest. Then support the fore-end with your thumb and forefinger only. This setup is easily practiced on upright beams at your local range, and once you get the idea, it's not only comfortable but quite stable.

In fact, all types of natural rests require a bit of practice, but not all ranges take kindly to their clientele running up and flopping down beside a fence post. Fortunately backyards work pretty well (with empty rifles), and if there isn't another option, living-room chairs aren't bad. The idea is to learn how to flop down beside a solid object of an odd size and get the rifle rested across it comfortably and steadily. With some imagination it can be learned in a few hours without firing a shot.

Most African game areas offer a wealth of natural rests in the huge termite mounds that dot the landscape—and the big ones even offer stalking cover. So long as you keep a lookout for snakes (which often occupy abandoned mounds), termite mounds are marvelous shooting platforms. However, some areas—like the floodplains of Zambia and Botswana and the savannas of the Serengeti—offer not only nothing to rest on but also no cover. Professional hunters commonly cut three poles five to six feet long, depending on the height of the shooter, and make a shooting tripod. It works perfectly, but in Africa it would be

Another good African trick is the shooting sticks, used to make a steady tripod rest. The only problem is that you customarily have a tracker along who isn't carrying a rifle. I don't have many hunting buddies who will carry along a shooting rest for me!

customary to have a tracker carry it. In the States that luxury is rarely available.

However, some hunters do carry a long walking stick that can serve as a great shooting aid. Colleague Sam Fadala is a big fan of the "Moses stick," and has often written about its use. I've tried carrying a stick, and it does work as a shooting aid. But toting something additional in hand just isn't for me.

There are also a number of commercially available options. Telescoping monopods, stick-in-the-ground bipods, you name it — they all work, depending on your style and temperament. One gizmo that I do believe in is the Harris bipod. This ingenious fold-up bipod attaches to the front sling swivel and has telescoping legs. The simplest model would be useful only in the prone position, but some models have legs that telescope long enough to use from the sit — and boy, do they help.

I don't use the Harris bipod in rugged country where a natural rest should be available. But in wide-open country, such as much pronghorn territory, it's a real godsend.

The last time I used one was in Montana. We had to crawl through half a mile of low sagebrush to get close enough to shoot. It was clear from the start that there was no chance to get really close, and little chance a natural rest would be available.

I crawled half a mile on hands, knees, and belly, losing a bunch of skin and gaining lots of cactus spines in the process. The closest I could get was about 350 yards, and I was glad I'd clipped on the Harris bipod before leaving the truck. It made quite easy a shot that would otherwise have been extremely difficult.

Some folks carry a shooting aid like the Harris wherever they go, and I don't have any problem with that. Personally, I prefer to save the weight and use a natural rest whenever possible. But whether you prefer your rest to be natural or manmade, learn to use one — it's the simplest, most sensible, and fastest way to improve your hit-to-miss ratio!

The Harris bipod is a great gadget for open-country hunting. It clips to the forward sling swivel, and the legs fold out of the way when not in use. With the legs extended, it's one of the steadiest shooting aids imaginable.

13

Shot Placement on Game

The ultimate objective of field shooting is to put the bullet in the right place—to quickly, cleanly, and humanely dispatch the animal you've selected to fill your tag. "Big game" means deer to most of us, and compared with much of the world's game, deer are relatively light-boned and their life-support systems are short-circuited fairly easily. On the other hand, deer (and all wild animals) are full-time survivors; flight is their natural reaction to danger, and if neither their central nervous system nor their circulatory/respiratory system is put out of action, a deer can sustain a simply amazing amount of damage and still make good an escape.

Unfortunately, that escape usually is only temporary. Deer can and do survive superficial wounds, even wounds that result in the loss of a limb. But generally any hit in the body from a modern centerfire rifle will be fatal to a deer or any other game animal—it's just a matter of when. Wounded animals die a horrible death. And in addition to humanitarian concerns, wounded and lost game is a tremendous waste of the resource.

Wounded animals that are lost are one of the dark sides of hunting. We don't talk about it very much in the sporting press. And we don't know exactly how serious a problem it is nationwide. But it's for sure that if we could eliminate the waste from wounded and lost game, we could all enjoy longer seasons and less restrictive bag limits. Unfortunately, there's no way to eliminate the problem altogether. As much as I hate it, and hate to admit it, I've lost a couple of animals along the way.

When it happens, it's certain that the bullet didn't hit the right place, and there's a better than even chance that the shot

This elk was taken with a .375 H&H, a cartridge that has proven itself adequate for elephant. The power of the cartridge is meaningless if the bullet doesn't get into the vitals to do its work.

shouldn't have been attempted. All hunters, whether outstanding field marksmen or poor shots, must have some idea of their limitations; what the excellent shot considers a routine situation might be a shot the poor marksman should pass up. But no matter what the circumstances, no shot should be attempted unless the shooter is quite certain that he or she can place the bullet in a vital area.

Without question, the most instantly fatal shot on any game animal is to the brain or to the spinal cord in the neck area.

Such a shot is guaranteed to drop the animal in its tracks, and will allow recovery of virtually all the edible meat. I know a fair number of very skilled hunters who specialize in head and neck shots, and they place their shots with the skill of a surgeon. However, these shots are not for me, and I don't recommend them for anyone except the highly skilled marksman who is willing to wait for the perfect opportunity.

Here are some good reasons. First, if you have any interest in saving the head and cape for mounting, you don't want to do the kind of damage a head or neck shot will do. Second, these shots are extremely tricky, with very small target areas and a high margin for error.

It isn't a case of hit or miss, either; if it were, I'd recommend these shots wholeheartedly. On a head shot, the brain must be reached to drop the animal. A slight head movement or an error in aiming, and the bullet is likely to go high and knock off an antler—which will do nothing more than give the animal a terrible headache. A miss that's a bit low, though, may blind the animal or break the jaw—and few deaths will be slower or more agonizing.

The neck shot is equally tricky. The bullet simply must sever the spinal cord. If it misses clean, great. More likely, though, is a flesh wound either high or low. A flesh wound above the spinal cord will probably

Under many, perhaps most, circumstances, the rifle certainly offers enough accuracy to make head and neck shots. I don't like them, since the slightest mistake can result in a horrible wound that may not be immediately fatal. I prefer aiming for the largest vital zone, the heart/lung region, where I have the most margin for error and where a solid hit will surely be fatal.

be a painful injury from which the animal will recover, but a low shot will probably cut the windpipe, again causing a slow, lingering death.

There are circumstances where head or neck shots are perfectly appropriate, but for me the only time to use them is at close range when obstructions prevent anything else. On a neck shot, there are a couple of special considerations. First, if the animal drops, keep your eyes on it and get to it quickly. A near-miss to the spinal cord will usually drop the animal instantly, but he won't stay down for long.

One time in Rhodesia I was tasked with shooting a number of impala, an antelope the size of a small whitetail, as rations for the work force on the ranch where I was staying. I was using an accurate .250 Savage, working in close and taking neck shots. It wasn't hunting; it was really grocery shopping. I would drop one ram, then follow the herd and try to get another the next time they stood. Twice in that day, neck-shot impala vanished before I got to them, and I haven't been too high on neck-shooting since then.

Sportsmen who hunt a wide variety of game also need to be aware that the exact locations of both brain and spinal cord vary significantly. In many ungulates the spinal cord dips very low in the neck, so unless you're shooting just behind the base of the ears, the center of the neck may not be the right spot. Many of Africa's larger antelope are particularly deceptive in this regard, and the American elk has an awful lot of non-vital neck surrounding the spinal cord.

The brain, too, can be deceptive. I once got confused on a midwinter bison; with all that long hair, I simply couldn't define the top of the skull. I shot just under the brain with a 250-grain bullet from a .348, and the

The closest buck is offering a perfect broadside shot, but shadows make the aiming point indistinct. Follow the rear line of the left foreleg about halfway up into the chest area, and you've got a perfect lung shot. You also will damage very little meat.

chase was on. I got the bull, but I would have been better off putting that first bullet in the heart/lung area.

Generally that's the case. I don't believe in fancy field shooting; I believe in putting the first bullet into a large area that you know you can hit and you know will cause rapid, if not instantaneous, death. Quite simply, that means a lung shot. An animal shot through the lungs is dead, pure and simple. He may cover a bit of ground, but generally much less than 100 yards.

The lung area on most game animals covers the center two-thirds of the chest horizontally. Vertically it lies between and just behind the shoulders. The best shot is a broadside one, of course, and on non-dangerous, relatively fragile animals such as deer I like to shoot just behind the shoulder, pretty much central on the body from top to bottom. That shot will mess up a bit of rib meat, but it leaves the shoulders alone and wrecks the lungs. Usually the animal will take a few steps, but he won't go far.

On heavier game, particularly tough game such as elk, I move the shot placement forward just a bit so that I'll break at least the on-side shoulder enroute to the lungs. And on dangerous game—be it boar, bear, buffalo, or whatever—I'll always make sure the bullet breaks heavy bone either before or after wrecking the vitals—or both.

The beauty of the lung shot is that it's not only surely fatal but also offers a tremendous margin for error. If you slip slightly high, you'll sever the spinal column above the shoulders, generally an instantaneously fatal shot. If you slip a bit low, you'll hit either the heart or the major blood vessels leading to and from it. If you hit a bit forward, you've got quite a lot of lung, shoulder, and spinal column. The only risk is hitting too far to the rear, and then you have a paunch shot and a long tracking job. If you aim *just* behind the shoulder, you still have a bit of room for error.

Other good, sure fatal shots? You can argue endlessly the advantages of the heart shot versus the lung shot. I prefer the lung shot simply because of the margin for error; on a heart shot you'll merely break a leg if you slip a bit low. However, the heart shot has a lot of fans, and I use it a fair amount of the time.

The heart generally lies very low in the chest, protected by the uppermost leg joint. For a straight broadside shot or one quar-

tering very slightly away, the aiming point is right at the corner of the "elbow." The heart shot has several things going for it. Obviously, it does the job. But it also offers a very definite aiming point, either the point of the joint or the distinct crease just behind. It doesn't leave a lot of room for error; too far forward and you're in the brisket, often a non-fatal hit and one that almost always results in a lost animal; too low and you're into muscle; lower yet and you break a leg high up—usually fatal, but not anytime soon. Hit too far back and you have a paunch shot with little immediate effect. Too high and you're square into the lungs, which is just fine.

The heart shot is nice on a stationary animal at relatively close range, just because of the definite aiming point. But don't expect the animal to drop; a heart-shot animal will frequently launch into high gear and travel up to 100 yards before piling up. In my experience, deer-size animals travel much farther with a heart shot than if hit solidly through the lungs.

The high spine shot has a few supporters, and it's incredibly deadly. Also a bit tricky, as the precise location differs in every species of game. However, if you sever the spinal column at the top of the shoulders, it's lights out. Likewise the base of the neck. I think most high spine hits are the result of slipping a bit high on a lung shot; I don't recommend that one, even though it's deadly. A shot to the base of the neck is superb, but I try it only on an animal quartering toward me; if I miss the vertebrae, the bullet will travel on into boiler room.

Sometimes you get lucky. Nobody shoots for the liver on purpose, but if you shoot too far back with a center-lung hold, you have a good chance of hitting the liver squarely. An animal so hit may travel a few yards before expiring, but he won't go far.

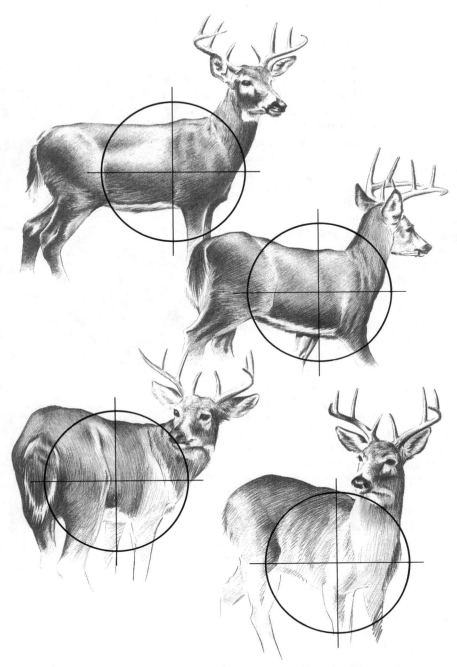

Shot placement on a broadside deer is simple, but deer don't often cooperate by standing just right. You'll more likely get a quartering shot of some kind. On animals quartering away, try to locate the off-side front leg, and follow its line up to the chest area to find your aiming point. You need to visualize where the vitals lie from any angle, and plan your shot accordingly. On strongly quartering-away shots, your bullet may actually enter the deer's body quite far back. On deer quartering toward you, keep your eyes on the on-shoulder; *that one protects the chest area that your bullet must reach.*

Spinal hits behind the shoulder should be avoided; they're only crippling, horrible to see, and destroy the backstraps—the best part of virtually every game animal. A possible exception would be a shot to the base of the tail on an animal moving straight away, but I'd save that one for a wounded animal that's getting away; there's just no margin for error whatsoever, and if you slip just a bit, your bullet will have to travel the length of the animal to reach the vitals.

Now let's talk about angles. Whether you choose to go for the heart or the lungs, the chest area is where you want your bullet to wind up. And the vital area never changes location—what shifts is the path your bullet must follow to reach it. The secret is to understand where that heart/lung region lies, and be able to visualize the path your bullet must take from any practical angle.

On shots quartering toward you, the aiming point varies from the point of the shoulder to the base of the neck. If the animal is facing directly toward you, the base of the neck or center of the chest is about all you have. It's a bit trickier if the animal is quartering away from you. The key is to keep your eyes on the *off-side* front leg. If you angle your shot with the intention of breaking not the on shoulder but the *off* shoulder, your bullet will plow smack through the chest region.

There's a catch, though. A slight quartering-away angle is a very good shot, offering the bullet virtually no resistance enroute to the heart/lung area. But a very strongly quartering-away shot asks a lot of a bullet. The bullet will have to enter somewhere along the back ribs, and chances are it will break two or three ribs before entering the cavity. Then it has to plow through some portion of the paunch, probably through the liver and through the diaphragm, and finally enter the boiler room. If you must attempt a strong quartering-

Here's an elk hunter's dream—a nice bull at close range. But there's really no shot here—an elk is simply too big an animal to risk trying to drive a bullet the length of the body to reach the vitals. The only sensible approach is to wait for the animal to turn, and chances are he will if you keep your cool.

away shot—what Elmer Keith called a "raking" shot—make certain you're using an adequate caliber and a bullet constructed to do that kind of work.

I made a fairly classic "raking" shot very recently, and it's worth telling about. It was on a good-size wild boar in New Zealand, but wild boars are the same the world over—sturdy and tough. I was way up on a hill, and the pig was feeding in a creek bottom about 225 yards below me. I was using a 7x57 with 154-grain bullets, generally on the light side for such work, but this was a new German bullet of wonderful construction, and I'd already shot enough game with it to trust it.

The pig was rooting around, and every time I had a good broadside shot, some brush intervened. He was just about to go around a bend and out of sight when he finally stood in the clear. It was a gray day, and he was a black animal; I couldn't really tell how he was standing except that he was clearly angled away from me. I concentrated on the off foreleg, putting the crosshairs just a bit above the center of his body. At the shot he took off, and since I didn't hear the bullet hit, I agreed with my host's comment that I'd missed. I hadn't; the pig ran 20 yards, then turned in a circle and fell over. The angle had been much steeper than I realized, but I'd plotted the course of the bullet perfectly. That little 7mm bullet, starting at only some 2,560 feet per second, entered behind the last rib, penetrated through the paunch, hamburgered the liver, passed through the heart, broke the off shoulder, and came to rest against the hide.

If you must attempt quartering shots at extreme angles, it isn't raw power that you need—it's that kind of bullet performance, and it's rare.

If I have an adequate caliber and I'm shooting a good bullet that I trust, I'll try a "raking" shot like that. On deer it's a rela-

The wild hog calls for slightly different shot placement in that the heart and lungs lie a bit farther forward than is the case with the deer family. A normal behind-the-shoulder shot will be just a touch too far back; the best shot is straight for the shoulder—and that's also the best way to anchor these tough customers.

tively certain thing, unless you're shooting a light-for-caliber fragile bullet. But I won't try a so-called "Texas heart shot"—an attempt to put a bullet in the vitals of a northbound animal from the south end. It can be done, especially if you're a bit overgunned for the game at hand and you're shooting very good bullets. But that's asking a great deal from even a good bullet. Besides, you're sure to make a terrible mess of the insides, and if you slip into the ham, you're going to mess up an awful lot of meat. Better to wait the animal out; sooner or later you'll get some kind of quartering angle. The only excuse would be on a wounded animal that's getting away, and then you simply must do the very best you can.

Animal anatomy is fairly straightforward, and if you stick with the basic heart/lung shot, you can't really go wrong. However, some animals are a bit tricky. For instance, wild hogs have a heart/lung area a bit farther forward than that of animals in the deer family. A classic behind-the-shoulder shot on a pig will actually be a bit far back; on pigs, go straight for the shoulder.

Some animals, such as American bison, African sable, and roan antelope, have a sort of shoulder hump created by long dorsal projections on the spinal column. This gives a false impression of the location of the lung area; on such animals you need to keep your bullets in the lower third of the body width. Heavily furred animals such as muskox can be extremely deceptive; with as much as 24 inches of hair all around the body, it's easy to shoot for the heart and hit nothing but hair. Very large animals such as moose are deceptive simply because of their size; it becomes quite easy to shoot at the whole animal.

When in doubt, find the front legs and then the shoulders. Those shoulders serve as armor for the machinery your bullet needs to reach. On a deer you've got an area nearly as large as a basketball; on elk, a big basketball; on moose, one of those "medicine balls" your high-school coach tortured you with. Concentrate on the vitals, visualize the path your bullet must follow, and you can't go wrong.

14

Bullet Performance

Next to choice of calibers, few subjects spark as many campfire arguments as bullet performance. When you get right down to it, it's really the bullet that does the work, not the cartridge or the rifle or, directly, the shooter. And it's generally the bullet that takes the rap if something goes wrong. Surely the rifleman couldn't have put the bullet in the wrong place, so the missile must have opened up prematurely and failed to penetrate—or perhaps it didn't open up enough and passed through without doing much damage. And so go the excuses.

Truth is, honest-to-God bullet failures are pretty rare. When wounded game gets away, I'm willing to bet the real culprit is sloppy shooting at least 99 percent of the time, even though we hate to admit it.

A good friend of mine is on the management team of a major bullet-manufactur-ing company. At one point in his career he was in the thankless position of answering customer complaints. Most of those complaints came from customers who had recovered bullets from their game and weren't happy with the way they looked. His favorite line in such discussions was, "At what point in the animal's death did the bullet fail?"

If a bullet is properly directed at the vitals of a game animal and it reaches them, then that bullet did just fine—regardless of what it looks like afterward. However, there are two definite schools of thought regarding bullet performance.

The one I personally adhere to wants a bullet to hold together and penetrate com-pletely—in one side and out the other. The opposite camp wants a bullet to expend all its energy inside the animal, maintaining that bullet energy soaked up by the ground

It's really the bullet that does the work, and hunters tend to be extremely demanding of their bullets. It's comforting when you recover a bullet from an animal and it looks like this Winchester Silvertip, right, recovered from testing media. Problem is that when something goes wrong, you never recover the bullet, so you've got a ready-made scapegoat that can't defend itself.

on the far side of the animal is wasted. Actually, this one can be argued endlessly, simply because both sides can claim plenty of right and wrong.

The idea of a bullet expending all its energy inside the animal is a good one. To accomplish this, expansion must be fairly rapid; in fact, some game bullets with quite good reputations darn near vaporize inside the animal—and the results are sure and sudden. This rapid expansion within the vital area causes tremendous damage to the soft lung tissue, can destroy the heart muscle altogether, and under ideal circumstances makes an animal drop as though it had been struck by lightning. The most spectacular deer kills that I've ever made—including head and neck shots—have been carefully placed behind-the-shoulder heart shots with a .22–250. Where this happened it was quite legal, but centerfire .22s are legal for deer in very few areas. Anyone who has seen a deer carefully shot with a

hot .22 centerfire would question the wisdom of such laws.

Encountering little resistance, the tiny 55-grain slug makes its way into the chest cavity and then comes completely unglued. There are many other examples of bullet energy being entirely expended in the animal, but I know of none more dramatic. The problem is that no hunter can count on being offered a steady behind-the-shoulder shot every time he shoots at a deer—and the folks who make the game laws can't count on hunters passing up shots their cartridges are inadequate to handle. As marvelous as they are on shots with no resistance, the hot .22s are a menace if the bullet must pass through heavy tissue or bone to reach the boiler room; they simply weren't designed to penetrate, and are likely to blow up on a rib or shoulder without getting through to the vitals.

As extreme as this example is, that's the problem I have with bullets expending all their energy inside the animal. You can't program a bullet to expand only in the chest cavity. On a good-size deer, if a bullet won't penetrate completely on either a behind-the-shoulder shot or a shot that catches just one shoulder, I'm worried about it; it just might not have the penetrating qualities or the ability to stay together that you simply must have on bad-angle shots.

It would be nice to expend all the bullet energy on the inside yet still have all the penetration you could want when you need it. The bulletmakers don't quite have that one figured. Actually, those folks have a terrible problem. First, they have to make bullets that will perform reliably at all manner of different velocities. A 180-grain .30-caliber spitzer, for instance, might be loaded into a .300 Savage, a .308 Winchester, a .30–06, a .300 H&H Magnum, or even a .300 Weatherby Magnum — a tremendous velocity spectrum. How one bullet can perform reliably and consistently over a velocity range like that I don't know.

The other thing is that hunters have been brainwashed by all these beautiful photographs of expanded, perfectly mushroomed bullets — and so everybody expects to find bullets that look like that in their game. A bulletmaker who makes the kind of bullet I like — a tough one that penetrates like gangbusters — has an image problem in that nobody is able to recover his bullets. They just keep on going, and nobody can say how much weight they retain. The famed Nosler Partitions are like that; you just don't recover them from deer-size game — and that's just fine with me.

On the other hand, the toughest bullet isn't always the best. Bullets that offer a great deal of penetration simply cannot inflict the same tissue damage as a bullet that expands more quickly and more fully. For penetration, the ultimate bullet is a full

If you look closely at this eland — a moose-sized African antelope — you'll see a lump behind the shoulder. That's an expanded 300-grain Sierra boattail softpoint, resting against the hide after breaking the opposite shoulder and wrecking the chest cavity — perfect bullet performance on so large an animal. There's also a tiny mark on the shoulder just to the left of the ear. That's the exit *from my second shot, a 300-grain A-Square Monolithic Solid, which also did exactly what it was supposed to do.*

metal jacket—and many African professionals still swear by "solids" for *all* game. At least they know exactly what they'll get, but a solid is clearly not the best for soft-skinned game.

Regardless of whether it opens quickly or slowly, *consistency* is one of the most important qualities of a bullet. One of my favorite bullets in the .375 H&H, for instance, is Sierra's big 300-grain boattail. Much tougher, deeper-penetrating bullets are available, but the Sierra has been amazingly consistent for me; I know almost exactly what it will do every time, and so I know where to place it and where not to place it.

These days it seems a surprising number of hunters are willing to pay a bit more for extra-special bullet performance; several semi-custom bulletmakers are doing a box-office business today, selling their bullets alone for up to $2 apiece. A couple of good examples are the Swift bullets, a partition-type (actually a bit more like the German H-mantle) that gives fantastic penetration; and Jack Carter's Trophy Bonded bullets. Carter's softpoint, called the Bearclaw, has a lead core bonded to a copper jacket, so weight retention is superb. His bullets mushroom fully with the jacket peeling back in massive razor-sharp cutting edges. The expansion is such that penetration, though adequate, is limited; on game of any substance at all, you'll recover your Bearclaw—and it'll look just like the pictures.

"Premium" ammunition, too, is popular today and usually features a bullet not readily available in standard-priced factory ammo. Federal was first with its Premium line, some loadings offering Nosler Partitions and others offering Sierra boattails. Now Winchester has followed with its new Supreme ammunition featuring some all-new boattail Silvertip bullets. Hornady's Frontier line, of course, features Hornady's excellent Interlock bullets. Weatherby has long offered Nosler Partition bullets in its factory ammo. And today some smaller ammo makers have gotten in on the act. Art Alphin's A-Square company offers an extensive line of hunting ammo with its own bullets. A brand new entry is Hirtenberger ammo from Germany. It's expensive, but it sure is good.

I think all this is wonderful, because there's nothing better than having an extra measure of confidence in your ammunition—so long as that confidence doesn't become overconfidence and lead you to attempt shots that are best left alone. Handloading is great fun, and the best part is cooking up the best load with the best bullet, and then going out and putting that load and that bullet to their intended purpose. But millions of hunters don't handload, and these "special" factory loads give everybody a chance to experiment and gain that extra bit of confidence.

Actually, though, there really aren't any bad bullets out there, but there are bullets designed for different things. The very

Here are six different .375 bullets recovered from game, including, on the right, a Hornady solid taken from an elephant. None of the softpoints look quite as pretty as they might if fired into testing media in a laboratory—flesh and bone are tougher on a bullet, and less consistent, than any testing media I'm aware of. Every one of these opened up, held together, and penetrated to do its work—otherwise it wouldn't have been recovered in the first place.

lightest bullets in any "normal" hunting caliber are usually designed for varmints. They're the ones that will get you in trouble on big game. The 110 to 130-grain .30 calibers, the 100-grain .270, the 125-grain 7mm bullets—these could indeed fail you on big game, but it wouldn't be the maker's fault, or the bullet's—they simply aren't designed for big game, but rather for very rapid expansion on thin-skinned varmints.

For deer-size game, stick with the middle bullet weights for that caliber: 150 to 165 grain in .30 caliber, 140 to 160 in 7mm, 130 in .270. For heavier game such as elk, go to the heavier bullets: 180 to 200 in .30 caliber, 160 to 175 in 7mm, 225 to 250 in the .338, and so forth. By following that very simple rule, your chances of a genuine bullet failure are almost nil.

Which isn't to say that the performance will always be exactly what you'd like. On deer-size game, my idea of perfect bullet performance on a broadside shot is to have both an entry wound and an exit wound, with the exit wound showing some bullet expansion—and I don't really care if the bullet had to break both shoulders to make its getaway or not. One of the big rationales given for wanting both an entry and an exit is that dual wounds offer a better blood trail. That's quite valid, but it isn't my reason. As I said, if I can get that kind of penetration on a normal shot on a deer, then I know I can trust that bullet on a larger animal or for a shot at a horrible angle. On elk I'd like to get an exit wound, but I'm not very likely to—there just aren't many expanding bullets that will go through an animal that size, unless the placement happens to be just so.

The next best thing to an exit wound is to find the bullet against the hide on the far side, nicely expanded and still intact. That's actually not uncommon. The bullet expends most of its energy by the time it gets all the way through, and when it reaches the tough, resilient hide on the opposite side, that skin stretches outward and soaks up the remaining energy, then springs back to trap the bullet.

One item mustn't be confused. Calibers are calibers and bullets are bullets, and going to a larger or faster cartridge doesn't automatically mean better bullet performance.

Fortunately I can't think of any American cartridges that don't have decent bullets available. The only problem is avoiding getting wrapped up in velocity hype. The magnums are great, but if you step up

These three bullets were recovered from three different wild hogs—a tough, heavy-boned animal. From left are a Winchester Power Point 100-grain .243, a Hirtenberger ABC 154-grain 7mm, and a Winchester 175-grain 7mm. Again, all three did their work perfectly.

from, say, a .30–06 to a .300 Magnum, take a step up in bullet weight as well. At the .300's high velocity, a 180-grain bullet will give more uniformly consistent results than a 150-grain bullet. In the 7mm–08 or 7x57, a 140-grain bullet is great. But in the 7mm magnums, you're better off starting with 150-grainers, and I personally never use less than a 160-grain bullet in a 7mm magnum.

The main thing, really, is to use a bullet of adequate weight-for-caliber, not one of the ultra-fast lightweights with more impressive muzzle velocities. And then, so long as you plan your shot so that the bullet winds up in the vitals, you'll get good bullet performance.

Just a few days ago I finished up that New Zealand hunt with some chamois and

Himalayan tahr hunting in the Southern Alps. I'd put up the 7x57 and was using instead a .30–06 with some of Winchester's new Supreme ammo, a 165-grain boattail Silvertip. They were performing with devastating results, getting into the vitals and wreaking incredible damage. I wasn't altogether satisfied, though, since I wasn't getting the kind of penetration I like. My guide, Stan Peterson, was ecstatic over them. "Look at that," he'd say. "That bullet got in there and really went to work!" He didn't want penetration; he wanted maximum damage where it counted—and he has seen more game shot than I ever will. So to each their own, and after all, in what part of the animal's death did the bullet actually fail?

I used a little 7x57 Mauser on this big New Zealand stag. Normally I prefer a bit more gun for game this big, but it's really the bullet that does the work, and the little Hirtenberger 154-grainer, traveling at only 2,560 feet per second, smashed both shoulders and kept on going.

15

Solving Mystery Misses

The sable is a large and beautiful African antelope; the coat of a mature bull is glossy black with white-barred facemask, and the deeply ridged horns curve back toward the rump in a magnificent arc. The sable is an animal of open glades, not a lover of thick cover like the equally beautiful kudu; he is generally not a difficult animal to hunt but is one of the world's most majestic trophies. I had never shot a sable, and I wanted one badly. A big herd was milling in some mopane trees just a few hundred yards away, and it looked like I would get my chance.

I belly-crawled through some dry yellow grass and cut the distance down nicely. The only problem that remained was to sort out a decent bull, for the brown cows carry scimitar horns as well, and in shadow, sorting them out is difficult. This time the sable did the sorting; a fine bull stepped out into the sunlight and stood facing me at about 150 yards.

There was nothing to rest against, and I supposed the bull had seen me creeping along. I wrapped my arm into a tight sling and sat, elbows braced over my knees. The bull never moved; I can still see the crosshairs of the .375 steady on the center of his chest as the rifle went off.

At the shot he was off and running, and the rest of the herd went as well with a big cloud of dust and clatter of hooves. But I knew his was a death run and we'd find him piled up just inside the trees. Except we didn't. We never found that bull, never found a drop of blood.

Eventually I got a very fine sable. But more than a decade later I can still see the firm, black crosshair wires against a black chest that gleamed in the sunlight. Everybody misses shots, and there's nothing wrong with an honest miss now and again. But what I call "mystery misses" come back to haunt you—those odd occasions when you feel you did everything exactly right and absolutely nothing happened.

Misses are painful, but they're acceptable if you learn something from them. Every miss should be carefully analyzed and the reasons for it—however ridiculous and embarrasing—etched into the brain. Did you leave the safety on when you had your best opportunity, and then miss when you finally got the shot off? Chances are you won't do that again. Did you overestimate the range? Did you shoot too quickly from an unsteady position when a good rest was right at hand? Chances are you worked hard to get that shot, and if you can't learn something from your mistakes, then neither this book nor anything else can help you.

Study the terrain, and you'll usually discover why you missed a shot that felt good. In country like this, the most likely reason is an unseen branch that deflected the bullet. If you know the rifle is on, it's worth the peace of mind to walk the ground between you and the game to see what you can find.

The problem with mystery misses, though, is that you can't learn from them because you don't know what happened. That sable is the one that haunts me the most. On virtually every other miss, even though I can't know exactly what went wrong, I can come up with a pretty good theory. I take missing seriously, and when it happens, I relive it over and over again. A good, honest postmortem is a healthy thing, as long as you don't overdo it. On some seemingly mysterious misses the answer is readily available; on others I've relived them for days, even weeks, before accepting an answer I can live with and learn from.

The main thing is never to accept a miss as an act of God. If you wobbled when you shouldn't have, admit it—and go back to practicing until you can call your shots with precision. Perhaps it was a true mechanical failure caused by your rifle being knocked out of zero. Any time I miss a shot and don't have a ready explanation, I first boresight the rifle. If it doesn't check out exactly right, I find a place to take a practice shot as quickly as I can. Usually I find that it wasn't the rifle—but at least I don't have to worry about it.

I check my ammunition, making sure all the ammo on hand is the same load I sighted in with. I check the scope mounts and bedding screws for tightness. If all those obvious things check out, I start to look to myself for the source of the failure. Usually, if you go over everything often enough, you can come up with something, and that makes it easier to go on to the next shot.

I still don't have an answer for missing the sable, and it still haunts me. The rifle was just fine; it's an old .375 with a 1–4X Redfield scope, and I've had it since I was 16. It has never shifted zero. In 1982 it (along with every other firearm I owned)

One of the great fears about a "mystery miss" is that it may not have been a miss at all. It's extremely important that you spend time looking for blood after firing any shot at game—and that you pick out some landmarks so you can find exactly where the game was standing. This little buck dropped right in his tracks, but it took an hour to find him on the grassy hillside.

was stolen in a burglary. In 1987 it was recovered in a local pawnshop—and it's still in zero. The distance to the sable was 150 yards; I paced it off. No reason for holdover, and I didn't—I just aimed at the center of the chest below the base of the throat and squeezed the trigger. There was no brush in the way, and I'm certain that neither the animal nor the crosshairs were moving when the bullet left the barrel.

The obvious answer is that I did indeed hit the bull, and he didn't bleed (which can happen, especially on a shot like that), and we simply failed to find him. But nobody

heard the bullet hit, and nobody saw any reaction to the big .375 slug. A good professional hunter, two magnificent African trackers, and I searched for hours on my insistence that it was a good shot, and collectively we agreed I couldn't have connected. The only answer is that I blinked, wobbled, flinched, or whatever, and just plain missed him. I've come to accept that, sort of.

Fortunately for my sanity, few misses are as perplexing as that sable. Generally you can come up with an explanation if you work at it.

Sometimes the ground will tell you while you're casting for tracks or blood. I mentioned a big Kansas whitetail I missed when I was a kid. There was a screen of light brush between me and him, and although I can't be certain, I'm quite sure in my own mind that the bullet was gobbled up by that bit of brush. The brush was about two-thirds of the way from me to the animal, which makes deflection extremely likely. But because of its location I didn't walk the ground to look for cut twigs.

Often in such cases, a careful look around will tell you everything you need to know. If you miss an animal and you find bullet-cut branches between you and where you were standing, you don't need to look any farther for an answer. You can kick yourself at will for attempting to shoot through brush, but you needn't stew over

A mistake in range estimation is the most common cause of a mysterious miss in open country. Generally a walk toward where the animal was standing and a search for blood will tell you everything you need to know.

a "mystery miss" — there's really no mystery at all. Sometimes you can get lucky and plow through an amazing amount of brush, but it's quite amazing just how little resistance is required to turn a bullet off course.

Poor range estimation is one of the most common causes of well-aimed misses. Generally this stays a mystery only if you fail to take a good hard look after you shoot. In unfamiliar country it's very rare for things to be as far away as they look. And with a modern flat-shooting rifle, an animal should be very, very far away before you need to start holding over in order to hit. And yet you see it done time and again, usually by hunters who aren't familiar with open-country shooting. I've done it myself, and I grew up shooting in open country. Before you allow daylight between your sights and the backline of a game animal, take a good, hard look. Chances are it will solve a lot of potential mysteries.

It's altogether too easy to lay the blame on your equipment, but once in a while a rifle will get out of zero. As I said, that's the first thing I check when I miss a shot and can't figure out why. Over the years I've had just three rifles come out of zero while actually hunting. One was obvious, but the other two were real mysteries for a time. On the obvious one, the rifle suddenly shifted its shots to about three feet high at 100 yards. It happened in Africa, and I suspected it strongly enough to immediately insist on finding a quiet place for a practice shot. It was worse than I thought, and a casual inspection showed a fresh ding on the objective bell of the scope. It might have happened in the Land Rover, or the rifle might have been dropped; this was my light rifle, and I hadn't been carrying it much myself. But there wasn't much mystery.

The other two situations were more subtle. One involved that Mannlicher-stocked 7x57 I mentioned earlier whose zero shifted radically with pressure from a tight sling. Had I practiced with the rifle from field shooting positions as I should have, I would have known. As it was, all I knew for quite a while was that I'd missed a relatively simple shot at the best pronghorn I'd ever seen. The next day I shot a nice buck with that rifle, and it was even more confusing since the bullet landed in exactly the right place at a much greater distance. However, on that shot I simply rested over a rock with my Stetson as padding.

It wasn't until I got back home and started experimenting on the range that I discovered what had really happened. It didn't put that pronghorn on my wall, but it did make me feel a bit better. Why did I bother to experiment? Well, I can call my shots pretty well, and when I had the crosshairs in exactly the right place and my partner called the shot way off to the right, I knew something was seriously wrong.

My third failure was pretty interesting. I was using a superbly accurate Savage 110 in 7mm Remington Magnum, and a couple of friends and I were hunting deer in the foothills of California's vast San Joaquin Valley. We had found a pocket of deep canyons that was stiff with deer, but it poured down rain from well before dawn until just before noon. We and our rifles got thoroughly soaked. We also didn't see many deer, though we knew they were there.

Toward noon it cleared off, and shortly after that we jumped a magnificent mulie in a deep, narrow cut. I dropped into a sitting position and promptly missed him; my bullet went way to one side. My partner, Payton Miller, instantly rolled the buck with as nice a running shot as I've ever seen.

This is a respectable pronghorn, but if the smile doesn't look forced, it should—this buck was taken after a haywire rifle caused a miss on the best pronghorn I've ever shot at.

After I got done slapping him on the back and admiring his deer, I got to worrying about my shot. I checked the boresight, and it was off quite a bit. Then I looked at the bedding, and one side of the channel was bearing on the barrel. Obviously it had soaked up the rainwater and had swollen. I resighted it for a temporary fix and shot a nice deer later on in the day. After I got home I got rid of that stock and replaced it with a fiberglass stock, the first synthetic one I ever owned. Some judicious stress-relieving and rebedding would have been cheaper and would have worked just as well, but I was looking for an excuse to try a synthetic stock and that was as good as any.

If you take enough shots at game, sooner or later you'll come to a situation that you just can't understand, even after you examine all the likely—and a few unlikely—causes. That sable is my nemesis, but I have another that's worse, since it involves a wounded animal that wasn't recovered.

I was sitting over a bear bait in timber country in Canada. A good bear was working the bait, so I stayed overnight in the tree stand on the off chance that he might be one of the rare morning feeders. It was a long, long night, fortunately not too cold, and the dawn came and went without anything happening. About midmorning I saw movement behind the bait, and out stepped a beautiful gray wolf. There was a log on top of the bait, and it was a measured 80 yards from me. He posed on top of that log, quartered toward me, and at the shot he fell over backward and thrashed furiously for a few seconds. I could see movement and the occasional leg or tip of tail, but the wolf had fallen over the bait and out of sight. Then all was quiet, and I was beside myself with excitement. I waited a few minutes, primarily to calm myself before I climbed down.

Finally I walked forward to collect and start skinning my wolf—in my view one of North America's greatest trophies. But nothing was there. No hair, no blood, no tracks. I worked the area all day and never found a trace. A few yards beyond the bait was a swampy area where tracking was impossible. But there was plenty of clear ground to the water's edge, and there was simply no sign in any direction.

I was shooting a .358 with big 250-grain semi-spitzers, and though the rifle wasn't particularly accurate, it was just fine for that kind of shot. I had a steady rest and a good hold, and I can still see the big animal falling back as if blown over by the big bullet. Did I miss him altogether? Did I pull the shot to one side and, since he was quartering to me, place the bullet past his vitals? Was that problem compounded by the big bullet not expanding, thus allowing the animal to make it to the untrackable swamp? But why were there no tracks, no hair, no blood, no sign of the thrashing that I know I saw?

I've often wondered whether I imagined the whole thing. The only sign anywhere was a fresh .358 empty on the floor of the tree stand. That's a real mystery miss, isn't it?

16

Bucks in the Brush

Whitetail deer are cover-loving animals, and that automatically makes close-cover hunting one of the most common situations in the hunter's world. Of course, the whitetail deer isn't the only animal that's hunted in the thick stuff; the blacktail of the West Coast often is, and so are elk and moose and a great many African antelope, particularly the spiral-horned tribe.

Regardless of which game animal you're after, the problem is simple: how to get a clear shot and, if you can't, how to get a bullet through obstructing brush.

The problem is so common that we've got a whole family of cartridges that are considered "brush cartridges." In general, these are large-caliber affairs with modest velocities. There's no firm definition of such a thing, but if you're thinking about cartridges like the .35 Remington, .358 Winchester, .444 Marlin, .45–70, and that ilk,

then your thinking falls in line with that of most riflemen. Calling such cartridges "brush rounds" gives the somewhat optimistic inference that they will penetrate more brush than, say, the .30–06 family of cartridges. Guys in my business haven't helped much; over the years we've used every imaginable permutation of the words "brush bucking" and "brush busting" to describe this type of cartridge.

Now let's look at the truth. No rifle bullet—regardless of weight, shape, caliber, or velocity—is particularly efficient at plowing through brush. Period. If anything stouter than a thin screen of dry grass stands between you and the vital zone of your game animal, there's absolutely no guarantee your bullet will get through. If it does get through, it could be deflected off course and land virtually anywhere—or it might get through exactly on course. It's

There's no point in trying to shoot through brush; the only sensible option is to try to find an opening. In timber it often helps to get low, beneath overhanging branches.

really a crap shoot, and there's no way to predict the outcome.

Over the years I've done a number of tests with a dowel box—a box that holds overlapping vertical dowel rods to simulate brush. Using this box, I've shot at targets with a wide variety of hunting cartridges, and the results consistently have been so haphazard that it's almost impossible to draw conclusions—except to say that nothing will reliably penetrate a thin screen of dowel-like saplings.

There are some interesting trends, though. First, it's long been said that high-velocity cartridges were among the worst at "bucking brush." That probably is true with very light, very fast bullets. But in the tests we've done, the 100-grain .243 and 7mm bullets from 160 to 175 grains have always done as well as anything else—and better than a lot of the so-called brush cartridges.

Next, a round-nose bullet is commonly believed to be better than a sharp-pointed (spitzer) bullet in brush. Not true, at least not in the testing I've done and witnessed. A long spitzer bullet, like those mentioned above and also a 180 or 200-grain .30-caliber, does better than a round-nose in those calibers, and beats the heck out of most of the brush cartridges.

In my tests I've never been able to get the .35 Remington to do very well; its short 200-grain bullets seem to be easily deflected and often hit the target sideways after coming through the dowels. The story is the same with the .358 and .348 with light, short 200-grain bullets, but a good deal better with longer, heavier 250-grain bullets. The .45–70 does pretty well, especially with the big, slow, 405-grain bullet.

Far more important than caliber is the location of the obstruction. If a thin screen of brush—or my dowel box—is smack dab in front of the target, the bullet will get through. It may hit the target sideways, and it may be off course, but it will get through. Move that obstruction just a few feet away from the target, though, and it becomes an open ballgame. Now the deflection—and there will be deflection—starts to take effect. The bullet might hit the target or it might not. And if it does, you have absolutely no control over where it hits. And though some cartridges are a bit better than others, they aren't enough better to make much difference.

I was hunting Cape buffalo along Zimbabwe's Bubye River in 1981. We'd tracked a small herd into extremely dense thorn, and finally saw black shapes moving through the brush ahead of us. I maneuvered around for what I thought was a clear shot and fired the right barrel of my double .470. At the shot the buffalo dropped, pole-axed — which surprised me, since I was aiming for the shoulder and shoulder-shot buffalo don't go down like that.

We walked up carefully, but there was no reason for caution. The buffalo was stone dead, and when we turned him over we found the bullet wound in the neck, nearly three feet forward of where I'd aimed. Moreover, the entry wound wasn't round. Instead it was the exact silhouette of a 500-grain .470 solid. The bullet had hit *sideways,* and by some stroke of luck had broken the animal's neck. This was curious enough to warrant investigation, so I back-tracked to where I'd fired from. It was only 60 yards. About 40 yards from the shooting spot, and therefore just 20 yards from the buffalo, was a small thorn tree with a branch neatly and freshly cut by a bullet. And if that was enough to deflect and cause to keyhole a 500-grain bullet at moderate velocity, you tell me the odds of getting a bullet through a real concentration of brush!

A round-nose bullet is often thought to be better than a spitzer for "bucking brush." Actually, dowel-box tests indicate the sharp-pointed bullet might stay on course a bit better. The round-nose will set up quicker in game, however, transferring energy a bit faster — in other words, it can mean a bit less tracking of wounded game.

A dowel rod box like this is often used in tests to simulate a bullet passing through brush. It yields interesting results — bullets that fragment, turn sideways, or never reach the target. If the box is placed a few yards away from the target like this, no bullet made can be relied upon to get through.

There are some things to be learned here. First, a scope helps. With that open-sighted double I actually thought the bullet's path was clear. With a scope you have a better chance of seeing small limbs that might be in the way. Second, if there's any brush at all along the route your bullet must take, you simply don't have a shot.

The only exception is an animal standing directly behind a thin screen. Under these circumstances it's far better to wait for a clear shot. But if the vital area can be picked out, most of us will probably give it a try. Generally, so long as the animal is directly behind the obstructing brush, we'll usually get away with it. As I mentioned, no cartridge gives a particular edge for this kind of work. However, you're better off with long, heavy-for-caliber bullets with high sectional density. Such bullets have a tendency (and only a tendency) to stay on course. You're also better off without too much velocity—but going to the heavier bullets available for that cartridge will usually take the velocity down a couple of pegs.

For this kind of work I like the traditional brush cartridges with heavy, round-nose bullets—but not for the traditional reasons. I like them because in heavy cover you will probably get just one shot, and after that shot—whether it hits or not—the animal will be out of sight. The traditional brush cartridges like the .348 and .358 hit extremely hard. With long, heavy bullets they're relatively stable and hit even harder. And round-nose bullets tend to start to open a bit quicker and transfer energy more rapidly. I just latched onto one of Remington's new .35 Whelen bolt guns. With a nice low-range variable scope and a round-nose 250-grain bullet at about 2,450 feet per second, it should be the ultimate heavy-cover rifle for deer, black bear, and wild pigs.

Browning's BLR in .358 Winchester is a magnificent brush setup, and this lovely cinnamon bear was standing in plenty of brush when I shot him.

Thinking about that Whelen rifle reminded me of something. Just last fall, through an odd chain of circumstances, I wound up going on two moose hunts, one in Alaska and one in southern British Columbia. Both turned out to be true brush-hunting problems but totally different.

In Alaska I was carrying the prototype for Remington's .35 Whelen with some untested 250-grain factory loads with round-nose bullets. We had spotted a bull a long way off, but he was on a thickly forested hillside with a lot of cows and some smaller bulls, and we knew he wasn't about to come out in the open. If there had been time, we might have waited him out for a day or two. But it was the last day of the season, so we went into the thick stuff after him.

We got lucky. We bumped one cow not 75 yards from the bull, but she went out the other way, and somehow we got right onto the bull without spooking everything in the world. He stood up at about 60 yards, but was behind an evergreen tree with just one big paddle sticking out. I waited a few seconds, and he took a step out, almost facing me but exposing a bit of shoulder. I hit him just inboard from the point of the shoulder, basically where the neck runs into the shoulder. Three-quarters of a ton of moose went over backward, and for a brief second I could see all four feet in the air. When I walked up I had to look at the little .35 in awe that it could do that.

Well, that's a perfect conclusion to a brush situation — wait for an opening, take the shot as quickly as you can, and hit the animal very hard with something that packs a punch. After that initial experience with the .35 Whelen, nobody should be surprised that I ordered one immediately!

The second moose situation, in southern B.C., was totally different. It was a hot, dry fall with no snow, and the game wasn't moving. There were moose around, but they were holed up in patches of house-high alders. In soft snow a man might burrow his way through them, but with dry leaves, forget it.

When I finally got a chance, the moose was in one of those patches, on a little rise, and I was on a hillside looking down. I could see his head and antlers and his backline. His black body was partly visible through the white alders, but it wasn't much of a shot. My outfitter, Lloyd Harvey, and I talked about it for a long time. The moose wasn't going anywhere right away, but it was a stalemate — I was sitting, lean-

In brush shooting, timing is everything. This is a nice woodland caribou, but it's pretty rare to see them in heavy woodland cover. This one presents a good shot if you take it right now. If you hesitate until he takes one more step, you've got no shot at all.

Savage's great Model 99, also in .358 Winchester, is another ideal brush setup. The 250-grain bullet has been discontinued in factory loads in favor of the lighter, faster — and much less efficient — 200-grain loading. That's unfortunate, but the .358 is still a fine choice.

ing the rifle over the lowest branch of a pine tree, literally in the only place from which I could see that moose. He was a long way off, but I was shooting a .340 Weatherby with 250-grain bullets. Few hunting bullets around have the sectional density of that one, and at the great distance I was shooting, the velocity would drop down. If anything had a chance to make it through that thin screen of alders, I was shooting it.

We talked about the range and agreed on a hold, and I sent the first bullet right over the bull's back. As I said earlier, if you're seeing daylight between your crosshairs and an animal's backline, think it over one more time! On a high miss the animal may not move, and this one didn't. I moved the crosshairs down and hit the bull three times in the shoulder/lung area. Finally, after the

The very fast slide action is a favorite of deep-woods hunters. This one is chambered for the .35 Whelen; with a 250-grain bullet, this cartridge should become one of the all-time greats for close-cover hunting.

last hit, he crashed into the willows, and we found him dead.

None of that was surprising; moose often display little reaction to even a solid hit, and at the distance and with the alders in the way, I couldn't be sure where I was hitting—so I kept shooting until something happened. The amazing thing was that the screen of alders had no apparent effect. Sometimes it's surprising what a bullet can get through. On the other hand, this obstruction was quite close to the animal, and sparse enough that it's quite possible none of my bullets hit a single branch, even though through the scope it appeared that the target was obscured.

Let's briefly discuss techniques for brush shooting. The most important thing, I think, is patience. If the target isn't clear, then you simply must wait until it is. If you start flinging lead through heavy brush, at best you'll spook everything within a mile; at worst you'll have an animal gutshot by a keyholing bullet. Learn to look for partial openings. In real brush you may never see the entirety of a stationary animal, and the classic lung shot you want might not be in the cards. Under such circumstances it's important that you understand the anatomy of the animal you're hunting. A neck shot or a high spine shot might be the only one you have—and either on a stationary animal beats heck out of any running shot.

On the other hand, if a vital area isn't clear, don't lose your cool and cut loose on what you can see. Wait, and let the animal do the moving. In brush, if you're close enough to see the animal, it can surely see you. Stay still and let him make the next move. That move might be instant flight, but a tentative step to see you better is just as likely. Be ready to take advantage of it!

In the thick stuff, the smart hunter is always looking for openings, shooting lanes that can be used if something breaks. All too often, though, the shooting opportunity in heavy cover comes with no warning, usually a crash of brush accompanied by a flagging white tail. And usually it happens when you're climbing over a log or struggling to the top of an embankment.

Generally a situation like that is a lost opportunity, period. However, these things often happen at very close range. If you can get the rifle up and on the animal, you have a chance. You have to do two things, though; you have to swing the rifle like a shotgun, concentrating not on the whole animal but on the vital chest area, and you have to find a clear spot to shoot as you're swinging the rifle, tracking the animal through the thick stuff. We're talking about quail-shooting ranges here. Lead isn't important, but as in shooting quail, keeping the rifle barrel swinging is critical.

I've pulled off a few such shots, but more often than not I've never gotten the gun up in time. Once, not too long ago, I did it all just right on the best whitetail buck I've ever seen, but I never pulled the trigger.

He was a huge typical 12-pointer with black antlers, a gorgeous buck. He jumped at extremely close range, but in four strides he would be gone. Somehow I managed to take in the size of the rack and get the crosshairs on him, but he kept his rear end directly to me and got away without ever offering a bit of shoulder.

At that range perhaps I should have tried a "Texas heart shot." Chances are I could have recovered the deer if I'd gotten one in him . . . maybe. I've thought about it a lot, but I probably did the right thing. A buck like that deserves better. And in brush the rules remain the same as they do in all hunting: you can't fire unless you're sure of your target and you have clear shot at a vital zone.

This lovely blond animal is one of the prettiest black bears I've ever seen — and I'm sure glad I didn't have a bear tag here, because this is no shot to be taking at a bear. Branches are in the way all along the bullet's path, and the chest is obscured by who knows what. There's simply no option here but to wait him out.

17

Long Range, Long Odds

Many years ago, accounts of 400- and 500-yard shots on game were bandied about somewhat freely. The average hunter was a bit less sophisticated than he is today, and his knowledge of ballistics was a bit sketchier. There were more people out there who were likely to believe such long-shot events weren't unusual. Today we've gone in the opposite direction. I can't speak for the entire sporting press, but in the magazine I edit, *Petersen's HUNTING*, I shudder when a contributor writes about a shot in excess of 300 yards. I usually edit the copy to read "the animal was a long way out," or words to that effect. A competitive publication has a firm rule that in print no shot will exceed 250 yards.

The exaggerations of yesteryear weren't reality. But neither is today's tendency to rule out the long shot. Shots at a quarter-mile and more do occur, and can be made

successfully. But they aren't commonplace, and must not be taken lightly.

Of course, that 440-yard figure does not necessarily define long range. A quarter-mile shot is long range, but the outer limits of your ability — or the capability of your rifle — may not extend nearly that far. If you choose one of the real close-range "brush" cartridges like the .35 Remington, .444 Marlin, or .45–70, 150 yards may be a long shot. If you prefer open sights, 150 yards is getting out there with any cartridge. I won't try to define at what point "long range" begins. For me, anything beyond 200 yards is starting to get long. Beyond that point I do some serious evaluation of whether I can get closer, and I also take a hard look at the equipment I'm using and how steady I can get to make the shot.

The animal makes a difference, too. If I'm using a powerful, flat-shooting rifle like a .338, I might try a bit longer shot on an elk or moose than I would if I were using a 7mm magnum or a .30–06. On deer I would shoot a bit farther with a .280 or .30–06 than I would with a .243 or .257 Roberts. I simply wouldn't shoot at some animals, such as big bears, beyond 200 yards with anything. And on Africa's thick-skinned game, I'd cut that in half at *maximum.*

Sometimes there's just no way to get closer. Although long-range shooting is risky and isn't recommended, there's really nothing wrong with taking a longish shot — if you know your rifle and your load, you have a steady position, and you've practiced shooting enough that you believe *you can do it.*

Generally speaking, for most hunters shooting at most game animals under most conditions, if the distance is such that you must aim over the animal to make a hit, the distance is simply too great to shoot. Period. There are so many variables involved, some totally beyond the shooter's control, that such shooting is extremely risky. And unfortunately, the risk isn't just a miss. The real risk is a wounded animal that isn't hit hard enough to be recovered — and at extreme range, the shooter may not be aware that a hit was made at all.

Extreme-range shots should not be attempted — whatever your personal extreme range happens to be. However, such shots will be attempted from time to time. And if you know your rifle, pay close attention to the shooting basics, take your time, and weigh all the variables, sometimes it's amazing what cool, competent shooting and a good rifle can accomplish.

From left, .240 Weatherby Magnum, .257 Weatherby Magnum, .264 Winchester Magnum, .270 Weatherby Magnum, 7mm Remington Magnum, 7mm Weatherby Magnum, .300 H&H Magnum, .308 Norma Magnum, .300 Winchester Magnum, .300 Weatherby Magnum. This selection of belted magnums represents some of the best choices for long-range work. At long distances the biggest problem is estimating the range; the flatter your cartridge shoots, the less you have to worry about holding over the animal to make a hit.

I should say that I make very few extreme-range attempts. Most of the ones I have attempted have been successful. Generally the only excuses for a long, long shot are that (1) you can't get closer, and (2) the circumstances are such that you believe you can pull it off. The fact that you're running out of hunting time and may not have another chance is not an adequate reason, although we all use it.

I just checked my game log, and I note a fair number of entries in the 300 to 350-yard range. I regard that as very long-range shooting on game, although not at the outer limits for a flat shooting rifle and a good shooting position. In nearly 25 years of fairly extensive and quite varied big-game hunting, my log reflects only seven animals taken at ranges approaching, at, or beyond an honest 400 yards. The circumstances and thinking surrounding some of these attempts are worth recounting.

I believe the longest shot I ever made was on a Colorado mule deer in 1982. He was a very large four-by-four, and I sat on a ridge glassing, watching him cross a valley below me and make his way up the opposite hillside. Although there was good snow cover, the hillside was covered with dense, man-high scrub oak. I watched the buck bed in a dense patch, and then tried to plan an approach. There wasn't one; it didn't appear that I had any chance to get closer.

I waited. It was a calm morning, but very cold. I thought I might freeze to death, but I did have a lovely flat boulder that made a near-perfect benchrest. I could see part of one antler and patches of hair now and again, so I knew the exact location of the buck. I did not know the exact distance, but I knew it was very far — I figured it to be 400 yards. I was shooting a .300 Weatherby with 26-inch barrel, a genuine long-range rig, and the 180-grain spitzers were leaving the muzzle at a chronographed 3,100 feet per second. I was sighted in just two inches high at 100 yards, which put me about 15 inches low at 400. I had a lot of time to figure it out, and when the buck finally got up from his nap and stood broadside, I knew pretty much what I wanted to do.

Unfortunately it was wrong. With a hold just a bit above the backline, the first shot hit well under the buck. I was lucky enough to get down out of recoil in time to see the bullet hit. That was unusual, but it was more unusual to hit low — generally you guess the range to be farther than it really is. When we got the buck down, we found that he was simply a horse, an unusually large-bodied deer that had thrown off my perspective. But I didn't know that; all I knew was that I'd missed low and the buck still stood.

I should have reckoned the buck was too far and quit shooting, but I didn't. Instead I raised the sight picture a foot and tried again, with the same result. Next time I lifted it a bit higher, and I could hear the bullet hit in the clear, cold air. We got the buck; the bullet had struck just under the heart, almost another low miss, and the buck left a blood trail a blind man could follow. I reckon the holdover was 20 inches above the body, and on a deer that size the bullet struck nearly 40 inches low. Which means the range was something in the neighborhood of 525 yards. It was great shooting, and it was a great buck — but I'm not very proud of it. I haven't tried anything like that since.

The best long shot I ever made, in my view, was in Kenya in 1977. We had found a fresh lion track, and we needed an animal for bait, and quickly. Remaining on my license for such purposes was a hartebeeste — usually plentiful, but on this day the gusty winds had the animals nervous

I believe this Colorado buck was taken with the longest shot I ever attempted on a game animal. I had lots of time and a good rest, and there was no way to get closer — all prerequisites for a long-range attempt. It worked out just fine, but I'm not sure I'd try it again.

and we couldn't find one. Finally we spotted a small herd far out across an open pan, and the bull stood facing me in a small patch of thorn.

I was on a roll then, shooting way over my head. I had started the safari with poor shooting, but at that point I'd shot the last seven or eight animals with an equal number of shots. My confidence was high, and I had come to regard my rifle, a straight out-of-the-box Ruger M77 in .30–06, as some sort of magic wand. I never hesitated in trying this shot. I took a good rest, held a

The pronghorn antelope is a classic open-country animal. Though pronghorns are often taken at longer-than-normal ranges, the hunter can usually stalk to within very acceptable shooting range.

Remington's Paul Spenard took this fine New Mexico pronghorn with a 6mm Remington mounted with a Harris bipod—a great open-country pronghorn rig.

body height high and a body width into the wind, and squeezed the trigger. The bullet hit just above the point of the brisket, and the animal turned and made 20 yards before piling up.

There have been some other hits at ridiculous ranges, and a few misses as well. Surprisingly, though, the misses have been far fewer than the hits. I think there are some significant reasons for this. First off, with very few exceptions, I've never tried a shot that I didn't think I could make—which means that at long range I have never shot at an animal that was moving at more than a slow walk. Another reason is that at very long range the game is generally undisturbed, and often is not disturbed by the passage of the initial bullet. If you can call

your shots, or have a buddy present who can, and if you keep your cool, you have a very good chance of being able to correct your errors. Of the seven legitimate 400-yard-plus shots that I've made, the first shot connected only on the hartebeeste and one other animal.

Lastly, even though I shoot a variety of different calibers, I'm a nut about knowing the ballistics of the load I'm using. If I never have to make another very long shot, that's just fine with me—but if I'm hunting country where it's even a remote possibility, I make sure I'm prepared, just in case.

One of the real tricks to consistently successful field shooting is quite simply to avoid long shots that require range estimation and guesswork. A good part of the holdover problem can be eliminated with careful sighting-in that maximizes the trajectory potential of your rifle, but we'll talk more about that later. First let's discuss some of variables that make long-range shooting so chancy.

For starters, the accuracy potential of both you and your rifle come into play. The magic minute-of-angle (MOA), a one-inch group at 100 yards, grows to a four-inch group at 400 yards. That isn't any problem; the vital zone of any big-game animal is much larger than four inches. But how many rifles actually reach MOA? Inch-and-a-half groups at 100 yards are more common, and that's six inches at 400 yards. Still

not a problem. Two MOA means eight inches at 400 yards, and here—strictly from the capabilities of your rifle—you're skating on thin ice with little margin for error.

In field shooting, though, there must be a margin for error. You aren't shooting from a benchrest. You might have a very good rest (and you damn well better if you're trying an extreme-range attempt!), but it's unlikely to be as rock-steady as the bench-

The problem with wind isn't really that it has an effect—it's in reading it and figuring out just how much effect it will have. Winds at a 45-degree angle cause half the drift of a 90-degree crosswind, while tailwinds and headwinds have no effect at all. But is the wind at the target the same as where you are? How can you tell? You can read the wind carefully, but it comes down to a best guess.

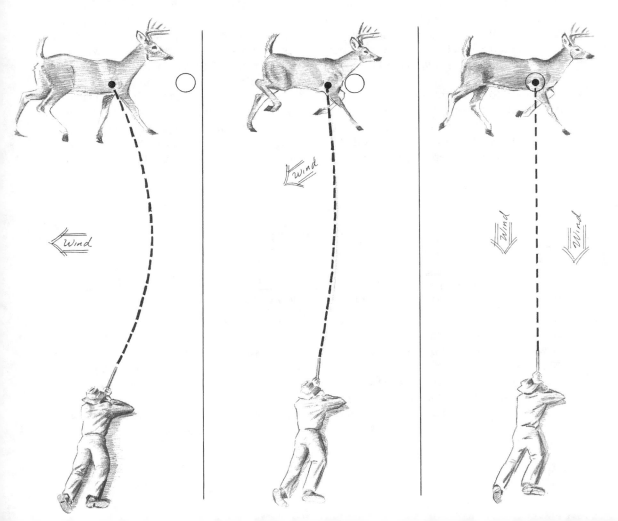

rest on the range back home. Nor are *you* as steady; you're bound to be excited, you might be shivering with cold, and you're very likely to be out of breath. Can you shoot to the accuracy potential of your rifle under such conditions? I can't. Which is another good reason not to try the really long shots.

The effect of wind on bullets is another major factor. It seems that long-range shooting and gusty winds go hand in hand. Whether you're in the mountains, on the open prairies, or on the treeless tundra, chances are you'll have to contend with wind. The chart shows the effect that varying wind velocities blowing at right angles to the bullet's path will have on popular hunting cartridges. You'll notice that at "normal" hunting ranges, winds of less than gale force aren't much to worry about. But at longer ranges, *any* wind becomes a significant factor.

It's easy to memorize tables. One of the best references around is Charles W. Matthews' *Shoot Better*, available from the author at P.O. Box 26727, Lakewood, CO 80226. This great reference, from a ballis-

tics expert who's also a computer whiz, will tell you everything you need to know about wind deflection, leads for moving targets, trajectories, and appropriate sight-ins for almost every factory cartridge in existence. However, neither his book nor anything else can give you the answers you must have in the field — you have to make the decisions yourself and place your sights accordingly.

As the accompanying chart shows, even a slight breeze starts to make a big difference as range increases. But even if you know the wind drift of your cartridge, bullet, and load, you must know three more things. First, at what velocity is the wind blowing? At best, this will be just an estimate in the field, a gut feeling. Second, at what angle is the wind blowing? Winds quartering toward or away from the bullet's path at a 45-degree angle cut the wind deflection in half; winds parallel to the bullet's path in either direction have no appreciable effect. And everything in between varies accordingly. Lastly, and most tricky, is the wind *at the target* blowing the same way as it is where you are? On the plains this is rarely a problem. But in the moun-

WIND DRIFT

| | | | Deflection in Inches | | | | | | | | | | | | | |
| | | | 10-mph Wind | | | | 20-mph Wind | | | | 30-mph Wind | | | |
Cartridge	Bullet Wt. (grains)	Muzzle Velocity (fps)	100 yds	200 yds	300 yds	400 yds	100 yds	200 yds	300 yds	400 yds	100 yds	200 yds	300 yds	400 yds
.243 Win.	100	2960	0.9	3.6	8.4	15.8	1.8	7.2	16.8	31.6	2.7	10.8	25.2	47.4
.25–06 Rem.	120	3010	0.9	3.5	8.2	15.2	1.8	7.0	16.4	30.4	2.7	10.5	24.6	45.6
.270 Win.	130	3060	0.8	3.2	7.6	14.2	1.6	6.4	15.2	28.4	2.4	9.6	22.8	42.6
.270 Win.	150	2850	1.0	3.9	9.2	17.3	2.0	7.8	18.4	34.6	3.0	11.7	27.6	51.9
7mm Rem. Mag.	150	3110	0.8	3.4	8.1	15.1	1.6	6.8	16.2	30.2	2.4	10.2	24.3	45.3
7mm Rem. Mag.	175	2860	0.7	3.1	7.2	13.3	1.4	6.2	14.4	26.6	2.1	9.3	21.6	39.9
.30–06	165	2800	1.0	4.1	9.6	18.1	2.0	8.2	19.2	36.2	3.0	12.3	28.8	54.3
.300 Win. Mag.	180	2960	0.7	2.8	6.7	12.3	1.4	5.6	13.4	24.6	2.1	8.4	20.1	36.9

tains it isn't unusual for the wind to be blowing in one direction on a ridge and in another in the valley below.

The most likely clues regarding the wind come from trees, grasses, shrubs. Watch how they're blowing all the way between you and your animal. A 10-mph breeze just stirs the more slender plants. A 20-mph breeze has things waving nicely; much more than that, and things really start whipping around. You simply must check the wind, and you must make some hard decisions as to what to do about it.

As tricky as figuring the wind is, the single most serious problem with long-range shooting (and with virtually all field shooting beyond 150 yards) is range estimation. Most of us are abysmally poor at it, and once an animal is far enough way that holdover is required, it is absolutely essential that you know the distance to your target within a few yards.

One good way to accomplish this is with a rangefinder. They used to be extremely bulky and unreliable, but today's rangefinders are extremely compact and, if you follow the directions exactly and calibrate them properly, quite accurate. I've played around with several from Ranging, and they do work.

Other good options are the various rangefinders built into riflescopes. These are generally built around extra stadia lines or some optical feature within the scope that is used to "bracket" a game animal from backbone to bottom of brisket. They work, if you pay close attention to what you're doing and *know the size of the animal you're hunting.* They're a bit faster to use than a stand-alone rangefinder, because while using them you're already looking through your scope. They aren't as precise as a good rangefinder, however, since individual animals within the same species can vary quite a bit in size.

A rangefinder is a great device, and modern ones are extremely accurate. I don't use a rangefinder in the field very often, but I think they're marvelous for learning to judge range.

These gadgets aren't for me, though. I usually have enough gear to haul up and down a mountain without adding anything more, and when I'm in the presence of game I have plenty else to worry about — like getting into a steady position and making an accurate assessment of the trophy.

I judge distance strictly by eye, using the "football field" method. Most of us know the length of a football field, and I estimate how many football fields will fit between the target and myself. At normal hunting ranges I can come pretty close, but at very long ranges it gets tricky.

I most heartily recommend a rangefinder to get started out right. Make a game of it, judging the distance by eye and then checking yourself with the rangefinder. Or do it the slow way — spend some time in the woods, in a park, wherever. Make your best guess, then pace it off. Judging range by eye is strictly a matter of practice, and that practice doesn't have to come during hunting season.

*The most common mistake in judging range is to overestimate, but a skylined animal is a notable exception —
generally an animal that's extremely visible is farther away than it appears to be.*

One thing to beware of is that your eyes will play tricks on you, especially in unfamiliar terrain with unfamiliar animals. Chances are you will overestimate; objects

There's absolutely no question that a sharp-pointed bullet shoots much flatter than a round-nose. Boattail bullets are the most aerodynamic of all, but their ballistic advantage over a spitzer isn't that significant. On the other hand, at long range you need all the help you can get!

viewed across broken ground — from one ridge to another, for example — often appear farther off than they are. There are exceptions; an animal on the skyline or in some highly visible position may actually be much farther away than it looks. Practice — not only during the off-season but also when you're sitting on a hillside taking a break. Question yourself about how far away an object is.

When it comes time to make a shot, it's your shot and your decision. But if you have someone with you who knows the country better than you, you're a fool if you don't ask him about the range. Generally you're a bigger fool if you don't listen to him, but I've seen competent guides be dead wrong in range estimation. Ultimately the decision of where to place the crosshairs is yours alone.

Long-range shooting is a very technical game, a game where ballistics come into play. Some cartridges shoot flatter than others, obviously, but a great many hunters forget that some *bullets* shoot flatter than others. If shooting at longer ranges might be in the offing, there's simply no comparison between the down-range ballistics of a modern, sharp-pointed spitzer bullet versus those of the old round-nose. The boattail shape, combined with a spitzer tip, is even a bit more aerodynamic than the spitzer, but not as significantly so as is commonly believed. On the other hand, at extreme range you need all the help you can get. The chart shows the difference a bullet shape makes, even if weight and velocity are identical.

Also under the heading of "all the help you can get" is sighting in your rifle properly so that you get the most out of the trajectory of your cartridge. But we'll discuss that in the chapter called "Getting Ready." For now we'll continue with another problem area—uphill and downhill shooting.

BULLET SHAPE COMPARISON

Cartridge	Bullet (grains, shape)	Velocity (feet per second)					Energy (foot-pounds)					Drop (in inches, 200-yd zero)		
		Muzzle	100	200	300	400	Muzzle	100	200	300	400	100 yds	300 yds	400 yds
.270 Win.	150 Spitzer	2900	2684	2478	2284	2100	2802	2400	2046	1737	1469	+ 1.7	− 7.4	− 21.6
.270 Win.	150 Boattail	2900	2707	2519	2339	2167	2802	2440	2114	1823	1564	+ 1.6	− 7.1	− 20.5
.270 Win.	150 Round-nose	2900	2537	2205	1905	1638	2802	2144	1620	1209	893	+ 2.0	− 9.2	− 28.3
7mm Rem. Mag.	175 Spitzer	2800	2614	2437	2268	2107	3047	2656	2308	1999	1726	+ 1.9	− 7.7	− 22.7
7mm Rem. Mag.	175 Boattail	2800	2643	2491	2344	2202	3047	2713	2410	2134	1884	+ 1.7	− 7.3	− 21.0
7mm Rem. Mag.	175 Round-nose	2800	2446	2124	1833	1576	3047	2325	1753	1306	966	+ 2.2	− 10.2	− 30.9
.30–06	180 Spitzer	2700	2488	2287	2098	1921	2914	2474	2091	1760	1475	+ 2.2	− 8.8	− 25.8
.30–06	180 Boattail	2700	2535	2376	2222	2075	2914	2568	2256	1974	1720	+ 1.9	− 8.1	− 23.2
.30–06	180 Round-nose	2700	2326	1989	1690	1425	2914	2162	1582	1142	811	+ 2.6	− 11.4	− 35.3

Data taken from Hornady Handbook of Cartridge Reloading, *3rd edition, and from* Sierra Bullets Reloading Manual, *2nd edition.*

18

Figuring the Angles and Other Problems

The buck was at the bottom of a big, open slide, and I was at the top. He was the biggest mule deer I'd ever seen—and he hasn't grown any smaller in my mind's eye as the years have passed. He was very far away, but I couldn't get any closer on the open mountainside. And yet I had lots of time. I examined the distance over and over again, and balanced that against the trajectory of the .264 Winchester Magnum I was carrying. It was a makeable shot, very much so; all I had to do was hold a slight bit of daylight between the horizontal crosswire and the buck's backline, and I'd have him.

At the shot he turned his head as if to look around for the buzzing insect, then he took four slow steps and vanished forever into a deep canyon. I went down to look for blood and didn't find any. But I did confirm

that the distance was everything I thought it was.

That buck bothered me a lot and could well have become one of those "mystery misses"—except that the answer was all too obvious. I'd held on the buck as though I was shooting on level ground, but I wasn't. That mountainside fell away at a 45-degree angle, and at that distance it was altogether a different shot than it would have been on the flat.

There are a number of ways to explain the effects of uphill/downhill shooting, but I've never been particularly happy with any of them. It's simple enough, yet one of those mystifying phenomenons that almost defy words. But I'll give it a shot. First off, it doesn't matter whether you're shooting uphill or downhill; the effect is exactly the same either way. No, shooting on the slant

There are so many variables in field shooting, and the difference in trajectory that an uphill or downhill angle will cause is just one more thing to worry about. But it does make a difference, and when you combine long ranges with steep angles, the difference becomes significant enough to cause a miss.

does not cause the bullet to "rise" more, and it doesn't go faster when fired downhill.

All bullets start to lose velocity and "fall" the instant they leave the muzzle. Two factors cause this: wind resistance and gravity. The aerodynamics of a bullet have a lot to do with its ability to retain velocity against air resistance, but nothing can alter the effects of gravity. If the rifle barrel was pointed exactly parallel to the earth's surface, the bullet would never reach the line of sight; it would start to drop immediately. When we sight in a rifle, we "cheat the act" by tilting the muzzle upward slightly in relation to the line of sight. By so doing, we haven't altered the workings of gravity in any way, but we have put the bullet's path to good use. Now, with the barrel tilted upward, the bullet will cross the line of sight at relatively short range, then continue to climb above the line of sight. Gravity is working on it all the time, and its path is curved from the instant it leaves the muzzle. Eventually that curve turns downward strongly enough that the bullet will cross the line of sight a second and last time. By then the bullet has slowed markedly. Gravity is really working, and the trajectory arcs downward faster and faster until the bullet finally impacts the ground.

That's what trajectory is all about, and how can it possibly differ when shooting uphill and downhill? Gravity acts in a straight vertical line from the earth's surface; it doesn't take into account the fact that the surface is far from flat. Regardless of the angle at which your shot is fired, all that matters as far as Old Man Gravity is concerned is the *horizontal* distance between you and your target.

Let's say my mule deer buck was exactly 400 yards downhill from me at a 45-degree angle. Think of a triangle, with the long leg running from me to the buck. The two short legs run vertical and horizontal—the vertical pull of gravity and the horizontal distance the bullet traveled. These two legs meet in a right angle directly underneath me, somewhere down in the mountain. As far as gravity is concerned, forget the actual distance. All that matters is the horizontal distance. In this case, if the long leg

of the triangle is 400 yards, then the short legs are slightly under 300 yards.

To be exact without giving a mathematics lesson (not my strong suit anyway!), you multiply the cosine of the angle, which is .707 for a 45-degree angle, by the length of the hypotenuse, which is the long leg. The exact horizontal distance is 282.8 yards. And if I wanted to hit that buck, I should have held as though he were 282.8 yards away, not 400. On the level, sighted about 2½ inches high at 100 yards, that 140-grain .264 bullet would have dropped something like 16 or 17 inches at 400 level yards. At 282.8 yards the bullet would have dropped about four inches. In other words, my bullet skinned right over him.

Now, it should be obvious that the distance must be long and the angle very steep before any correction needs to be made. When these conditions occur, the trajectory is stretched out. In theory, if you were shooting at a buck from a vertical cliff and he was directly below you, the distance wouldn't matter—your bullet would travel in a straight line. But wait—remember that the path of your bullet and your line of sight aren't exactly parallel; we've tilted the barrel slightly upward to force the bullet's path to cross the line of sight.

So if you have the misfortune to shoot at

TRAJECTORY DIFFERENCES AT VARIOUS ANGLES

Cartridge	Bullet Wt. (grains)	Muzzle Velocity (fps)	Trajectory (200-yard zero, drop in inches)											
			Horizontal			15°			30°			45°		
			100 yds	300 yds	400 yds	100 yds	300 yds	400 yds	100 yds	300 yds	400 yds	100 yds	300 yds	400 yds
.270 Win.	130	3060	+1.5	−6.8	−20.0	+1.6	−6.6	−19.3	+1.7	−5.9	−17.3	+1.9	−4.8	−14.1
.30–06	165	2800	+2.0	−8.7	−25.7	+2.1	−8.4	−24.8	+2.3	−7.5	−22.3	+2.6	−6.2	−18.2
7mm Rem. Mag.	150	3110	+1.4	−6.7	−19.9	+1.4	−6.5	−19.2	+1.4	−5.8	−17.2	+1.8	−4.7	−14.1

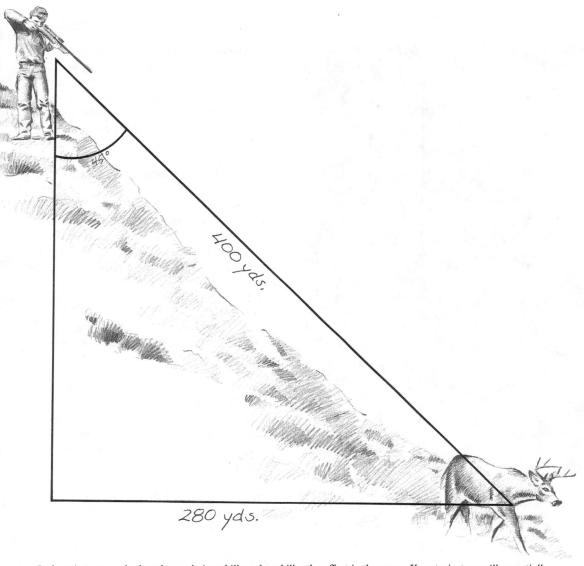

It doesn't matter whether the angle is uphill or downhill—the effect is the same. Your trajectory will essentially follow the trajectory curve of a bullet fired at the horizontal *distance to your target.*

an animal almost directly above or below you, keep in mind that your bullet will cross the line of sight at short range, as usual— but it may never cross it again, because of the stretching out of a vertical trajectory. Even at a modest distance like 200 yards, on a near-vertical shot I would hold a

couple of inches below where I wanted to hit.

How do you figure the angles in the mountains? Well, you really can't. Few of us carry surveyor's equipment with us. And it's not necessary to be able to figure an angle exactly, or know its exact effect. You

In field shooting, snap judgments are necessary. There often isn't a lot of time, and no way to figure the exact angle and the difference it might make to your bullet's flight. Fortunately the differences aren't significant; it's enough to remember to hold just a touch lower than you would on level ground.

do need to remember that it makes a difference, and when the distance starts getting long and the angle becomes steep, aim a bit lower than you normally would. If your rifle is accurate and your position steady, the size of an animal's vital area should be sufficient to ensure a solid hit at sensible shooting distances if you give this angle question a passing bit of attention.

Most of the areas we have discussed in this and the previous chapter are quite critical in the ability to hit game. Range estimation is the most important, but if you consistently ignore wind drift and steep angles, you will surely come to grief eventually.

Now let's talk about a couple of worrisome subjects that are most assuredly not critical. Hunters come in all shapes and sizes. Some are just natural-born worriers, and over the years I've gotten quite a few letters asking about the effects of altitude and temperature on trajectory.

Perhaps I shouldn't make light of these concerns, for the letter writers are dead right — altitude above sea level and air temperature do influence the ballistics of your hunting cartridge. But the horror stories circulated about these effects are just that, and I suspect they've been used as excuses for missing often enough that a lot of folks believe them.

Air is "thinner" at high altitude. That's a fact. Thus it follows that air resistance to the path of a bullet is less. That's also a fact. Tremendous increases in elevation will have the effect of stretching out your trajectory slightly. If you travel from sea level to Nepal to hunt blue sheep at 18,000 feet, your rifle will indeed shoot a bit flatter than you're used to. But if you travel from sea level to, say, elk country at 4,000 to 7,000 feet elevation, the difference might be there — but it's unlikely you'll notice it.

Incidentally, the reverse would be true as well; if you live on top of Pike's Peak and travel to Oregon to hunt blacktails on the coast, chances are your rifle won't shoot quite as flat as it did at home. There are so many more significant factors, however, that a change in elevation isn't one to worry about.

Far more important is the necessity to check the zero on any hunting rifle after traveling a great distance — whether you have changed elevation or not—especially if you use commercial transportation of any kind. Your ability to hit game is in much more danger from the airline baggage-smashers than from any change in elevation!

Temperature is less significant than altitude. Extremely low (and extremely high) temperatures do indeed have an effect on the combustion speed of propellent powders. In extreme cold the burning rate is a bit slower, and the bullet will travel a bit slower; the reverse is true at very high temperatures. The surface of the earth gets neither cold enough nor hot enough, however, to make a difference noticeable in the field under any but the most unusual circumstances.

One warning, though: ammunition should not be left out in direct, hot sunlight. Air temperature won't make a noticeable difference, but metal-cased cartridges roasted in hot sunshine can become very hot indeed, in more ways than one. It would be most unusual for an unsafe situation to develop—but it's possible, especially if you start out with handloads a bit on the warm side pressure-wise.

How much difference does air temperature make? Well, if you sight your rifle in at about 70° Fahrenheit and then travel to the Arctic to hunt muskox at minus 30, you can count on losing about 100 feet per second. From a normal mid- to high-velocity load, that equates to something like three to four percent—nothing to worry about. Moving from a temperate or cool climate to a very hot area is a greater consideration, not from the standpoint of trajectory but from that of firearm functioning.

My load development for an African hunt is usually done in 50° to 60° weather, and I know that I could have 90° to 100° middays over there. The last thing you need is sticky extraction caused by a bit of unex-

Air is indeed thinner at high altitude, and bullets will encounter less resistance. But the differences are so slight that altitude variances are the last thing a mountain hunter should have on his mind when he lines up on game.

pected pressure, so I don't handload to the top of the charts for African hunting; I make sure there's a bit of room for unexpected pressure just in case. With factory loads there's absolutely no worry; plenty of safety margin is built in.

Check your rifle's zero when you change location, climate, and altitude as a matter of routine. This ritual is a good basic check and will alert you to genuine problems such as a scope getting knocked out of alignment—which will shift things much more than any climatic change anywhere on earth possibly can.

19

Shooting Running Game

Earlier in this book I mentioned my good friend John Wootters' astute comment about shooting at game from the offhand position. He followed that up by saying that the second best thing we could do for America's game conservation efforts would be to convince hunters that their rifles would not fire unless their intended quarry was standing perfectly still.

Shooting at moving game is indeed difficult, and shooting at running game with any degree of consistency is beyond just difficult. Taking ill-considered shots at moving animals is undoubtedly a principal cause of wounded and lost animals.

Without question, the best plan is to stalk in reasonably close to an undisturbed animal and take a well-aimed shot at a stationary target. Or use a well-located stand, or whatever hunting method you prefer— but get yourself into position and take your shot before the animal takes flight. That isn't always possible, but there's the chance that if you don't fire, a spooked animal will stop and give you a stationary shot. No running shot in the world, at any distance, is as good a bet as a standing shot. Many times I have stopped a stalk and set up a shot when I could have gotten much closer; I'd rather shoot from a bit farther away than risk spooking the animal and either passing up the shot or taking a running shot.

It's unreasonable to rule out running shots, however. Once in a while we're going to try them, and once in a while they'll work out perfectly. The competent field shot will do everything he can to avoid such a situation, but be ready to handle it if it arises and is a reasonable situation.

What's a reasonable running shot? Heck, I don't know. I know I've tried some

When a pronghorn looks like he's just loafing along, he's likely to be moving 30 miles per hour. Shooting at moving game is always to be avoided, and in particular never *shoot at a running animal in a herd — it's too easy to hit the wrong one.*

things that I had no business trying. A prime example is pronghorn antelope. There's no faster animal on this continent, and it's believed that only the cheetah is faster in the entire world. A pronghorn that has turned on the afterburners can hit 60 miles per hour.

Once, when I was a kid and didn't know better, I turned loose a .243 on a running buck. He was crossing at right angles, and he wasn't close. For argument's sake let's say he was 300 yards out. He hadn't really put on the afterburners, but I suspect he was doing a nice, sedate 30 miles per hour. The computers tell me the correct lead would have been about 15 feet. I did lead him, but not nearly enough. He was with a herd, and my bullet landed squarely on the neck of the second doe behind him!

It was a good lesson; it's been a lot of years since I shot at a running pronghorn. No matter how good the hold feels, it's sheer folly to shoot at any animal moving in a group. Even if you figure the lead exactly right and establish it perfectly, there's no telling where the bullet will land if you slow down or stop your swing as you fire.

I made the same horrible mistake fairly recently, and I'm still embarrassed and ashamed. I'd seen a very large mule deer bed in a low bench with two does, but I couldn't find him. Finally I did, or he found me. He barreled up out of there, and I got the crosshairs on him and swung smoothly. It was just perfect — the sight picture looked ideal, and he was the buck I thought he was. He was also just 40 yards away, quartering up over a grassy ridge.

I shot, but nothing happened; he got over the ridge, and when I got to the top I could see him far down in the next canyon, obviously unhurt. But there on the ridge was a freshly shot doe. I still don't know how I did it; I never saw her at all. Fortunately I could legally take a doe, and later that day I caught up with the same buck and shot him. So it wasn't the disaster it could have been, legal and otherwise — but it was an incident I wish I could forget.

And yet, in spite of these foibles, I'm pretty darned good at running game. I know some guys who are better but not very many. Nobody is 100 percent reliable on running shots — which is why they should be avoided. Not feared, but avoided.

If you must try one now and again, there are some basic principles to follow. First

I made a nice running shot on this fine buck and was happy to get him — but the first time he jumped I just plain missed him and hit a doe on his far side. If I hadn't been in an area where a bonus doe was legal, my hunt would have been over and I'd have been in a jam.

and foremost is that the rifle barrel must be moving when the shot is fired. This "swing" is as critical in rifle shooting as in shotgunning. If you stop the barrel as you finish your trigger squeeze, the shot will fall behind — even if the sight picture looks perfect. So, when confronted with a running shot, pick the animal up with your sights; swing with it; get ahead of it as required, establishing your lead; keep swinging; and squeeze the trigger. Simple to say, hard to make yourself do.

The next principle is the lead. Again, as in shotgunning, your sights must be aimed at the spot your animal will be when the bullet arrives, not where it is now. There is no way to even establish a guideline as to how much lead is required; on fast-moving

animals crossing at right angles at some distance, the appropriate lead may put your sight picture clear out of the scope's field of view — which means the shot is quite impossible.

Charles Matthews' *Shoot Better* will give you the basic lead for any given cartridge — and the lead depends on the speed of your bullet as well as the speed of your target. Most computer ballistics programs will give you the same information. However, target speed and angle are the really critical unknowns, and they're virtually impossible to figure accurately by eye in a fast-breaking field situation.

A target at right angles requires the most lead; a target going straight away requires no lead. Quartering angles between those two extremes require some degree of lead. In general, if the animal is far enough away that you need to do some mental arithmetic to figure the lead, it's too far to be shooting. How far is that? I can't say. Like most decisions that must be made in field shooting, that's up to the judgment of the hunter.

I missed this running buck, but Ron Smith dumped him a few seconds later with one of the finest running shots I've ever seen. It can be done, and sometimes it's appropriate to try — but running shots should be avoided like the plague if at all possible.

But it isn't very far, certainly not much more than 100 yards for many of us, much less than that for most of us.

The big problem is that even on running game, you simply cannot shoot at the whole animal. You must concentrate on the vital zone, and that's where your bullet must land. And if you aren't certain you can do that, you simply shouldn't make the attempt. Of course, that is speaking of unwounded game; if a wounded animal is escaping, then any shot that's remotely possible simply must be attempted.

There are ways to improve your skills on running game. Shotgunning is one of them; good, experienced shotgunners are gener-ally reasonably competent at running game. Both trap and skeet are helpful, but for this application I'd give the nod to skeet. The extreme leads required on the center stations are more in line with what the rifleman might face, and the sustained swing is the game of skeet.

In areas where it's possible to do so, off-season jackrabbit shooting with your big-game rifle is the best training ground there is. You won't hit many of them, but you'll learn how to lead, swing, and follow through with the swing after the shot is fired. Second best is any rabbit hunting with a .22 rifle. In target games, the Olympic running-boar event is magnificent prac-

Successful shooting of running game with a rifle isn't materially different from hitting flying game with a shotgun. It's essential that you keep the rifle barrel moving, establish your lead, swing with the target, and make certain that you fire with the barrel moving, following through afterward by continuing your swing.

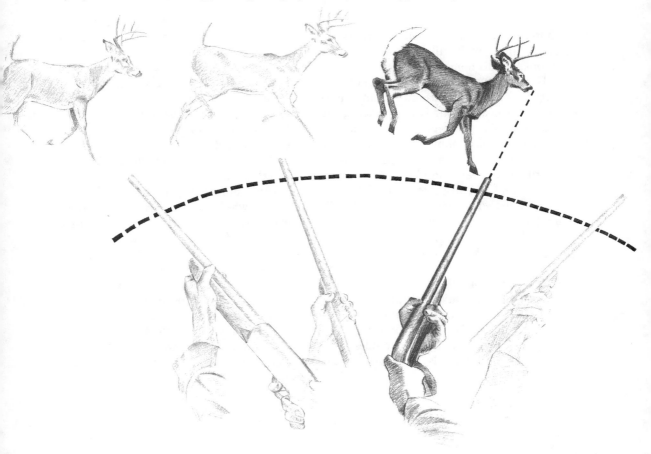

HOW MUCH LEAD?

Cartridge	Bullet Wt. (grains)	Muzzle Velocity (fps)	Lead (in feet, 10-mph target speed)				
			50	100	150	200	300
.30–30 Win.	150	2390	1.0	2.0	3.1	4.4	7.3
.30–30 Win.	170	2200	1.0	2.2	3.4	4.7	7.6
.35 Rem.	200	2080	1.1	2.3	3.7	5.2	8.7
.270 Win.	130	3060	0.7	1.5	2.3	3.1	5.0
.270 Win.	150	2850	0.8	1.6	2.5	3.4	5.4
7mm Rem. Mag.	150	3110	0.7	1.5	2.3	3.1	4.9
7mm Rem. Mag.	175	2860	0.8	1.6	2.4	3.3	5.2
.30–06 Spr.	165	2800	0.8	1.7	2.5	3.5	5.5
.30–06 Spr.	180	2700	0.8	1.7	2.6	3.6	5.6

Values given reflect a target speed of 10 miles per hour. For differing target speeds, multiply values shown by target speed and divide by 10. Example: With the .270 Win. 130-grain load and a deer traveling at 25 mph 200 yards away, multiply 25 x 3.1 = 77.5 divide by 10 = a lead of 7.75 feet. Values shown reflect target traveling at right angles to the bullet path *only*. Targets traveling directly toward or away require no lead. Forty-five-degree quartering angles should be multiplied by 0.7.

Data taken from Shoot Better *by Charles W. Matthews (Bill Matthews, Inc., Lakewood, CO, 1984).*

tice. I'm told that America's best in that sport, Randy Stewart, is absolutely deadly on running whitetails in the southern woods he calls home.

However, there are but a handful of running-boar ranges in the entire country. Fortunately you and a buddy can make a good substitute. All you need is a safe place to shoot with a piece of high ground and a few worn-out tires. Rig a cardboard or fiberboard target frame inside each tire, and affix a standard bullseye target to it. It takes two people; your buddy gets up on the hill and rolls the tires across your front. The bounding, leaping targets move much like a spooked buck. The tire-rolling trick will give you a healthy respect for moving targets—they're *tough!*

The best justification for taking running shots is when unexpected close-range encounters occur. You know the kind I'm talking about—a huge buck explodes from underfoot and bounds away with great leaps. The first problem is that most hunters will be caught unprepared, with rifles slung and heads hanging down. If there is potential for seeing game, especially up close and unexpectedly, that rifle must be in your hands, and you must be alert and looking, ready for action. Still-hunting through heavy cover isn't a casual stroll through the woods; it's a mentally demanding exercise that requires you to be keyed up and ready at all times.

If you are ready, you've got half the battle won when a buck jumps. At close range, lead becomes inconsequential; just a touch ahead of the shoulder is plenty. More important is to swing the rifle with the animal—*don't* point and shoot. Pick out the vital area, concentrate on it, swing the rifle with it, get just a touch ahead, and let the shot go. Sounds simple, but it's not.

If still-hunting in heavy cover is your style, running shots will probably come to you more frequently than to the stand

Some running shots are not only impossible but also downright suicidal. There are a couple of good bulls in this herd of Cape buffalo, but nobody would be foolish enough to let fly into a running herd like this!

hunter or the open-country hunter. There are some characteristics that make a rifle well-suited for this kind of work.

First and foremost, the stock must fit; when the shooter puts the gun to the shoulder, the sights absolutely must align instantly. Basically, the rifle must point where you're looking without any adjustment. Any action style can do this; it's a question of balance and stock fit. Choice of sights depends on what the shooter is most comfortable with. I believe that a low-power scope is the best for this kind of work. You don't need high magnification, and the single sighting plane and the instant alignment of the crosshairs are very important. The "plex"-type reticle is very good, but I think a good, bold dot is the very best reticle for running game. I haven't used one

much, but I have made a few running shots with the dot, and there's something about putting that dot on a moving animal that's, well, comforting. If close-cover whitetails were my game, I'd have a 2½ or 3X fixed-power scope with a dot.

Although light rifles are pleasant to carry, a rifle with some weight — especially in the barrel — is a help for running game. Under all circumstances, heavier rifles are easier to hold steady than light ones, but on running game the heavy rifle makes it easier to keep the swing going.

Tubular-magazine lever guns are good that way; the loaded magazine puts extra weight out in front, and although the rifle is light, it's a bit barrel heavy, and that helps you swing through your target. The best rifle I've ever had for running game was my old .375 with a 1–4X Redfield scope and a very stiff barrel. Once I got it swinging, it just wouldn't stop, and I can recall a number of well-placed running shots made with that rifle.

One of the best running shots I've made lately was on a Cape buffalo, and like most running shots, I question whether it should have been made or not. We'd been on a bachelor herd of four bulls for hours, and we'd jumped them in the thick stuff a half-dozen times without seeing more than dust or their backsides disappearing into the next patch of thorn. Finally we lost the tracks in an island of heavy bush, and when we came out on the far side, we realized the buffalo were now behind us. We went back in, and the buffalo flushed like quail with a tremendous racket.

We ran through the brush and spilled out into the open just as the buffalo crossed in front of us. The outrider was a good bull, and I never thought about the consequences of blowing this particular shot. I was carrying a double .470, and nothing mounts and swings like a double that fits. I ran to the right to get clear of a tree, pulled up short, and swung the big rifle like a 20-gauge double shotgun on a very large, very black quail. I remember swinging it fast and getting the bead down in the notch and just a bit ahead, and then the rifle went off. The buffalo pitched forward on his nose, sliding 30 feet in a great cloud of dust. It was spectacular, but I'm glad I don't have to do it that way all the time. Far and away the best technique for handling a running shot is to wait until he stops!

20

Dangerous Game — A Different Business

Depending on which author you read (and believe), it could be easy to get the idea that the woods are full of creatures lying in wait to claw, gore, bite, trample, and eat you. It's true that there are a number of animals that can be dangerous, especially in Africa but also in North America. In most cases, though, I think the danger to the hunter is overrated. I have shot three African lions and something over a dozen Cape buffalo, along with the rest of the so-called "big five." I've also shot both brown and grizzly bear, a passel of black bears, and a great many wild hogs. I've never had a seriously close call, but I have had three fairly major problems. One was with an African lion that another hunter had shot but hadn't killed; and two were with wild hogs. I had wounded one of them myself, and my stepson had wounded the other one.

I don't think my experience means that I'm either particularly lucky or particularly good; I think it's most unusual to have a problem with any game animal. Most sticky situations occur because somebody made a terrible mistake—bad shooting, poor choice of equipment, or poor judgment at a critical time. In almost every instance of a serious charge by a game animal, you can find strong evidence of hunter error if you examine the facts.

I know good professional hunters who have been badly mauled—once. They'll usually tell you where they screwed up if you push them. I also know many top professional hunters who have never been touched by an animal, and they intend to keep it that way. In the professional guiding trade, scars from an animal mauling aren't a badge of honor; they're a badge of incom-

Of the truly dangerous game animals that I have experience with, the African lion is the only one I'm actively afraid of. Lions turn my knees to jelly, and with some justification — if you make a mistake on one, you might not walk away from it. That is why low-percentage shots simply must not be attempted.

petence, if only a momentary lapse. And so it is with us amateurs.

I'm often asked about my favorite kind of hunting or favorite kind of game. That's a tough question, because I genuinely like virtually all types of hunting, and I enjoy game animals on their own merits. In other words, I don't try to compare pronghorn hunting with whitetail hunting. I suppose that at bottom line I enjoy deer hunting as much as anything; few thrills match the sight of a big buck. But there's a special thrill to hunting dangerous game. Mind you, I don't actually expect to get chewed up, and I certainly don't want to. But hunting has a special flavor of tenseness, of total awareness and concentration, when you know that you simply cannot make a mistake and get away with it.

The hunting world is shrinking today, especially where very large animals and the great predators are concerned. A quarter century ago in India one could hunt tiger and gaur, the huge Asian buffalo, and in Africa it was possible to hunt the entire Big Five — rhino, elephant, lion, leopard, and Cape buffalo — on a single safari. Here in North America we had brown and grizzly bear, as we do today, and polar bear hunting was also readily accessible. It isn't the same today, but excellent opportunities remain to hunt truly dangerous game.

Tiger hunting is over with, probably forever. So is hunting short-tempered black rhino in Africa. The Cape buffalo remains quite huntable, probably at lesser expense than ever before. Cats and elephant are still huntable today, but safaris for them are

The Alaska brown bear is the world's largest predator—fully three times the size of the largest African lion—and one of the most dangerous game animals. Any rifle looks small against such an animal, and it's sheer folly to tackle a bruin this size without an adequate rifle. This bear was taken with a .375 H&H, a good choice.

more specialized and more expensive than in days gone by. White rhino are huntable at great expense, but they're more docile than the black rhino—I think you'd have to mess up very badly to get into a really dangerous situation with one. Relatively new on the scene is Asiatic water buffalo and banteng (another Asian bovine) hunting in Australia. These transplanted herds offer good hunting, and though the animals aren't as truculent as Cape buffalo, full-out charges do occur.

Here in North America, thankfully, the situation hasn't changed as radically. We still have excellent hunting for both brown bear and grizzly bear, and populations of both are on the increase.

We also have excellent black bear hunting in many parts of the U.S. today. And make no mistake, the black bear can be a tough customer. He is rarely considered dangerous in the sense that a grizzly is dangerous. But like all bears he is extremely

unpredictable and must not be taken lightly. Continent-wide, the number of black bear maulings vastly exceeds the number of grizzly/brown bear maulings, although that's partly a function of population. I know two black bear guides who have been seriously mauled by fairly small bears. In both cases the bears had been wounded.

In the wild hog we have another potentially tough customer. Interest in hog hunting seems to be growing by leaps and bounds in the U.S. as pig populations expand, and that's good—I think hogs are a vastly underrated game animal.

The pig doesn't see very well. But there's nothing wrong with his hearing or sense of smell. He's also very tough. Once mature, a wild boar in North America has no predators whatsoever, save man. An unprovoked charge is extremely rare, but if you harass him or hurt him, you can have a real fight on your hands. I'm hard put to classify a

The white rhino is a huge beast, but actually quite docile, though you simply don't take any chances with game in this size category. Body size alone dictates the use of a very powerful rifle.

pig up there with a grizzly bear. But he's another animal that must not be taken lightly.

When you talk about dangerous game, you're actually talking about situations that make a *potentially* dangerous animal *actually* dangerous. And in that context, it must be remembered that any wild animal is potentially dangerous. A bull moose in the rut, for instance, is out of his mind. Rutting moose have attacked trains and logging trucks, and the hunter who calls up a moose in this mood must be prepared to deal with three-quarters of a ton of mindless rage.

Even a deer has the equipment and strength to do serious and permanent damage to a man—and although it's quite rare, men have been seriously injured and even killed by wounded deer.

The first rule of thumb with any animal that has been shot is to approach with extreme caution, from the rear. And be ready. Animals generally considered to be non-dangerous, I approach from the rear with rifle ready; and once I get close, I watch carefully for any signs of life for a few moments. At this point you can generally see where the bullet went in or came out, and that will give you a good idea of whether the animal is still alive or not. If there are no signs of life, I circle to the front, and with a round in the chamber and the safety off, I extend the rifle muzzle and touch the animal's eye. It's at this point that a stunned animal may possibly leap up, and if that happens I'm ready to pull the trigger.

If there's no reaction at all to a touch of the eye, the game is over. If there's a slight reaction, then the animal hasn't quite expired. I back off and wait a few seconds longer, then try again. If there's still a reaction, it's time to consider a finisher. I almost never carry a handgun when hunting with a rifle, so I usually place a finishing shot through the lungs, carefully avoiding the shoulder so as not to damage any more meat than necessary. Obviously a neck or head shot will do the trick, but in my business I generally want to get good photos of the animal, even if I don't want the cape to have the animal mounted—and I don't like to inflict the kind of damage a rifle will do at close range.

With truly dangerous animals the general procedure is the same. Once you've approached from the rear, stand and watch for several minutes—and be ready. If you have a partner or a guide with you, have him throw a rock or a stick or a dirt clod and hit the animal. If there's any reaction, don't hesitate—shoot—especially on very large animals such as grizzly or buffalo that

All bears should be treated with great respect, including black bears. Two guides of my acquaintance were badly mauled by smallish black bears that had been wounded.

are tough to stop once they get adrenaline pumping. From the rear like that, the best course is to break the spine. Or you can circle slightly to the side before doing the rock-throwing, so as to have a clearer shot. If there's any rise to the ground, make certain you're on the uphill side. Even if you've circled around enough to have a clear shot at the chest, forget about that area. If a finishing shot is called for, break the backbone, the neck, or the shoulders.

On dangerous game—or any game for that matter—don't approach haphazardly.

That's how I got into trouble on a wild hog not too long ago. My stepson had hit a big boar a bit too far back with a .30–06. I thought he had run on through a low saddle, so Paul and our guide/host, Tom Willoughby, ran up there to try to intercept him. I went straight down into the brush where the pig had vanished, to try to pick up tracks. I wasn't hunting, so wasn't carrying a rifle. As an afterthought I had grabbed Paul's pistol, a police .38, just in case a finisher was needed.

I found the pig lying in a thick chaparral bush, looking very sick. I worked in behind him and carefully lined up on the spine from about eight yards. The bullet didn't penetrate, and I suddenly had the pig's undivided attention. He was hurt and I could have gotten out of his way, but instead I forgot what I was carrying and stood firm to shoot it out with him. I shot him in the head five times, and all but the last bullet (which entered through the right eye) flattened out against the skull without penetrating.

As I said, you get into trouble only when you screw up, and we'd screwed up by the numbers. The animal hadn't been hit properly in the first place. It happens to all of us, but it's still a mistake. Second, and most serious, I went in on the wounded pig casually, without an adequate firearm.

On dangerous game, these mistakes must be avoided. So let's look at both of these areas. First, shooting at dangerous game is a bit different from shooting at nondangerous game. Late in a hunt, with an adequate rifle and cartridge, a low-percentage shot at a nondangerous animal may be attempted, and can be understood and forgiven. Not on dangerous game. Shots simply must not be attempted unless the shooter has a clear shot at a vital zone and is completely confident the shot can be made. The conse-

This is my stepson, Paul Stockwell's, excellent wild boar—the one that came close to eating me. I simply goofed up, compounding the mistake by walking in nonchalantly without an adequate firearm. It would have been embarrassing to get hurt by a California wild hog—but it almost happened.

quences of doing it wrong are simply too great. If the animal is wounded, you and your partners must go after him. If you can't find him, then you've left a wounded, angry beast that might well take it out on the next unsuspecting human to come along.

All the shooting basics we've discussed earlier apply here but even more so. The shot at a dangerous animal must be taken calmly and deliberately, and it must be a shot that has almost no chance of going awry. Even at that, dangerous game will be wounded and must be followed up—but not as often as will happen if marginal shots are attempted.

The other consideration regarding actual shooting at dangerous game is that if the animal doesn't go down immediately, you must keep shooting. An African professional hunter once stated that his American clients tended to be very good field shots,

but they had a bad habit of "admiring their shots." Instead of quickly following up a hit (or miss) with another shot, they had a tendency to wait and watch for the initial shot to take effect.

I understand that, because I'm guilty of it. If I'm shooting from a very steady position and have confidence in the rifle, I don't shoot again on deer-size game if I'm certain the bullet has gone in the right place. On a heart shot, I know the animal is likely to run 60 to 100 yards; on a behind-the-shoulder lung shot, I know the animal might run or might just stand for a few seconds. But I know he won't go far, and I don't like to mess up the meat by taking a running shot that might hit anywhere. Not on dangerous game. *Never* on dangerous game. On animals that have potential for hurting you, you must get another cartridge into the chamber instantly; and if that animal isn't down, you must keep shooting until he's down or out of sight. In the latter case, wait half an hour before following up, and reload your rifle completely before you start.

On buffalo the most typical situation is a broadside shoulder-heart shot. Time and again the animal will receive the bullet, then turn his tail to you and head for the thick stuff. I like to make that initial shot with a softnose from a big rifle, but I follow it up with a solid up the rear when the animal turns—and another if I can get another shot before he's gone in the brush. Chances are that first shot will have done the trick, but I'm not willing to bank on it. On dangerous game, keep shooting. Cartridges are cheaper than hospitals.

In the previous chapter I mentioned a shot I made on a running buffalo. A good argument could be made for not attempting such a shot. But a couple of things favored my giving it a try. First, I had a rifle

On really dangerous game, shoot again. Americans have a bad habit of "admiring" their shots—waiting to see the results before shooting again. You simply must not take chances on the really dangerous animals.

ideal for that kind of shot—fast-swinging and well balanced. Second and most important, it was plenty big enough for the job at hand; it was a .470 Nitro-Express firing a 500-grain bullet. I would not have attempted that shot with a .375, period. After the buffalo went down, I ran forward quickly, loading the fired barrel as I ran. I stopped 20 yards short of the buffalo as he lay on his side, his back to me, and put another 500-grain solid through the spine

and down into the chest. Everything worked perfectly, but part of what made it work was a plenty-big-enough gun.

On dangerous game, I don't believe in half measures. The rifle and its cartridge must be adequate for the job. No, it isn't necessary to use a cannon. But it is necessary to use a rifle you can shoot well, that functions perfectly, and that throws a bullet that will penetrate to the vitals and disconnect the animal's life-support systems.

I won't discuss what I consider adequate for various animals; we did that earlier. I suggest, however, that whatever cartridge you choose, you pay careful attention to the bullet you select. Dangerous animals— whether bears, boars, or buffalo—tend to be very heavily muscled. They're hard on bullets, and you must select a tough bullet that will get in there and do its work.

The other hog that gave me trouble was a classic example. I was deer hunting in Texas, and just at dark a very large hog stepped out in front of my stand. It was too late to judge antlers on deer, so I decided to shoot. I shot him at 20 yards, right on the point of the shoulder as he quartered to me, with a 7mm Remington Magnum, more than enough gun. But I was using a fast 150-grain deer bullet, and at that close range the bullet opened too quickly and failed to penetrate. I found that out later.

At the time, all I knew was that the pig took off like, well, a scalded pig, and it was getting dark fast. I couldn't wait, because of the fading light, so I went into the gloomy scrub oaks after him. I found him, or he found me. I pressed the muzzle against his side as I jumped out of his way, and that did the trick. Lesson? Right rifle, wrong bullet. For dangerous game of any type I can think of, with the possible exception of leopard, whatever caliber you choose, go for the heavier, stoutly con-

The proper way to approach a dangerous animal is from the rear, and preferably not alone. At this point one of the hunters should toss a stone while the other covers; at the slightest movement, fire.

structed bullets. Velocity is wonderful, but it does you no good if the bullet opens up before it gets to the boiler room.

As a last note, it's surprising how many hunters go after dangerous game with a rifle that doesn't function properly. On *any* hunting rifle, but particularly one for dangerous game, make absolutely certain the rifle feeds from the magazine every time. I've gotten three different big-bore bolt actions from three different (and very good) makers, and none of them fed reliably from the magazine without some gunsmithing. It would have been all too easy to

go to the range and sight the rifle in by single-feeding into the chamber and then gone in on a dangerous animal, never knowing the rifle wouldn't feed. Check it out, and before you go hunting, run every cartridge you're taking along through the magazine and into the chamber.

Most hunting situations require a full measure of a very simple ingredient — common sense. If it's there — and if the hunter pays attention to it — he will rarely run into trouble. If he goes off half-cocked, well, things could get a whole lot more exciting than he bargained for.

21

Getting Ready

Proper preparation is the key to the success of almost any human endeavor. Sallying forth to put venison in the freezer is no different. And it really doesn't matter whether you plan to knock over a nice forkhorn whitetail on the back 40 or shoot a 40-inch Dall ram in the Alaska Range. Preparation is still the key.

This book is primarily about field shooting. If it were about hunting, then I could ramble on about equipment, pre-season scouting, studying of topo maps, and all the other preparations that make for a successful hunt. But since our purview here is shooting, this chapter will cover just two items that must be prepared—the rifle and the shooter behind it.

Let's get the rifle ready first. Many hunters do some practice shooting throughout the year, so their rifles are more or less always ready. On the other hand, many of us don't touch our rifles from the end of one season until just before the next one starts. And if you shoot throughout the year, the rifles you shoot during the offseason may not be the same ones you hunt with. So let's say that the big-game rifle hasn't been fired in some time, and it's time to get it ready for opening day.

First off, don't wait until the last minute. If you have a problem, you'll need some time to correct it. I'm kind of a rifle nut, and I have more rifles than I can reasonably use in a season (or several seasons). As I mentioned earlier, I also use manufacturers' rifles on a trial basis a fair amount of the time. So, though I may have a couple of rifles available that would work, it seems I have to make a couple of trips to the range to get a rifle ready literally every time I go hunting.

It also seems that every time I get ready for a hunt, something goes wrong with at least one of the rifles I plan to take. If I'm

Once the rifle is sighted in, get away from the bench. Sensible practice — for field shooting — should include firing from a wide variety of formal and impromptu shooting positions. Any position that might conceivably be used in the field should be practiced as extensively as possible.

lucky it's something simple enough that a little re-zeroing will do the trick. All too often, though, it's something more major, like a scope-mount screw shearing off.

So start plenty early. If you haven't fired your rifle in some time, imagine the worst possible thing that could go wrong, and head to the range in plenty of time so that, if it happens, your local gunsmith can fix it.

Before you even think about firing the rifle, do a couple of things. First, clean the barrel with a copper brush and a good solvent, and swab it out with clean patches until they come out as clean as they went in. Its pre-trip cleaning is the last one my rifle will get until the hunt is over (unless I get water in the barrel or something like that). A rifle may have a slightly different point of impact with a freshly cleaned barrel than it will after being fired a few times.

Next, give the rifle a good going over. Check the stock for cracks, particularly around the tang. Check all the mechanical features to ensure they're functioning properly. *Without* loading the rifle, make sure the safety functions properly, and then, with the barrel pointed in a completely safe direction, run several cartridges through the magazine to make sure the rifle feeds properly.

Check the screws to make sure they're tight — not too tight, but held securely in place. Loose floorplate and trigger-guard screws are often the culprit when a bolt-action rifle suddenly shifts zero or shoots erratically. Pay special attention to the scope-mount screws and the screws on the scope rings. Now, I'm famous for doing this — if you try to tighten them too much, you'll surely twist them off, and then you're in for a trip to the gunsmith. Too tight is just as bad as not tight enough. You can't really lean into the screwdriver or Allen wrench, but they should be good and snug with no play whatsoever. I always use Loctite as an added measure of security, especially on heavy kickers.

All right, you know the rifle is functioning properly and the sights are on nice and tight. Now it's time to give some thought to the load you're going to use. I've given some guidelines for bullet selection elsewhere in this book, so I won't go over it again. Suffice it to say that you want to pick a bullet that is constructed for the kind of game you'll be hunting, and is of adequate weight for that game. You'll also want to give some thought to bullet shape. If you'll be hunting in open or semi-open country, you'll surely want an aerodynamic sharp-pointed bullet if your rifle will handle one safely (tubular-magazine rifles must be used with flat-pointed bullets). If a longish shot is most unlikely, then you might prefer to use a round-nose.

Regardless of what bullet type you select, chances are you'll have a lot of choices available to you. If you handload, the options are endless. I usually select a bullet that has the qualities I think I need for a particular hunt or a particular animal. Then I go to my loading manuals or my notes from previous use of that bullet — or to my buddies who may have used that bullet — and I come up with several loads, using different powders, for that bullet in that cartridge that offer the velocity levels I want to achieve. I load up only a few of each, and make a trip out to the range to see which load groups the best in this particular rifle. Every rifle has a mind of its own; a load that groups extremely tightly in one .30–06 may not group worth a darn in another .30–06. But by experimenting a bit, you can usually turn up a good load fairly quickly.

The hunter who doesn't handload has the same task ahead of him. Let's say he's planning a mule deer hunt in the high country and has decided that a sharp-pointed 165-grain bullet will be the best choice in his .30–06. At least four companies offer factory 165-grain .30–06 loads. I'd get a box of each, or at least as many as I could find locally. Then I'd see which one shot the best in my rifle, especially if it was the kind of hunt where I knew I might need all the accuracy my rifle had to offer. They may all shoot the same, but generally one or two loads will outshoot the others in a particular rifle. If you want all the accuracy your rifle will deliver, it pays to experiment whether you handload or not.

Pinpoint accuracy isn't important in all hunting situations. Let's say that instead of high-country mule deer, you're going whitetail hunting in thick woods a few

This 7mm Remington Magnum of mine is normally very accurate, but every rifle is a law unto itself, and no two will shoot exactly alike with the same load. Here are 10 different groups with 10 different factory loads — none the same size or in the same place. Part of getting ready is deciding what bullet weight and shape are best for the game you plan to hunt, and then experimenting to find what load your rifle likes best that offers that type of bullet.

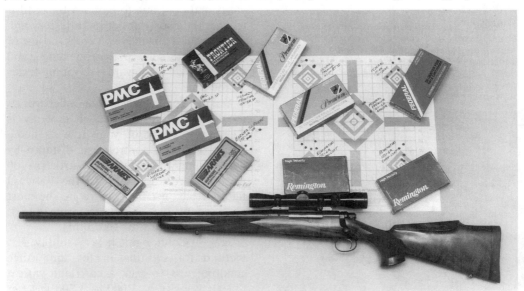

miles from your house. You don't think your shots will come at more than 75 yards, and your open-sighted .30–30 is all the rifle you need. In that case, choice of ammo isn't terribly important. You probably won't want the light 125-grain .30–30 load, but you could take your pick of any of the 150- or 170-grain .30–30 factory loads, and your choice wouldn't be wrong. You could experiment to find out which shot best in your rifle, but chances are any of them will be plenty good enough.

Now that you know what load you want to shoot, you need to zero in your rifle. We talked about this earlier, but now there's an added wrinkle. You're actually going hunting, so you want to sight in your rifle for the country and the game you'll be hunting.

If you're going to that same woodlot we just talked about, it's a simple chore. You aren't expecting a shot of any length, and you don't believe there's any reason to prepare for one. So you sight your rifle to be dead-on at 100 yards. Now, your scope, if

I selected a .340 Weatherby for this moose hunt, but in anticipation of a close shot I chose a 250-grain round-nose bullet. The shot was actually quite long, and although I made it all right, I would have been much better off with a spitzer bullet. The lesson? Unless you're certain your shots will be close, stick with spitzer bullets.

you're using one, probably sits 1½ inches above the center of the bore; if you're using iron sights, it's half that distance. With almost all cartridges in use today, your bullet will thus be climbing slightly to reach its dead-on position at 100 yards. It may climb a bit more after that, but shortly beyond 100 yards it will start to drop, and you'll be low if you hold dead-on much beyond that.

But that's OK — you're expecting a close-range shot, and it could well be one of those fast-flushing deer we talked about earlier. You want your rifle to be as close to dead-on as you can get it. Actually, when I shoot open sights I sight the rifle to be dead-on at 50 yards; 100 yards is a bit beyond my capabilities with coarse open sights.

But suppose you're going after that mountain mulie buck. In that situation your shots will probably be longer, and you'll want to maximize the trajectory your rifle has to offer. If you tilt your rifle barrel up slightly in relation to your line of sight, your bullet will climb through your line of sight at close range, usually 20 to 30 yards from the muzzle. It will strike high at 100 yards and continue to climb a bit until it reaches the high point of its trajectory arc. Then it starts down. It will cross the line of sight again at some point downrange, and then continue downward — dropping faster all the time.

You can control where that bullet crosses the line of sight. Its second crossing is where you speak of your rifle as being "dead on." You control that distance by determining where your bullet strikes at 100 yards. There's no magic in the 100-yard figure — that just happens to be the most common distance on most shooting ranges. There are several ways to do this.

Jack O'Connor put it very simply. His method for sighting in for long-range shooting was to pick a cartridge with a muzzle velocity of 3,000 to 3,200 feet per

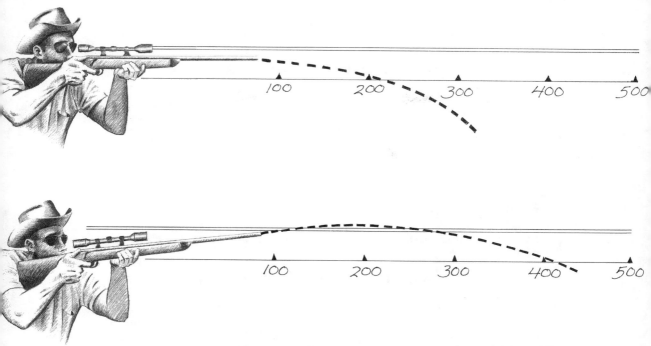

If the line of sight and the line of bore were exactly parallel, the bullet would never cross the line of sight, and thus a rifle could never be sighted in. Instead, the bore is tilted up slightly in relation to the line of sight, causing the curved path of the bullet to cross the line of sight once at close range and again downrange where the rifle is said to be "dead on" at that certain range.

second. He sighted it in to be exactly three inches high at 100 yards, and then he grouped the rifle at 200, 300, 350, and 400 yards so that he knew exactly what the rifle was doing at those ranges. He reckoned that a rifle with a good aerodynamic bullet at these velocities, so sighted, would print two to four inches high at 200 yards, dead-on between 250 and 300 yards, and seven to 14 inches low at 400 yards. Not a bad way to go.

Few of us have access to known ranges beyond 200 yards (often it's tough to find a 100-yard range!). So many of us have to rely on the 100-yard sight-in and trust the tables and other references for the rest.

Rather than pick an arbitrary two- to three-inch-high sight-in at 100 yards, I prefer another method called "point-blank range." Although the term is subject to interpretation, "PBR" means, in this con-

text, the maximum range at which you can shoot at a game animal without holding your sights under the vital zone at close range or over the vital zone at long range. You can pick your own vital-zone size, by the way. On smallish game like pronghorn (which can measure as little as 14 inches from backline to brisket), you might not want your bullet to rise more than three inches above the line of sight, and your maximum point-blank range is that point at which it falls three inches below the line of sight.

On larger big game, four inches above and below establishes a good window. For elk in wide-open alpine country, a 10-inch window (the bullet rising five inches above and falling five inches below the line of sight) isn't out of line.

Whether you handload or not, the various reloading manuals, especially Sierra's,

SIGHT-IN TO BE DEAD-ON AT 250 YARDS
Factory Ballistics

Cartridge	Bullet Wt. (grains)	Muzzle Velocity (fps)	Trajectory (drop in inches)				
			100	200	250	300	400
.25–06 Rem.	117	3060	+ 2.6	+ 2.1	0	− 3.6	− 15
.270 Win.	130	3110	+ 2.5	+ 2.2	0	− 3.6	− 16
7mm Rem. Mag.	150	3110	+ 2.3	+ 2.1	0	− 3.5	− 16
.300 Wby. Mag.	180	3165	+ 2.4	+ 2.0	0	− 3.4	− 15

A perfectly good way to sight in your rifle is to determine that you want it to be dead-on at a given distance, in this case 250 yards. To do that, you must have either access to a range extending that far or accurate ballistics charts that tell you where to put your sights at 100 yards.

POINT-BLANK-RANGE SIGHTING-IN
Factory Ballistics

Cartridge	Bullet Wt. (grains)	Muzzle Velocity (fps)	Trajectory (drop in inches)				Dead-On Range (yards)	Max PBR (yards)
			100	200	300	400		
Sight-In for 6-Inch Window								
.270 Win.	130	3110	+ 2.6	+ 2.3	− 3.4	− 15.7	253	295
7mm Rem. Mag.	150	3110	+ 2.6	+ 2.3	− 3.3	− 15.3	254	297
.30–06	165	2800	+ 2.8	+ 1.6	− 6.3	− 22.6	230	269
Sight-In for 8-Inch Window								
.270 Win.	130	3110	+ 3.2	+ 3.6	− 1.4	− 13.0	281	329
7mm Rem. Mag.	150	3110	+ 3.2	+ 3.6	− 1.3	− 12.6	283	331
.30–06	165	2800	+ 3.5	+ 3.0	− 4.1	− 19.7	256	299
Sight-In for 10-Inch Window								
.270 Win.	130	3110	+ 3.8	+ 4.8	− 0.4	− 10.7	305	357
7mm Rem. Mag.	150	3110	+ 3.8	+ 4.8	− 0.6	− 10.2	307	360
.30–06	165	2800	+ 4.2	+ 4.4	− 2.1	− 16.9	278	326

Another good way to sight in is to use the Point Blank Range concept to maximize the trajectory of your rifle. In this method, you pick the size "window" of your trajectory; the examples here show 6-, 8- and 10-inch windows. Data taken from Shoot Better *by Charles W. Matthews (Bill Matthews, Inc., Lakewood, CO, 1984).*

include superb ballistic tables that will tell you where you stand with your cartridge and bullet. Bill Matthews' *Shoot Better* is largely based around this PBR concept, and it tells you everything you need to know *for factory loads.* The chart shows some examples, but selecting the exact sight-in for your rifle is beyond the scope of this book.

As an example, let's look at Jack O'Connor's favorite .270 with the 130-grain load. We'll use the tables for Federal's fine Pre-

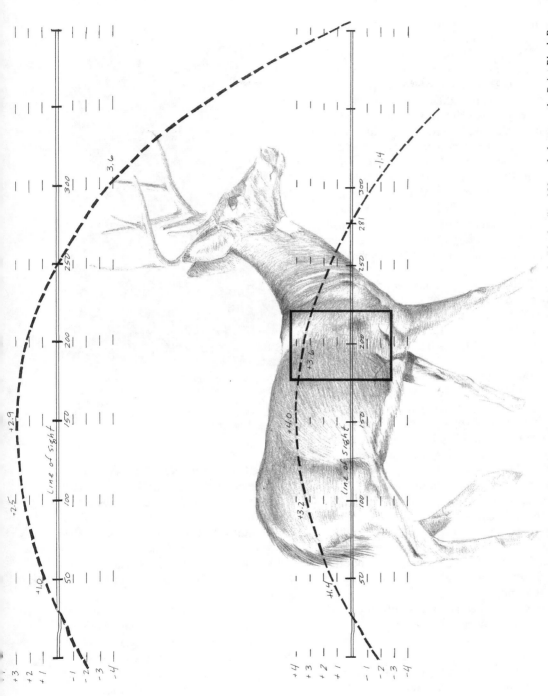

Two ways to maximize the trajectory curve of a 130-grain .270 Winchester. Top, sighting in to be "dead on" at 250 yards; bottom, the Point Blank Range concept, in this example establishing an eight-inch "window."

mium 130-grain .270 with a boattail bullet. If we sight in to be two inches high at 100 yards, we'll be almost half an inch high at 200 yards, about seven inches low at 300 yards, and 21 inches low at 400 yards.

That's a decent sight-in, but instead, let's say we're pronghorn hunting and we want a point-blank range based on a six-inch window. Thanks to computers, we can find out that we need to sight in to be 2.6 inches high at 100 yards. At 150 yards we'll be three inches high, the high point of our trajectory. At 200 yards we'll be 2.3 inches high as the bullet starts back down. It will cross the line of sight at 256 yards, our "dead-on" point, and at 300 yards we'll be three inches low.

Shifting to an eight-inch window (four inches above and below the line of sight), we sight in 3.2 inches high at 100 yards, four inches high at 150 yards, and four inches low at 335 yards. And that, my friends, is a long way to shoot without worrying about holdover!

It's obvious that you can play around with your rifle's trajectory quite a bit, and also obvious that, by varying your 100-yard zero, you can simplify field shooting quite a bit. There are still two major considerations. First, whatever the trajectory of your cartridge, you simply must have a working knowledge of it at all ranges at which you might attempt a shot. And even more important, you must have the ability to put that bullet where you want it to land.

So let's talk about getting the shooter ready. Once you've sighted in your rifle and you're happy with your sight-in, you have to get yourself ready to take advantage of any shooting opportunity. There are two parts to this preparation: physical and mental.

The physical part centers mainly around shooting practice. It should also be said

A good part of getting ready should include getting in proper physical condition for the kind of hunting you'll be doing. Hunting is more enjoyable when you're in shape for it, and your chances of success are greatly enhanced.

that the better your overall physical condition, the better you'll hunt — and the better you'll shoot when a chance comes along. You won't shoot well if you're dead tired. Before hunting season is the time to shed unwanted pounds and do some walking and/or jogging. But be sensible — don't start on any exercise program before seeing a doctor.

In terms of shooting practice, the best thing you can do is get away from the benchrest. Once you've sighted in your rifle the way you want it, the bench is of no further use to you, except possibly to check and recheck that zero as hunting season nears. Instead, practice from sitting, kneeling, and offhand. Too much shooting isn't a particularly good thing, so don't overdo it. Make sure that you wear plenty of padding and good hearing protection.

It's a good idea to set up a "course of fire" that you follow in every practice session. Some of us can take more recoil than others, but a good training regimen would be a minimum of 20 rounds once a week. I would fire five rounds sitting, five kneeling, and five standing — and take a good break between each position. The last five rounds should be used leaning against whatever impromptu rest your range offers. A support pillar for a range shed works well, or perhaps you can kneel behind the bench itself. Vary this one, and practice getting steady and getting your shot off quickly. If you start a program like that a couple of months before hunting season, you'll be amazed at how your confidence level increases as your group sizes decrease.

Practice sessions don't have to be on the range. Varmint shooting, small game, or plinking does wonders. Even if you can't use your big-game rifle, do use the same positions — and especially take every opportunity to recognize and quickly use a natural rest.

Hunters who dwell in urban areas may not have the opportunity to do a lot of shooting of any kind. That's no excuse for not practicing. A lot of what should — and *must* — be practiced can be done at home. Getting into and out of shooting positions, getting the sling in place, even sight alignment and trigger control can all be practiced at home with an empty rifle — in front of the television if you like. The Marine Corps calls such dry-firing practice "snapping in," and it is just as beneficial and important as actual trigger time.

Important, too, is mental preparation. Although a great deal of skill and effort are involved in locating and closing with a game animal, and shooting skill is involved in connecting with a shot, hunting is a mental exercise, too — especially in the final moments.

In those final moments you can talk yourself out of or into success. It's up to you. A technique that's in vogue today among sports psychologists is called "visualization." Physical practice remains important, of course, but visualization is a

A great deal can be learned about your rifle from a steady benchrest, and it's advisable to mix in some shooting for groups along with field shooting practice. The problem is that too many hunters tie themselves to bench shooting to the exclusion of practicing other positions.

means of "psyching yourself up" in which you imagine — visualize — yourself as being successful in your sports. The runner visualizes himself breaking the tape at the time he's striving for; the high jumper pictures himself going over the bar at the height he's shooting for.

It works for hunters, too. I've done it for years, without knowing there's a name for it. Basically, I picture the animal I'm going to be hunting. I picture it from all angles at all distances, and I visualize where I must place the sights to be successful. And then I imagine the path of the bullet, all the way to the target area. Finally I visualize myself with that animal, successful.

There's no mysticism involved in this; it's rare when the actual shooting situation resembles what I've imagined. But the power of positive thinking is simply amazing. Undoubtedly you're going to be thinking about your upcoming hunt, and if you think about how you'll feel if you blow it, you're one step closer to doing exactly that.

Instead, concentrate on success. And visualize the animal you're after. Form a clear mental picture of where his vital zone lies from all angles. In the field, keep that mental game going. Chances are your opportunity won't come exactly when you think it will. It will come when you least expect it, and you must be ready, both mentally and physically. The consistently successful hunter is an incredible optimist. He *believes* the buck he's looking for is right around the next bend in the trail, just over the next ridge, or right here under his nose. He keeps looking through the last hour of the last day, and if he doesn't get a shot, well, he's already looking forward to next year. He also knows, deep down in his soul, that when that opportunity arises — from whatever angle and whatever reasonable distance — he'll be able to pull off the shot. He knows his rifle and his load, he has practiced from every conceivable position, and in his mind's eye he has *seen himself do it* a thousand times. He's ready.

Hunting is very much a mental game. The months of planning and dreaming that precede any hunt — and the long hours of glassing and waiting during the hunt — can be spent in mental preparation that gets you ready to make a successful shot. Or that time can be misspent as you talk yourself out of a successful shot before the opportunity ever arises.

22

Gun Safety in the Field

Hunting is an exciting sport, and there's nothing wrong with getting excited. Statistically, hunting is also a very safe sport, much safer than high-school football, for instance. However, it does combine potentially dangerous elements—that wonderful excitement, plus firearms, plus uncertain footing in rough terrain. Nothing, but nothing, is worth an accident.

I have lost several acquaintances to hunting accidents, although only one incident was firearms-related. One gentleman I knew fell off a sheep mountain in Russia; it was a freak accident, but he may have pushed himself a bit too far on uncertain footing. The bushplane is a common conveyance in much remote hunting country, and I've known many hunters who went down in light planes. Here, too, somebody—perhaps the victim, perhaps not—likely pushed it too far. You can't be in a hurry in rough country, whether you're on foot, on a horse, or in a boat, 4WD, or airplane. Sometimes you'll have to wait out the weather, and whoever or whatever is waiting for you back home just might have to keep waiting.

Even though, in my experience, firearms accidents are the rarest of hunting accidents, they happen. And they're the saddest of all since there's absolutely no excuse for them.

We all know the basic safety rules, and they apply in the field as well as on the range. There's a fine line between being ready for a shot and being unsafe; it's great to be always ready, but there's no excuse ever to be unsafe.

With most accidental discharges that occur during hunts, the most common problem is that the gun was loaded in the first place. Safeties are wonderful things, but they're mechanical devices. They can fail, although they rarely do. Much more common is for the gun to be knocked off safe by a passing branch or whatever.

I follow some rules of thumb. No loaded firearm should ever be placed in a vehicle. Generally it's illegal, and it's also asking for disaster. Under some circumstances, where legal, cartridges might be carried in the magazine in a vehicle, but *never* in the chamber. Likewise, a rifle should *never* have a cartridge in the chamber when it's in a saddle scabbard. And I'll go one step further—if you're going to carry the rifle slung on your back, unload the chamber. I've had several different kinds of safeties brushed to "off-safe" on a slung rifle, and it's a small next step for a piece of brush to catch the trigger. If you take a fall with a slung rifle, that muzzle is out of control and can go anywhere.

Generally, I carry a cartridge in the chamber only when I'm completing a stalk, or I'm in cover where I think a shot might occur at any moment. If that's what I'm thinking, that rifle is in my hands, not slung. If I have to negotiate an obstacle, or if I'm in steep country where I might take a tumble, the cartridge comes out of the chamber.

I'm a bit of a nut on this, and I check my chamber constantly. I also pay close attention to my partners' chambers. It's amazing how many times you'll find a cartridge in them when one shouldn't be.

The next thing is to watch where the muzzle is pointing at all times. That sounds a bit too obvious, but it isn't. If you and a partner are traveling single file on a narrow game trail and your rifle is carried in one hand, where is the muzzle? If you're second in line, chances are it's pointing at your buddy. How about going up a steep hill with the rifle slung? When you bend for-

Traversing rough country is dangerous enough, and a sling minimizes worry about where the rifle barrel will point if you slip. If the rifle is slung or if the footing looks unsteady or you have an obstacle to negotiate, there should be no cartridge in the chamber. I have a round in the chamber only when I'm expecting to get a shot any second.

ward and your partner is uphill from you, where does your muzzle point? At your buddy. In all types of terrain, you must be aware of where the business end of your rifle points. I once ran a photo in *Hunting* of myself crawling through some horrible thorn in South Africa. I was crawling with

Pay close attention to the direction of your gun muzzle when you're in awkward positions. Crawling like this, traveling on narrow trails, or climbing steep hillsides often naturally points your gun muzzle in a dangerous direction.

the rifle butt-forward, and a reader took me to task for being unsafe. Not true. I was crawling behind another man, and the only way I could keep that muzzle from pointing at his rear end was to reverse it.

Fence crossings are a traditional danger area, and the rules apply: unload your rifle and lay it down a few feet away with the muzzle pointing in a safe direction. Pick it up after you cross the fence.

Part of being "muzzle aware" is to make certain that it doesn't get plugged up with snow or dirt. That's a problem with slinging a rifle muzzle-down, as some hunters prefer; stumble a bit, and your barrel can be plugged with mud. Actually, anytime you take a tumble you need to look at your barrel and make certain it's clear. It's a good idea to check it periodically under any circumstances. A friend of mine was hunting gaur in Thailand when a wasp started to built a nest in the muzzle of his .458! I don't know if it would have caused the rifle to blow or not, but I wouldn't want to be the guy to find out. Saddle scabbards are particularly bad for picking up debris and depositing same in the rifle barrel.

A good fix for all of this is to carefully seal the muzzle with electrician's tape before starting every hunting day. It takes just

Snow has a bad habit of finding its way into an unprotected gun muzzle. If it turns to ice, it can cause a dangerous blockage. The cure is simple—just put a fresh piece of tape over the muzzle before starting the day's hunt. And of course, check the muzzle every time you take a tumble.

a second and will neither increase pressure nor change your zero. The air within the barrel blows the tape off long before the bullet reaches it, or so I'm told. This trick saves the hassle of digging snow and dirt out of the muzzle.

Mechanically, there are few things you can do to make a rifle safer than it is as it comes from the factory. In these days of product liability lawsuits, you can take as given that a factory-supplied safety is functional. Personally, I feel more comfortable with the safeties that block both the firing pin and the trigger, like the old Mauser-

type safety. Trigger-blocking safeties are effective, however. More important is to take a hard look at how positively that safety engages. A number of factory rifles have perfectly functional safeties that are much too easy to inadvertently brush to the fire position. I trust safeties, to a point— but I trust an empty chamber much more.

One area to watch out for is rifles that have been messed with. A trigger job is a great thing, but if you go too far, you might create a monster that will go off if you jar it. For field use, I don't like a too-light trigger. If you're going to have a trigger pull lightened, have it done by a good gunsmith who knows exactly what he's doing. And if you buy a used rifle that has been altered in any way, have that same good gunsmith take a look at the trigger group.

Another thing that should go without saying is to make absolutely certain of your target before you fire. Flame-orange clothing helps, but even in flame-orange country there could be a hunter out there who refuses to wear it. You're excited while you're hunting, and you want to see game. Your eyes have a frightening tendency to see what you want them to see. Take a second look, and make absolutely certain you're seeing what you think you're seeing. And make certain you know the location of your hunting buddies at all times. The common technique of driving for big game is one of the most dangerous of all tactics. It makes sense to hunt with people you know and trust — and even then, be absolutely certain you know where everybody is. In thick country, if you don't know where your buddies are, you simply must not fire.

A word on flame-orange clothing. I don't like it, and I hate to wear it. But I hate getting shot at worse. It's good stuff, worth its weight in gold. Wear it, and carry some extra along with you. If you need to pack out an animal on your back, tie some flame-orange flags to the antlers and legs.

It's amazing how your eyes can play tricks on you. One time I was sitting on a ridge while my hunting partners made a drive up through the valley below. I looked down the slope and thought I saw Todd Smith coming up the hill toward me. He went out of sight in a little fold, and I relaxed. A few moments later I saw movement below me, much closer, and there was

Safety-wise, hunting is just like most other activities — you're at the most risk when you get tired. A tired hunter with his head down, rifle slung, and a cartridge in the chamber is an accident looking for a place to happen. Mind your gun barrel always, but keep your chamber clear unless there's a good reason for it to be otherwise.

a nice buck feeding on acorns. I watched him for a few moments, and then I shot him. And then I remembered seeing Todd very clearly, and my heart thumped wildly until I got to the buck. It was a full half hour before Todd reached me, and he came in from a different angle. I hadn't seen him at all; I'd seen the buck walking uphill straight toward me. But I'd expected to see Todd coming from that direction, and I saw him. Many hunting accidents are the result of just the opposite of that situation.

23

Keeping It Working

I wish I were at least a passable amateur gunsmith. Truth is, though, that I'm quite hopeless at most kinds of mechanics. I've often dreamed that one day I'd run off to Africa and become a professional hunter. But a good professional hunter simply has to be a topflight mechanic as well as a decent gunsmith.

Even if you're all thumbs like me, you may need to do a bit of backyard gunsmithing now and again to keep your firearms working in the field. And you definitely need to do some planning to ensure that you don't get caught in the back of beyond with a thunderstick that doesn't work.

Obviously, if you're hunting close to home, a gun problem isn't all that significant; you may lose the rest of that day, but it's no big deal. If you've traveled a great distance to hunt, however, it can be a very big deal indeed, whether you're stuck in a high-country camp in Colorado or one in Mongolia. If your rifle isn't working, you'll be sitting there kicking yourself.

First off, as you're preparing for the trip, make certain everything works properly. I think this is the third time I've said so in this volume, but I'll say it again—run all the cartridges you plan to take through the action(s) of your rifle(s). Inspect all the cartridges carefully for dents, dings, spent primers that somehow got into your primer feed tray, etc. And of course make certain they're the right cartridges for your rifle. A friend of mine was guiding a pig hunter one day, and got him in nice and close on a big boar. The hunter fired, and the rifle sounded like a huge bell ringing. My buddy turned to look, and the rifle was a shambles. The hunter had somehow mistaken a .280 Remington cartridge (at that time called 7mm Express) for a 7mm Remington

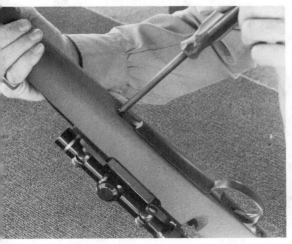

Loose action screws are a common culprit when a rifle's accuracy suddenly becomes erratic. Keep them nice and snug, and make sure your kit has screwdrivers that will fit the screws of your rifle.

Magnum. Fortunately nobody was hurt, but the rifle was ruined.

Next, if you are going a significant distance to hunt, I strongly recommend taking along a spare rifle. Generally you'll be going with a buddy, or perhaps a party of three or four. Not everybody needs to bring two rifles, but there should be a spare rifle with every party. On two different occasions I've gotten off commercial airplanes to discover that my rifle, all nice and snug in a hard case, was broken in half.

The first time it happened was on a black bear hunt in Arizona. My buddy picked me up after my one-hour flight to Tucson, and we drove like mad up to the San Carlos Reservation and made camp in the dark. Only then did I open my guncase. The stock on my .300 Weatherby was splintered; it looked as if it had been dropped off a five-story building. The other rifle in the same case was untouched, and it was fortunate there was another rifle in the

case—I had the only bear tag, and my buddy didn't bring a rifle. Two lessons—take a spare, and inspect your guns before you leave the airport.

The second occasion was on an African hunt. I had a Remington .30–06 from the firm's custom shop, a beautiful rifle. But on arrival it had become a take-down model, broken cleanly at the wrist. My .375 instantly became my light rifle on that trip.

Breakage during transportation is far from the only thing that can happen to firearms. Last year in Botswana my stepson and my father-in-law each took a light rifle and planned to share a .375 between them. After a few days the stock on my father-in-law's .30–06 was broken in half, courtesy of a hard bump in the Land Cruiser, and the long Mauser extractor of the .375 separated from the bolt collar. They commandeered my .375, which was a bit inconvenient since it was a left-hand bolt, but we managed just fine. One more disaster and we would darn near have run out of rifles!

A good hard case is the best travel protection you can get for your rifle, and usually a rifle can go anywhere in one and not even shift zero. But every once in a while a disaster can happen, so it's important to have a spare in camp if you've traveled any distance to hunt.

This lovely Remington was shipped in a very good hard guncase. What happened? Who knows, but it makes sense to prepare for the worst and have a spare around.

An out-and-out mechanical problem like we had with that Mauser is rare. It's happened to me only once before, on a Savage 99 that just plain froze up with a fired cartridge stuck in the chamber. I never did get it cleared until after I got home. Unless you have some gunsmithing skills and bring along some tools and a few spare parts — like ejectors, extractors, firing pins, and such — a genuine mechanical failure often means that you have to reach for the spare rifle, or trade off with your buddy.

A serious mechanical problem is pretty rare, though. If something is going to get damaged, chances are that it will be either the stock or the sighting equipment. One of the most useful things a hunter can throw into his duffel bag is a big roll of the strongest plastic tape he can buy. With it you can repair boots and waders, seal off your gun muzzle in a rainstorm, and, in a pinch, put a broken gunstock back together. It won't look like much, but it can be done.

The next most useful item a hunter can bring along is some form of alternative sighting equipment. Maybe a horse rolls on your rifle, or your riflescope simply gives up the ghost. Having iron sights in place on your rifle is a sensible move. If you don't have a detachable scope mount, make certain you bring along the screwdrivers or Allen wrenches, or both, that you'll need to remove the scope.

It's a bit of an old wives' tale that iron sights are more dependable than scopes. Once upon a time that was true, but today's scopes and mounts have become extremely rugged and reliable. And since most shooters use scopes, at least on general-purpose flat-shooting rifles, iron sights have become almost cosmetic rather than functional.

I have seen scopes take a bashing and get knocked out of zero, but that happens to iron sights as well. And I have seen a scope or two get broken when a horse rolled on them (no big surprise — the stocks broke, too!), but although it has happened to me on the range, I have never had a scope fail in the field. On the other hand, I have had iron sights on two different, rather expen-

sive bolt actions from respected manufacturers actually fall off the rifles on hunting
trips. If your backup is going to be iron
sights, check them out carefully. Sight
them in as you do the scopes, and make
sure they're securely in place.

A better option — one many hunters are
going to today — is to carry a spare scope in
your duffel bag. It should already be set in
rings that are compatible with the mounts
on your rifle. With some mounts you can
actually have it pre-zeroed; in other cases
you'll have to sight it in when you switch
scopes. I've gone this route myself lately,
especially on hunts in remote country. So
far I haven't had to use the spare scope, but
it sure is comforting to have on hand.

What do you do if your iron sights fall
off? Well, if you can find them, that's another good use for the electrician's tape.

Aside from a spare rifle and/or a spare
scope, there are a few other things the
smart hunter won't leave home without. Of
great importance is some kind of scope
caps. I'll be honest — I don't use them a lot.
But in rain and wet snow, you simply must

have scope caps that you can get on and off
quickly. If the snow or rain is really blowing, you won't want to remove the scope
caps until you're actually ready to shoot.
There are good commercial ones available
that flip up at a touch. But my favorite
scope cover is a piece of inner tube, sliced
off so it's like a big rubberband. It keeps the
lenses completely dry, and if you need to
get the rifle into action in a hurry, all you do
is pull the rear of it back and to one side
and let it go. It will snap off, and you're in
business. I cut them a bit generous, because
in a pinch a little square of that rubber also
makes a great fire starter.

I don't carry a spare rifle sling; if my
sling breaks, the electrician's tape can fix it.
And if not, a piece of rope will work. I do
pay attention to the sling swivel studs and

A small cleaning kit, including a jointed rod, is an essential item on any away-from-home hunting trip. The rod is needed not only to clean the rifle if the weather turns bad but also to get snow and mud out of the barrel if you take a spill.

There's nothing like a roll of electrician's tape. It can protect a muzzle from snow and rain, make a quick fix on a broken stock in a pinch, and even hold iron sights on a rifle — but I wouldn't want to bet on the groups!

make sure they aren't working loose. One of the easiest ways to break a scope is to have the forward swivel stud come loose while the rifle is slung. The rifle pitches back and always lands smack on the scope. And for some reason there's always a big rock right where it lands.

As I mentioned, I'm not a nut about gun cleaning. However, I always carry a cleaning rod, patching material, solvent, and oil. If you get some gunk down your gun barrel, you must clean it. And if you get really wet, you should clean your gun barrel. It's amazing how quickly rust will form if you don't. Under those circumstances, it's essential that you pull the action out of the stock and get the hidden metal parts completely dried and then lightly oiled.

To accomplish this you will need screwdrivers that fit the action screws. All manner of ingenious compact cleaning kits are available these days. Many have a pull-through cleaning rod—not a solid affair but a cable of some type that is dropped through the barrel, fitted with a brush or patch, then pulled back through. They're great for cleaning, but I like to have an honest-to-God cleaning rod available in case mud or snow gets packed in the barrel and I have to literally drive it out.

A lot of hunting, particularly in North America, is done in extremely cold weather. When the mercury starts edging toward zero, normal lubricants become sluggish. Much lower than that and they can freeze up to the point that your firing pin won't fall. If you anticipate severe cold, strip your rifle down, especially the bolt and trigger assembly, and degrease it carefully with rubbing alcohol or any degreasing solvent. Then use some dry graphite to very lightly lubricate the moving parts.

In very cold weather, don't take your rifle inside your tent, cabin, or wherever you're

To prepare for subzero weather, it's critical that all liquid lubricants be removed from the rifle, especially the bolt. They'll freeze up and prevent the firing pin from falling. Degrease with a good solvent, then lubricate very sparingly with dry graphite only.

staying. It will sweat something fierce, and the exterior of the scope will fog up unbelievably. Cover the rifle, but leave it out in the cold.

Under the opposite conditions—very warm climates, such as desert hunting, early-season hunting, and much African hunting—rust can form very quickly, usually caused by the salt from your sweaty hands. Under those conditions daily maintenance, such as a thorough wiping down and a light cleaning and oiling, is a must.

In the field, use common sense. Don't leave your rifle lying where it might get knocked around. You might not care about the scratches, but you sure don't want the scope to get knocked off. If you're hunting from horseback, never walk away from the horse for any reason without taking the rifle out of your scabbard. If you don't need the rifle with you, carry it off a safe distance and hang it in a tree. But don't ever leave a horse alone with your rifle; that will be the time he'll choose to scratch an itch by rubbing up against a tree or rolling.

If you're riding in a pickup truck, keep your hands on your rifle and mind where the barrel is. I just heard about an incident in which a truck hit a bump and a hunter's eye was put out by an out-of-control gun muzzle. If you'll be riding around in a truck, the best course is to take an inexpensive soft gun case and keep the rifle in it.

Today's hunting rifles are extremely durable tools, and it doesn't take much to keep them happy and working. On the other hand, if you're just the slightest bit unlucky, it's amazing how little it takes to mess them up completely. So carry a few simple tools and a cleaning kit—but make sure some kind of a spare firearm is available!

Horseback hunts are wonderful, but don't trust the horse with your rifle. If you leave your horse for any reason, never leave the rifle in the saddle scabbard.

24

Buck Fever!

The malady we call "buck fever" has stricken hunters ever since there were hunters. It manifests itself in many ways. Sometimes it resembles malaria, except that the shakes are worse. Sometimes it can be confused with a manic-depressive state that generally calls for a padded room. Unlike most human ailments, it occurs only in the presence of game. And sometimes its effects are pretty weird. Normally it interacts with the sighting mechanism of the hunter's arm and causes bullets or arrows to fly all over the landscape. But in its most virulent form the firearm may actually cease to function and, of its own volition, eject all of its unfired cartridges on the ground. In a related form of the disease, the firearm and the hunter amalgamate into a tightly frozen mass.

Buck fever isn't a serious disease; generally nothing dies from it, although those who suffer from it wither slowly from embarrassment if there are any witnesses. The truth is that every hunter suffers from it sooner or later.

It is simply excitement in its purest form — excitement so intense that the nerves and muscles and reactions are overridden and very odd things happen. There's certainly nothing wrong with excitement. That's what hunting is all about, and if you don't get excited in the presence of a beautiful game animal, you're much better off playing tennis or golf.

On the other hand, there's such a thing as too much of a good thing. A little buck fever goes a long way, and if it pushes you out of control, then it isn't fun any more. And you're also not safe to be around.

But in small doses, well, that's what we're out there for. I'll be honest; I get a small dose of buck fever every time I'm in the presence of game. My heartbeat speeds up, my breathing gets ragged, my palms sweat—all classic symptoms. It's that kind of rush that keeps me climbing one hill after another and explains why our family bank accounts never quite balance. My buck fever is generally controllable. Or, to put it better, over the years I've learned what I must do to keep it under control.

Basically, I play games with myself. In general, buck fever sets in hard just as you start to get ready to take a shot. During those moments, I'm fussing with my equipment, keeping my mind and my hands occupied with things that will help my shooting. I'm getting into a tight sling or a hasty sling; I'm casting around for a rest, and then making it better by adding a hat or a backpack or a rolled-up jacket; and finally I'm really concentrating on the shooting basics. I concentrate on my breathing, on the sight picture, on my trigger control. And if I'm paying attention to all those things, I simply don't have time for buck fever to set in seriously.

The chapters on shooting positions, shooting basics, use of the sling, and finding a good rest weren't meant to be taken lightly; all of these things combine to make a good field marksman. All of them also have a dual purpose—to keep the shooter's mind occupied and to keep him calm and cool while he gets ready to take his shot. Whether you like the techniques I've described or not, you have to admit that they make more sense than standing up on your hind legs and emptying a magazine into a hillside.

If you're with a buddy, it helps to talk each other through a shot—provided, of course, that the target animal is out of earshot. The kicker on that, though, is that your buddy needs to keep calm. Buck fever is infectious, and I've seen overexuberant guides infect their clients with it in a heartbeat. If your hunting partner can keep his voice low and even, no matter how excited

This wasn't a very difficult shot, but I still get a healthy dose of nervous excitement every time I get close to game. To ward off the jitters here, I fussed with my equipment, getting into a sling and taking a rest against the tree. Yes, I could have made this shot without a rest, but my habits work for me and I don't like to break them.

he really is, he can help a great deal. The things he might say would include helping to pick out the exact animal in a group, estimating range, suggesting an aiming point on the animal, or urging you to wait until the animal turns to offer a better shot. Such advice is free; you don't have to follow it. You're even welcome to get angry and tell him to shut up. That's to the good as well. You can't be angry with your buddy and have a bout with buck fever at the same time.

A good guide will always attempt to talk his client through a shot. His range estima-

There's nothing wrong with a little friendly coaching, regardless of the experience level of the participants. But such kibitzing must be calm, quiet, and constructive.

tion may not be infallible, but if he's in familiar country, chances are good that his judgment is better than yours. He may ask you to take a shot that you're not comfortable with; that's your call one way or the other. But so long as he's not the excitable type who starts jumping up and down in the presence of game (like you want to!), a little quiet coaching never hurts. I have

a fair amount of experience shooting at game, and I've never turned down that kind of kibitzing.

Bob Morrison, a bear guide in Alberta, let me in on a great secret, and it has some interesting anti-buck-fever applications. He hunts where cultivated fields meet unbroken forest. In the evening the bears often come out in the open to feed along the edges of monstrous barley fields. As daylight fades he glasses field edges, and if a suitable bear shows, the stalk is on. He gets the wind right, and relies on slight folds in the fields, plus a bear's poor eyesight, to make the stalk. He stalks in the field because it's too noisy in the adjacent timber. It's nerve-wracking—you might have to cover a mile of open field literally in sight of the bear most of the time. Morrison found that he was losing a lot of bears to buck fever—many clients were far gone with the disease before the stalk was half over.

He came up with a simple trick. If he starts to feel that the client is nervous (and a good guide can feel it, make no mistake), he turns to him and whispers, "I'll keep my eyes on the bear. Tap me when we've covered 100 yards."

At the end of that 100 yards he asks him to keep track of the next 100, and so on. According to Bob, it works like a charm. The idea is to occupy the hunter's mind so that the jitters can't come in. He's concentrating as hard as he can on placing his feet silently, plus he's now counting steps. He doesn't have time to get nervous. (Since Bob told me that, I've counted steps a couple of times. It works when you're alone just as well as under the direction of a guide!)

There's a high, horribly rough canyon in Arizona's Catalina Mountains that has been a magic place for me. I've taken several good Coues whitetails out of it, includ-

This is my best-ever Coues buck, one of my most prized trophies. He was in some thick junipers with a doe, and we had to wait him out. I think I did my best job ever of controlling buck fever on this deer, and I was just as proud of myself as I appear to be.

Two years later, in the same canyon, with the same hunting buddy and the same rifle, I didn't do quite so well on this pretty little eight-pointer. In fact, buck fever got the best of me, and it's a miracle that my shots landed in the same county as the deer. But after all, buck fever is just excitement, and that's part of what we're out there for!

ing my best one. I figure I've done both my best and my worst job of controlling buck fever there.

The first time we went in there, we glassed from a high promontory and saw several fine bucks. Toward midmorning we made our move on a real monster, the kind of Coues buck I'd been looking for but never expected to find. It was a rough stalk, down and then back up again over several deep, rocky cuts. Finally we made our way to the ridge overlooking the canyon bottom where we'd seen the buck. The rut was on and he was with some does, so we expected him to be there.

He was, but we didn't see him for quite a while. The does were there so the buck had

to be as well. Nervousness grew with each passing minute, and I was darn near beside myself.

Finally the buck showed, in a little patch of cedars. And he was everything a Coues deer hunter dreams of. I crawled a few yards closer to take a rest against an oak; this buck was about 225 yards away, and that's a long shot on these little deer — especially in my frame of mind. I made the tree, got into a tight sling, and sat with my supporting hand braced against the trunk. The buck was behind the cedars now, so I had to wait him out. Finally he stepped clear, quartering to me. I could have waited for a better angle, but the Remington 7mm Magnum I was using is extremely accurate, and I knew the jitters were just moments away; I'd held them off as long as I could. I got the shot off, and the buck went down. The bullet entered on the point of the right shoulder and exited the left ham. I talked to myself throughout that episode; I wish I could remember what I said, 'cause it sure worked.

Almost two years later to the day, I was in the same canyon with the same man, ace Coues deer hunter Duwane Adams. And I was carrying the same rifle. We spotted a very nice eight-point buck with some does and made a nice stalk on him. This stalk was much easier; all we had to do was sidehill around, and we had enough cover so that we got within about 125 yards. The slope was such that I couldn't use a rest, but I got into a nice, tight sitting position and waited for the buck to turn broadside. He

did so after a few seconds. And then buck fever took over.

The rifle barrel turned lazy eights in the air, and I couldn't keep the crosshairs on the whole deer, let alone where it counted. I finally got the shot off and missed him clean. He was after a hot doe, and he scampered a few steps and stood again. And the jitters got worse. The gunbarrel was totally out of control now, and I was shaking like a leaf. That shot missed, too. Probably didn't even come close. Somehow the third shot connected, but it must have been a pure accident.

What happened? Heck, I don't know. I can't really remember. I suspect I was a bit overconfident and probably didn't play the games I should have played to occupy my mind. I should have known—all deer get to me, especially those hard-won little Coues deer. But it's OK—I don't get that excited all that often, and it's a good experience to realize that every bit of the excitement is still there. But it's better if you can keep it under control!

25

The Anatomy of a Shot —
Putting It All Together

As you can see from the foregoing chapter, I consider myself to be in a state of controlled panic when I'm shooting at game. It's all right to be nervous — you're supposed to be nervous — but you do have to keep it under control. Concentrating hard on the shooting basics — on getting into position and getting good and steady — is as good a way as any to push the panic aside. But there's a bit more to it than that when push comes to shove.

Back in the good old days, the sporting press called it "the moment of truth." It's too bad that saying has become trite, because it's accurate. No matter how long you are afield, eventually it comes down to you, your rifle, and generally just one cartridge. That single squeeze of the trigger determines success or failure, and that's the way it is.

Is success really all that important? We hunt for different reasons, of course —

and generally for several reasons rolled into one. Hunting is an excuse to be in lovely country, to get closer to nature, and observe beautiful animals. It's also a challenging, enjoyable exercise — both mental and physical.

For most of us the important part isn't whether we come home with game or not; few of us can be considered subsistence hunters today. And I wouldn't care to place a price tag (or have my wife see one!) on the venison in my freezer. The great Spanish philosopher Ortega Y Gassett wrote that "We don't hunt in order to kill; we kill in order to have hunted." We aren't birdwatchers or tree huggers. We're hunters, and I'm not ashamed of it. And if you can tell me truthfully that you really don't care whether you hit or miss when that "moment of truth" arrives, then you've vastly different from any other hunters I've ever met in the woods.

Being successful in the field isn't the most important thing; if I don't get a shot, that's fine. But if I get a shot, you can bet that I want it to be a good one — and I do everything I can to make sure that it is.

I care. I've missed my share, and will again, and it bothers me. I don't sulk for days, but it eats on me. When that final encounter between me and the game I seek arrives, I want to be successful more than anything in the world.

To make that happen, you must do a great many things all at once, and you must do them exactly right. There's a great deal of airspace around a game animal, and that space has a tendency to soak up bullets if the shooter commits the slightest error.

In this book we've talked about many things: selecting rifles and cartridges; the basics of good shooting; how to find and use a rest in the field; where to place shots on game animals; how to prepare mentally as well as physically; how to hold buck fever at bay. All these things come together for that single trigger squeeze. These and one thing more — timing.

Now, it isn't always possible to plan the shot you will get. Let's say you're walking through thick timber and a whitetail buck jumps up from under your feet. You didn't plan that shot, but it's the only shot you have at the moment. And timing is critical. Chances are you must shoulder your rifle and fire in a matter of seconds, before the buck is gone into the thick stuff. You can't look around for a rest; you can't stop and take several deep breaths. But you can remember to mount the rifle to your shoulder, chambering a round and/or releasing the safety as you do so. And you can remember to get the rifle barrel swinging, get it on the animal, and keep it swinging as you squeeze the trigger.

If you do those things, you'll have your buck, taken with a shot you'll always remember. Jack O'Connor wrote that a running buck offered just as big a target as a standing buck, and that's obviously true. If you're ready, and if you've practiced for just such an event, you can pull it off — especially if you *believe* you can.

Many, perhaps most, shots are much more deliberate. Instead of walking through the woods, you're in a tree stand, watching a game trail, and a doe steps tentatively into view. She looks behind her, and you know a buck is coming. Slowly, slowly, you shift the rifle so that it rests nicely on the branch you tied into place for just this event. You put the sights on the half-hidden form.

Do you shoot, or wait? That's up to you, and I can't answer it for you. If you think you can get away with it, you wait until the buck steps into the clear. And perhaps you wait a bit more until he turns broadside. You know how the wind is blowing — or you should. You know how well you're camouflaged — or you should. You know what the doe is doing — or you should. Is she nervous now? Is she still coming on? How much of

This was a dead-cinch shot, and it could have been taken at this instant. But the deer were undisturbed, and the angle was terrible. I had the wind in my favor, and I knew that sooner or later the buck on the right would turn and give me the broadside shot that I like. I waited 15 minutes or so, but finally he did turn and I got the ideal shot. I stayed ready that entire time, and could have fired at any instant if the deer showed signs of alarm.

the buck can you really see? Does your bullet have a clear path to the vitals? If it doesn't, you must wait. And now the jitters come. Don't let them. Concentrate on your sights. Take a deep breath, then another. Relax your body. The sight picture and that buck are all that matter. He's taking a step. He's in the clear. You've imagined this a thousand times, and you can do it.

Stalking situations are more deliberate yet, in that you choose the place from which you will shoot. You know, or should know, your capabilities with your rifle, so you know how close you would like to get. And you don't want to stop at the outer limits of your capabilities; you want to get as close as you can.

On the other hand, you're stalking an undisturbed animal. The last thing in the world you want to do is bump that animal and be faced with a running shot. But you're looking at the terrain, and you know where you want to go. And where is that? The closest point you can reach that will keep your scent away from the animal and offer a clear view, a clear shot, and — you hope — a steady rest.

The real secret to successful stalking is picking landmarks. With the possible exception of nearsighted beasts like bears and pigs, you must remain out of sight of the animal throughout the stalk. In a stalking situation, you've already spotted the animal, probably from afar with binoculars

In a stalking situation you simply must stay flexible, ready to shift position as many times as necessary to get the shot you want at the animal you want. On the other hand, you mustn't expect perfection; you must have a sense of how close you can get and how far you can push it.

and/or spotting scope. You must not begin the stalk until you know what the animal is likely to do. His activity must tell you that he's going to stay in the general area where he is now, or head in a specific direction that will let you intercept him. You must watch from afar until you know these things, and then you can begin your stalk. While you're stalking, you don't know what the animal is doing, and you can't worry about that. If he does something unexpected, so be it; you'll blow the stalk for sure if you keep checking on the animal enroute.

You must guide yourself by landmarks — a certain rock formation, a hill with a distinct shape, or a particularly tall tree. Once you get there, chances are the ground will look entirely different from its appearance at a distance. It will have folds and ridges,

and it will probably be confusing as hell. So you must have a definite destination in mind from which, if everything goes according to plan, you'll be able to shoot.

It's possible that you can even pick out from afar the rock or log that you will use as a rest. Or you might have to do that as you crawl to your chosen vantage point. But whatever the situation, you must have a plan in mind. And as you complete your stalk, go over in your mind again and again what you must do.

After that, it's all the same as any other shooting situation. Find a rest, or get into a steady shooting position — or both. Locate the animal. Concentrate on the basics. Get a good sight picture.

But wait. That plan you made several hundred yards back might not be the best one now. The ground looks different. The distance is greater. Can you get closer safely? Then do so. Make a new plan. Once you're close enough, wait for the right moment; if the animal is undisturbed, don't rush the shot, and don't take a bad angle.

I stalked two bucks not long ago, a youngster and a good one. It went like clockwork; the wind was in my face, and the deer were feeding in a little cut. I crawled onto a grassy knob about 150 yards above them, pushed my backpack in front of me, and then pushed the rifle into place on top of it. The deer were still feeding, and the youngster was standing nicely broadside. The better buck, though, had found something particularly succulent. His head was down, and his rear end was to me. I waited. The shot was makable; I think I could have taken out his spine. But everything was perfect, and there was no reason to rush. The jitters came, and I concentrated on my sight picture. The jitters went, and I waited some more. "My" buck took a few steps forward, quartered slightly, and I almost fired. Then he stepped behind a

Often on a stalk you will cover vast distances, all the while completely out of sight of your game. It's essential to pick landmarks toward which you can work. I had picked out this distinctive boulder from more than a mile away, and this caribou bull was still feeding behind it when I got there. After a close look I decided I didn't want him, but it was a great stalk.

bush and put his head down to feed with even more relish. I waited some more, and the jitters came and went again.

A good quarter-hour passed, and finally the deer stepped out, head down, broadside. I put the crosshairs just behind his shoulder and squeezed the trigger, and I did admire that shot. I knew exactly where it went, and although several seconds passed with no reaction, I knew the deer was dead. He was.

Things don't always go quite that smoothly. I will never forget my "moment of truth" during the Lander (Wyoming) One Shot Antelope Hunt. I was on a writer's team with *Field & Stream*'s Dave Petzal, captained by Bill Quimby of *Safari* magazine. During the sight-in sessions I had seen how well they could shoot, and I was worried about holding up my end. The Lander hunt is a friendly competition. There aren't any prizes. The medicine man of the Shoshone tribe blesses each hunter's single bullet (each hunter also has plenty more unblessed bullets in case he screws up), and they sally forth. The winning team

dances the victory dance with the Shoshone braves; all the losers dance with the squaws. You don't shoot with your teammates, but with a hunter from another team. You flip a coin for first position, then from dawn on you alternate hours until you fire your shot.

I had the first hour, but it was nearly over before we saw a buck antelope—two bucks actually, and one of them was pretty decent. I bailed out of the truck and belly-crawled several hundred yards. The antelope were in a little swale, and though there was no cover, the ground rolled enough to let me close to about 200 yards. I had picked a stretch of long-forgotten fence as my mark; once I crawled under it, I should be almost in sight and certainly within range.

I reached it and crawled under it but still could see nothing. Ahead of me was an abandoned post, four inches square and sticking about six inches out of the ground—an ideal rest for a prone position. I crawled to it carefully and peered around it. Both bucks were there, about 200 yards

It's absolutely essential that the complete field marksman be able to call his shots — to know with near certainty exactly where the animal was hit. This bear offers quite a reasonable shot, but after receiving the bullet, chances are he'll be in the woods in one jump. That first shot must be right — and you must know where it lands. After taking this photo I shot the bear, and that's exactly what happened — one jump and gone, and then I waited before following up. The shot did go where I called it, right behind the shoulder; the bear went 40 yards.

away, still in the little swale that now opened before me.

I rested my hat on the old post, then laid the fore-end of the rifle across the top. I was shaking, my palms were sweating, and my heart was trying to leap out of my chest. I took several deep breaths, concentrating on breathing and sight picture. I would have liked to wait a long, long time, but the situation wouldn't have gotten any better. I concentrated harder, and the sight picture steadied.

The buck took off at the shot, and I saw dust kick behind him and seemingly above

him. I didn't pause to admire this shot. I worked the bolt and put the sights on him. He was running as only antelope can run, but he was moving dead away, so it would have been easy. But I hesitated just long enough to recall the sight picture I'd thought I had — and the hesitation was long enough. In that instant he somersaulted into the sage, shot through the heart. I didn't know it, but Petzal and Quimby already had their pronghorns; we danced with the braves that night.

An important part of that moment of truth comes after the shot. If the animal is still up, and if you have a clear shot, shoot again. If the animal goes down, watch him carefully and be ready. Once you're sure there's no movement, *carefully* pick some landmarks that will guide you to his location. Remember that the ground will look much different once you get there. If the animal has gone out of sight, carefully recall your shots. The complete game shot is able to call his shots, to know with almost complete certainty whether he has hit his animal and, if so, where. Relive the placement of your sights when your shot or shots went off. What do you think happened? Did you hear the bullet hit?

Even if there was no indication of a hit and you're certain you missed, go look for blood. Pick out landmarks just as if you had a downed animal, and work your way to them. Drop your hat or an orange

Too many almost-perfect shots go wrong in the followup. Even with the most perfect bullet placement, few animals drop in their tracks; most must be followed, even if just a few yards. And often there will be no blood for the first few steps. Wait a few minutes, take careful landmarks, then move to where you last saw the animal — and be ready! Most of the time you'll find your game down, but every once in a while the bullet won't have gone exactly where you wanted it to.

streamer where you think the animal was standing, then work in circles until you find blood or are absolutely certain you missed.

If you have blood, the best course is generally to sit and wait for half an hour. If the animal isn't pushed immediately, he may not go very far. He should stiffen up a bit from his wound, and if he's still ambulatory, you may have a decent shot at him if you don't rush things. But that isn't a hard and fast rule. If there's a vantage point nearby, you may want to make for it and wait there. But don't move away from that initial blood trail without marking it with something you can readily find.

Too many almost-perfect shots go wrong in the follow-through. If the animal isn't lying dead where you shot at him, don't assume anything. Be completely ready, and if you have blood, take any possible shot that he gives you. You have a wounded animal now, and your obligation is to find him and bring him to bag. Above all, don't panic now. Keep in mind all the shooting principles, and be ready to put them to use at any second. Tracking wounded game is nerve-wracking, exhausting work, but take it very slow and keep alert. If you have a blood trail, your chances of recovering the animal are very good.

All of us are going to have to follow a blood trail at some point. I wish it could be otherwise, but nobody is going to shoot perfectly all the time. We'll have some memorable hits, but there will be a few forgettable misses and almost-misses scattered in. The trick is not to forget those misses, or dwell on them unduly, but to learn from them. If each provides a lesson learned, and if we pay attention to our shooting and practice good shooting techniques, those misses will eventually become few enough to really forget. And it's a lot more pleasant to remember the shots that went where you wanted them to go.

Index

Grolier also offers merchandise items.
Please write for information.